Future Publics

Future Publics

Democracy, Deliberation, and Future-Regarding Collective Action

MICHAEL K. MACKENZIE

OXFORD
UNIVERSITY PRESS

OXFORD
UNIVERSITY PRESS

Oxford University Press is a department of the University of Oxford. It furthers the University's objective of excellence in research, scholarship, and education by publishing worldwide. Oxford is a registered trade mark of Oxford University Press in the UK and certain other countries.

Published in the United States of America by Oxford University Press
198 Madison Avenue, New York, NY 10016, United States of America.

Library of Congress Cataloging-in-Publication Data
Names: MacKenzie, Michael K., author.
Title: Future publics : democracy, deliberation, and future-regarding collective action / Michael K. MacKenzie.
Description: New York, NY : Oxford University Press, [2021] |
Includes bibliographical references and index.
Identifiers: LCCN 2021008108 (print) | LCCN 2021008109 (ebook) |
ISBN 9780197557150 (hardback) | ISBN 9780197557167 (updf) |
ISBN 9780197557181 (oso) | ISBN 9780197557174 (epub)
Subjects: LCSH: Democracy—United States.
Classification: LCC JK1726 .M34 2021 (print) | LCC JK1726 (ebook) |
DDC 320.973—dc23
LC record available at https://lccn.loc.gov/2021008108
LC ebook record available at https://lccn.loc.gov/2021008109

DOI: 10.1093/oso/9780197557150.001.0001

1 3 5 7 9 8 6 4 2

Printed by Integrated Books International, United States of America

For Maude, of course.

Contents

Preface

This project has been propelled by both hope and dismay. I began working on *Future Publics* more than 10 years ago while doing my PhD at the University of British Columbia under the supervision of Mark E. Warren. At the time, I was cautiously optimistic that democracies as we knew them would continue to improve. Over the last few years my optimism has diminished considerably. I am worried that once-stable democracies are increasingly vulnerable to existential threats: the rise of demagogues, racial and ethnic tensions, the rejection of truth, declining levels of trust, increasing income inequality, xenophobic nationalism, and the use of digital technologies to undermine, rather than enhance, inclusion and deliberation.

On a personal level, I am—like many of us—daily confronted with the neglect and failures of previous generations. I am an Assistant Professor of Political Science at the University of Pittsburgh. I live with my wife and four-year-old daughter in a pleasant, mixed-income neighbourhood that is near—but not too near—the campus. We walk, bike, and shop in our local area and we have access to a functional (if not great) public transit system. We live near two large parks (Schenley and Frick), and up the hill from the Monongahela River. It should take 20 minutes to walk (with a four-year-old) to the river near our house, but there is no safe or pleasant way to do so because the neighbourhood is bisected by a busy, multilane roadway. There is a sidewalk, but it is largely unused because it is mere inches from where the cars, trucks, and buses go whizzing by. The irony is that in order to enjoy the natural landscapes within walking distance of our home we would need to drive to get there, thereby making a small contribution to destroying the nature we wish to enjoy.

And much of the nature that is meant to have been preserved in our parks has, in fact, been destroyed. In Frick Park, near the river, there is a small creek (or "run" as they are called in Pittsburgh). It's in a deep ravine that muffles the noises of the city: the traffic, car stereos, motorbike engines, and trains. The forest provides some pleasant shade on summer days, and a cool breeze often blows down the ravine. We would like to spend more time there with our daughter, but the creek has a foul smell because the city has allowed the sewage system to drain into it whenever there are heavy rains (which is quite often in Pittsburgh). The creek is also littered with plastic waste: shopping bags, toys, bottles, and many unidentifiable pieces of trash. I find this situation deeply depressing, and an indictment of the past. We should be able to walk to the park without risking our lives in traffic, sit in the shade, and swim in the creek. It would not have been terribly difficult or costly for previous generations to have preserved these goods, even in urban environments—goods that nearly every generation before ours would have enjoyed without much thought. Now that these goods have been ruined, it will be costly and difficult—albeit not impossible—to resuscitate them.

There are, of course, many other examples of humanity's failures to think and act in future-regarding ways. The earth's life-support system is being threatened by the burning of fossil fuels. We impose public debts on future generations without sufficient thought whether they will benefit from our borrowing. We build nuclear weapons that might destroy us, and nuclear power plants without thinking enough about what we will do with the waste they produce (which will be deadly for tens of thousands of years). We embrace new technologies without thinking enough about how they are likely to reshape our societies and our futures, or how they might (or should) be controlled through regulation. We allow ourselves to be constrained by constitutions that were written by—and for—previous generations. We are willing to spend public money on disaster relief, but not on taking proactive steps to help protect ourselves from disasters. We let our education systems and school buildings crumble, and our health systems falter, even though maintaining and strengthening them would be less costly than rebuilding them in the future. Most wealthy countries have done little (or nothing) to mitigate income inequality even as their economies have grown. And most shameful of all, we have allowed the evils of racism and other forms of prejudice to persist and reproduce themselves every generation.

Many of us think about the future as something that has to be predicted rather than shaped or created through our own individual and collective actions. One reason for this is that most of us have almost no influence over the larger forces that will shape our shared futures: societal drift, general inadvertence, invention (e.g., technological developments), market forces, and the actions of the rich and the powerful. In this book I argue that we can rectify this situation only by making our democratic systems more inclusive and deliberative. This claim challenges the conventional wisdom that democratic systems are structurally myopic because of the short-sighted preferences of voters, the political dynamics of short electoral cycles, the fact that future others who will be affected by our decisions cannot be included in our decision-making processes, and the reality that democratic processes are often captured by powerful actors with dominant short-term objectives. All of these are real barriers to future-regarding collective action, but inclusive and deliberative democratic processes are also the only means we have for making our shared futures together in collectively intentional and mutually accommodating ways.

In March 2020, just after I finished writing this book, the World Health Organization officially declared the COVID-19 outbreak a global pandemic. Within weeks of that declaration the world—our worlds—changed dramatically. Activities that used to be routine, such as going to the grocery store, taking the bus, going to public events, sending our children to school, going for dinner with friends, or flying around to visit people or attend academic conferences, have been changed beyond all recognition or curtailed altogether—along with our expectations for how ordinary life ought to function. It is easy to think of the pandemic as an act of nature: pathogens are naturally occurring, continually evolving, and they have always threatened the survival of humanity and other species. But the COVID-19 pandemic is, sadly, another example of our neglect of the futures we are creating. Consider this statement from Joel E. Cohen that was published in the journal *Science* in 1995, and which now seems disturbingly prescient:

> As more humans contact the viruses and other pathogens of previously remote forests and grasslands, dense urban populations and global travel increase opportunities for infections to spread: The wild beasts of this century and the next are microbial, not carnivorous. (Cohen 1995, p. 341)

The irony is that while urban density is a problem *during* a pandemic, regulating or preventing suburban sprawl would help mitigate the destruction of forests and grasslands, and thereby help keep us away from those pathogen-carrying species that we have so thoughtlessly intruded upon.

The world has struggled to mount a coordinated global response to the COVID-19 pandemic, but governments have acted swiftly—if unevenly—to address the problem by restricting travel, banning large gatherings, forcing businesses to close, and regulating our social interactions. These restrictions may be effective (it is too soon to tell), but it is certain that they have weighed more heavily on some people than others. However stilted and uneven they have been, our collective responses to the pandemic prove that we can act swiftly to address global problems, even when such actions require paying significant near-term costs—which is precisely what must be done to address many of the long-term problems we face.

At the same time, many experts and political leaders have thought about the pandemic as a short-term issue that requires a rapid response. In doing so, they have not thought enough about the potential long-term consequences of the actions we are taking to address the problem. Future generations will have to pay the massive public debts we have incurred during the pandemic. Some governments, such as Hungary's, have used the pandemic as an excuse to further undermine—or eviscerate—democratic institutions. Many millions, or perhaps billions, of people may be thrown into poverty because of the global economic slowdown. Public goods that are needed to fight climate change and other problems, such as urban density and public transportation, may be shunned and underfunded in the future, and social distancing rules threaten to lacerate the fabrics of our collective lives in ways that may be hard to repair. How do we balance the desire to protect people from something like COVID-19 with all the negative long-term consequences associated with whichever actions (or inactions) we take to address the problem? From a democratic perspective, collective decisions about how to balance irreconcilable concerns can only be made legitimate, and thus acceptable, if they are made in adequately inclusive and deliberative ways. The example of COVID-19 thus illustrates one of the central themes of *Future Publics*: we cannot navigate through the present—or through any crisis situations—and get to better futures if we do not have institutional mechanisms for ensuring that public decisions are made and guided by the publics they are meant to serve. Anything less will get us futures that have been created by drift, inadvertence, unchecked market forces, or powerful actors pursuing their own short-term interests and particular (or peculiar) visions of what desirable futures might be like.

If we are honest with ourselves (and we are not very often), we cannot expect humanity to last forever. In *Republic*, Plato makes a distinction between becoming and being. The realm of becoming is where we live, where everything is always changing, improving, or decaying. The realm of being is the world of ideals—and knowledge—where things exist in unchanging forms. Living, as we do, in this world, we are always changing. We are always in the process of dying, for example, even when we are growing into the prime of our lives, just as our political systems are always in the process of improving or decaying (or, more accurately, improving in some respects and decaying in others). Adopting a long-term perspective compels us to admit that this great experiment in living on earth, at least, cannot go on forever. But this conclusion, which must be true, is also beside the point in many respects. Future-regarding action, as I understand it, should be aimed at balancing the legitimate concerns of the present with the potential interests and concerns of the future. This involves striving to make better—healthier, happier, more fun, productive, inquisitive, creative, and loving—lives for people and other species now, without undermining the potential for future others to also enjoy those goods. We need to acknowledge and value the fantastic improbability, variety, and beauty of life as we know it so that we might be compelled to act in ways that make it possible for life to continue for as long as possible, in whatever forms it takes. We have a role to play in this because we now know that humanity has the power to either help preserve or destroy human life—and many other lives—on earth. The human experiment might last for hundreds of thousands of years, achieve great things and, most importantly, allow billions of future others to flourish and enjoy the things we have enjoyed, such as love, friends, family, parenthood, nature, music, literature, philosophical inquiry, or the satisfaction and challenges of creative or competitive pursuits. Or the human experiment may come to an end because of our own conscious or inadvertent, individual and collective actions or inactions. This book is addressed to those who care enough about the future to think and hope that it should be the former and not the latter: we should strive, while we are here, to make futures that are better and not worse for future others, both humans and nonhumans alike.

Michael K. MacKenzie,
Pittsburgh, Pennsylvania
August 2020

Acknowledgements

I could not have written this book without the help, support, feedback, and criticisms of many people. My most heartfelt thanks go to Theresa Webber for her love, support, and encouragement, and for all the sacrifices that she has made for me and for our little family. Our daughter Maude brightens every day with her enthusiasm for life, love, and nature. She has been my lodestar throughout the writing process, even though she was not yet born when I first started this book. I would also like to thank my parents, Ursula and Ken, my sister Kathryn, and all my friends for accepting the fact that this project has, in many ways, monopolized my time and taken me away from them.

I owe a debt of gratitude to all those who have helped me explain, refine, and revise the arguments that I make in *Future Publics*. My PhD supervisor, Mark E. Warren, has provided just the right amount of encouragement and criticism over the years. Alfred Moore has diligently read multiple drafts of every argument in this book, and although I take ownership of any errors or lapses of judgment, our lengthy discussions helped shape my thinking in numerous, untraceable ways. Michael Goodhart has been a wonderful friend, colleague, and mentor. He has provided substantive (and timely) feedback whenever I have requested it, and he has helped guide me through the publication process. I will try to repay him by supporting others as he has supported me. Thanks are also due to the many other mentors that I have had during my time in academia, including, but not limited to, André Bächtiger, André Blais, Joanne Boucher, Fred Cutler, Archon Fung, Joan Grace, Elisabeth Gidengil, Alan M. Jacobs, Christopher Leo, Allen Mills, Jonathan Rose, Jim Silver, Stuart Soroka, and Allan Tupper.

Special thanks are due to those who took the time to participate in my book workshop at the University of Pittsburgh in November 2018: Jonathan Bruno, Stuart Candy, Robert Cavalier, Simone Chambers, Tim Dawson, Michael Goodhart, Jonathan Kuyper, Andrew Lotz, Tamar Malloy, and Celia Paris. Your feedback, suggestions, and thoughtful critiques helped turn my dissertation into a book. Additional thanks go to all my colleagues at the University of Pittsburgh for creating a productive and stimulating intellectual environment. Matt Avina, Rian Litchard, and David McCoy were careful, diligent, and critical research assistants.

I would also like to thank those who organized the academic workshops where the ideas in *Future Publics* were first presented: Gustaf Arrhenius, Iñigo Gonzalez-Ricoy, Axel Gosseries, Michael Morrell, Jón Ólafsson, Maija Setälä, Graham Smith, and Inés Valdez. Special thanks go to Jonathan Boston, Didier Caluwaerts, Sean Finn, Andrew Lotz, Maija Setälä, and Graham Smith for all the conversations we've had about how to make our democratic systems more future-regarding. Your critiques and suggestions have added both substance and style to the final product.

Lastly, I would like to thank Angela Chnapko at Oxford University Press for giving me feedback on my book proposal at the 2016 Association for Political Theory, First Book Manuscript Workshop, and for her support for the project since then.

PART I

CONCEPTUAL BACKGROUND

1
Introduction
The Democratic Myopia Thesis

1.1. Introduction

We often ignore or dismiss the potential interests of our future selves and future others when we make collective decisions. We burn fossil fuels even though doing so is unsustainable and damaging to the earth's life-support systems. We produce nuclear waste that will exist for thousands of years even though we do not know how to store it safely for that long. We build cities that encourage, and often require, people to live in unsustainable ways—to drive everywhere instead of walking, cycling, or using public transportation. We embrace new technologies, such as genetically modified seeds and artificial intelligence, without making future-regarding collective judgments about how these technologies should be used, nurtured, and regulated, or whether they should be permitted. We spend millions of dollars responding to natural disasters, but we typically spend very little to prepare for them (Healy and Malhotra 2009). We produce plastic waste that will not decompose for thousands of years; it is polluting our water systems, our bodies, and killing fish and other animals that we rely on for food. A lot of that waste comes from single-use products such as plastic bags or other packaging materials (Geyer et al. 2017). We are, in effect, willing to harm our future selves, future others, and many other living things for thousands of years in exchange for a few moments of convenience. To add to this, most governments make budgetary and borrowing decisions without adequately considering the potential interests of future people. In the worst-case scenario, we borrow money from future people, including our future selves, to do things that will harm them.

The things that we do—individually and collectively—*will* shape the future. This is an ontological observation. We shape our natural environments and the social, cultural, and political worlds in which we live. We invent new things. We procreate or decide not to. All of our actions (and inactions) will affect the future, but there is something different about the modern period.

Future Publics. Michael K. MacKenzie, Oxford University Press. © Oxford University Press 2021.
DOI: 10.1093/oso/9780197557150.003.0001

Unlike most previous generations, we now know that we have existential power over the future. We have the power to decide whether humanity—and the world—has a future. Karl Jaspers (1961) called this the "new fact." For Jaspers, our existential power over the future is epitomized by the invention of the atomic bomb, which is "novel in essence" because it contains within it the power of self-destruction—"it is now possible for life on earth to be wiped out by human action" (p. 1).

More recently, scientists have argued that we are in a new geological era called the "Anthropocene." As Steffen, Crutzen, and McNeill (2007) explain, in the past, the "human imprint on the environment may have been discernible at local, regional, and even continental scales, but preindustrial humans did not have the technology or organizational capacity to match or dominate the great forces of nature" (p. 614). Today, humanity "is, in one way or another, becoming a self-conscious active agent in the operation of its own life support system" (p. 619). The problem is that while we know our actions might have existential consequences, we do not know how to act in collectively intentional, future-regarding ways to get the futures that we think we might want for our selves and future others.

There is also evidence that the pace of human activities—the rate of social, economic, cultural, technological, political, and environmental change—is increasing. According to Steffen, Crutzen, and McNeill (2007) "the human enterprise" after World War II suddenly experienced a "great acceleration" (p. 617). At this time, human activity and productivity in nearly every field started to increase exponentially: population growth, petroleum consumption, economic development, foreign investment, the number of automobiles, urbanization, water use, the damning of rivers, international travel, communications, and, in general, technological change.

One of the consequences of this "great acceleration" is that each generation is becoming less like the previous one increasingly quickly, and this makes the life experiences of the present different from those of the past and the future (Toffler 1970). In contrast, for most of human history, each generation inhabited a world that was very similar to the one inhabited by the previous generation. Arthur M. Schlesinger (1999), for example, estimates that while modern humans have lived on the earth for only about 800 lifetimes, there has been more scientific and technological change in the last two lifetimes than during all the others put together (p. xii).[1] As Benjamin Barber (1998)

[1] For example, premodern humans used palm-sized stone tools called Acheulean hand axes for more than a million years, and the design of these tools changed very little over that period of time.

has pointed out: "Whilst for thousands of generations life for a cohort of grandchildren roughly resembled life for their grandparents, in our century there is enough change in a decade to confuse people in the fifteen years it takes to grow up" (p. 574). William E. Scheuerman (2004) has called this the "social acceleration of time." Toffler (1970) called it "future shock."

These two observations about the modern period—we are now aware of our own existential power over the future, and the worlds we live in are changing increasingly quickly—make future-regarding collective action both critically important and especially difficult to do. As Schlesinger (1999) has observed, the "law of acceleration hurtles us into an inscrutable future" (p. xiii). The social acceleration of time makes it harder to understand what the long-term consequences of our actions are likely to be—and the rapid pace of change in so many different areas of human life means that we have to think holistically about how we are, or might be, affecting the future by our mere presence in the world.

There is something intuitively problematic—something deeply wrong or unjust—with the situation that we are in. We know that what we do will affect and possibly harm the future, but we find it difficult to act in collectively intentional, future-regarding ways. We have cognitive biases against the future—we tend to think more about our immediate needs and less about the potential interests of our future selves and future others (e.g., Kahneman 2011; Caney 2016)—but most of us also care about the future. We worry about own futures and the futures that we will, or might, leave for others (e.g., Scheffler 2013, 2018). Many of us want to make the future better but we do not know how to do so.

What is particularly disturbing is that some of our most cherished institutions—our democratic systems—appear to be part of the problem, not part of the solution. Elected officials rarely look past the next election, or the one after that, to address problems that will have long-term consequences. Voters are often focused on their own near-term interests and concerns: they may be aware of longer-term problems, and they may wish to fix them, but when forced to choose, they are often unwilling or unable to forgo near-term benefits for future potential gains—especially future benefits that they might

Indeed, according to Matt Ridley (2010) the "bodies and brains of the creatures that made Acheulean hand axes changed faster than their tools" (p. 49). This seems incredible from a modern perspective—but historically, minor, minimal, or imperceptible technological and cultural change between adjacent generations is more the rule than the exception.

not live long enough to enjoy. On this account, democratic systems are functionally short-sighted. Democracies tend to focus on the present not when they are working badly but when they are working well: when they are sufficiently responsive to the immediate needs and demands of affected publics. This argument, which I call the "democratic myopia thesis," is a sort of conventional wisdom: it is one of those things that many scholars and pundits take for granted as a truth about democracy without subjecting it to adequate critical scrutiny.

In this book, I aim to rethink the democratic myopia thesis. I do not conduct empirical analyses to determine whether existing democratic regimes are more or less short-sighted than authoritarian alternatives. Instead, I challenge the assumptions that have been made by proponents of the democratic myopia thesis about what democracy is and what it might be.[2] Democracies *are* often bad at making long-term decisions, but democracy—and in particular deliberative democracy—is also the only means we have for making our shared worlds, and thus our futures, together. In this book, I seek to articulate a deliberative democratic theory of future-regarding collective action that focuses on the world-making, and thus future-making, potentialities of democratic decision-making processes. It is true that our existing democratic systems typically fail to adequately empower us—as both individuals and collectivities—to make the futures we think we might want, but we nevertheless need inclusive, deliberative democratic processes to make our shared futures in collectively intentional, mutually accommodating ways.

In this chapter, I outline the democratic myopia thesis as I understand it. Although it is often presented as a single argument, there are at least four interrelated but conceptually distinct claims that have been made by proponents of the thesis. The first draws on the observation that voters are often short-sighted. The second emphasizes the political dynamics of short electoral cycles. The third concerns the fact that future others who do not yet exist cannot be included in our decision-making processes, even though they will be affected by our decisions. The fourth deals with "democratic capture"—or the undue influence of powerful minorities, such as economic elites, who may have dominant short-term interests and the power to pursue them at the expense of the longer-term interests of society more generally. Scholars and pundits often fail to make distinctions between these different

[2] For an experimental test of some of the theories develop in *Future Publics* see MacKenzie and Caluwaerts (2021).

components of the democratic myopia thesis, but it is important to do so because each component of the thesis raises its own set of challenges and is associated with different possible solutions to the problem.

In assessing the democratic myopia thesis, many scholars have come to the conclusion that democracies are incapable of effectively dealing with long-term problems such as climate change. In response, some have argued in favour of authoritarian alternatives to democracy (e.g., Bell 2016; Heilbroner 1991; Ophuls 2011; Ophuls and Boyan 1992; Randers 2012; Shearman and Smith 2007). Theses scholars argue that authoritarian rulers will be better able to impose unpopular but necessary near-term costs and restrictions on the actions of otherwise unwilling publics and powerful economic actors.

I accept certain components of the democratic myopia thesis, but I reject the idea that authoritarian governments are likely to get us the futures we might want. Authoritarian responses to the democratic myopia thesis would constitute an abdication of our collective, future-making capacities. Authoritarian leaders would be empowered to make our futures *for* us rather than *with* us. But modern societies—and the futures that we will create—are impossibly complex. The present is diverse, and the future will be too. As such, it is not clear what we should do now or how we should respond to any specific public problems with potential long-term effects or consequences. We will need inclusive, deliberative democratic processes to make judgments about what we should or should not do as collectivities, precisely because there will be many legitimate but potentially conflicting concerns associated with any course of action (or inaction). It strains credulity to think that any one individual or set of supposedly superior rulers might be capable of identifying the appropriate ends of a society *as a whole*. The only sources of information about the appropriate ends of a society or group of people are those people themselves (e.g., Saward 1998, Chap. 2). If this is the case, it is implausible to imagine a small, and necessarily unrepresentative, group of authoritarian rulers making desirable futures for us: futures that adequately accommodate all the various and often conflicting interests and concerns of both existing and future people. Fortunately, there are, I argue, democratic responses to each component of the democratic myopia thesis. In this book I argue that we need to think politically—and not just philosophically—in order to properly understand the challenges of acting in future-regarding ways; and we need to act democratically—and deliberatively—if we hope to get the futures we want for ourselves and future others.

1.2. The Democratic Myopia Thesis

1.2.1. Myopic Voters

The most common, and widely cited, component of the democratic myopia thesis has to do with the idea that voters are functionally short-sighted: voters, and people generally, are primarily concerned with their most immediate needs and only tangentially or abstractly concerned with the future. This is a problem because voters are the ultimate source of power and legitimacy in democratic systems. As Edward Tufte (1978) has argued, there is, in democratic systems, "a bias toward policies with immediate highly visible benefits and deferred, hidden costs—myopic policies for myopic voters" (p. 143).

Although it may be possible to encourage individuals to think more carefully about the future, this tendency to discount or ignore the future is seen as a largely immutable component of the human condition. It is grounded in our cognitive psychology, and it is not therefore *just* an epiphenomenon of our cultural practices, political institutions, economic systems, or philosophical or religious beliefs.[3] Dennis Thompson (2010), for example, emphasizes these aspects of the human condition in his description of the democratic myopia thesis. "Democracy" he explains "is partial toward the present. Most citizens tend to discount the future, and to the extent that the democratic process responds to their demands, the laws it produces tend to neglect future generations. The democratic process itself amplifies this natural human tendency" (p. 17).

If there is a "natural human tendency" to favour the near term over the long term, democratic systems will tend to be short-sighted; not when they are working poorly but when they are working well—when they are adequately responsive to the immediate demands, needs, and concerns of affected publics. In democratic systems, leaders who want to maintain power will thus face strong incentives to adopt policies that have demonstrable net benefits within the next one or two electoral cycles, and similarly strong incentives to discount or ignore future potential problems if fixing those problems would require imposing near-term costs on unwilling publics. As Jørgen Randers (2012) argues: "The short time horizon is a serious challenge if society needs to spend now in order to avoid a problem in the distant

[3] See Hershfield (2011) for a concise but detailed review of the literature on future discounting and cognitive psychology.

future. Short-termism works actively against wise policy in such situations. And since short-termism tends to dominate among the voter mind-set, it also tends to dominate the mind-set of politicians" (p. 165).

If voters were less myopic—if they were sometimes willing to pay near-term costs for future potential benefits—elected politicians would be able and incentivized to pre-emptively address future potential problems. But, as the argument goes, people are not like that. Most voters, most of the time, will favour their own immediate needs and concerns over those of their future selves and future others.

1.2.2. Short Electoral Cycles

A related problem—and the second component of the democratic myopia thesis—has to do with the fact that democracy, as Matravers and Meyer (2011) point out, "is government *pro tempore*." In democratic systems, "rulers exercise power for a limited period of time, after which they stand for re-election and reappointment, or retire from office" (p. 19). When representative democracy is working well, voters can exchange one set of ruling elites for another, if they wish to do so, every election cycle. Regular elections help keep rulers accountable and responsive to the concerns of affected publics, but they can also make it difficult for elected governments to make credible long-term commitments. Ruling elites often have shared worldviews and similar material interests, but they do not always agree on policy objectives, and they have strong incentives to distinguish themselves from each other during election campaigns. When rulers are regularly replaced by other elites in elections, there is a danger that the policies adopted by one government will be overturned or dismantled by the next. Given these dynamics, it may be difficult for democratic societies to maintain long-term policies, such as carbon taxes, long enough for those policies to do any good. The threat of policy oscillation—or policy disjunctures—can also make it more difficult to convince political actors to support long-term policies in the first place. Those who would, in principle, support long-term policy initiatives may be unwilling to do so if there is a credible threat that those policies will be abandoned by future governments. It is one thing to spend personal, political, and public resources on future benefits; it is quite another thing to spend those resources on future benefits that might never be realized.

The *short electoral cycles* and *myopic voter* components of the democratic myopia thesis are related to each other in practical terms, but they are, in fact, conceptually distinct. In order for elected leaders to act in future-regarding ways, it will be necessary for them to obtain support from their voting blocks, and this can be difficult if voters are, generally speaking, myopic. The regularity of elections—and the ever-present possibility that one set of rulers will be replaced by another—creates additional complications for the future-minded politician. It is not enough to convince voters to support long-term policy initiatives; to engage in effective long-term action, it is also necessary to ensure that public support for long-term policies is maintained as circumstances, needs, expectations, governments, political alliances, and even the individuals who make up a polity change over time.

In short, the political dynamics of short electoral cycles combined with the (usually) myopic views of voters makes it difficult for democratic societies to engage in future-regarding collective actions. This is a fundamental challenge for democratic societies because it suggests that we cannot have good (i.e., responsive and accountable) democratic systems if we want to solve long-term problems. Our democratic systems will be short-sighted *when* they are working well: when governments are regularly replaced, when elites are kept accountable, and when the system as a whole is responsive to the changing needs and expectations of affected publics.

1.2.3. The Exclusion of Future Others

A third, and often neglected, component of the democratic myopia thesis has to do with the fact that future others who do not yet exist cannot be included in our decision-making processes, even though they will be affected by our decisions. Given this situation, the potential interests of future others may be ignored, dismissed, or trampled upon with relative impunity by contemporary political actors. As Tremmel explains:

> If only [those] future individuals, who are born in the next 200 years, could vote on energy policies, this would create a huge majority which would facilitate a quick shift to renewable sources of energy. If only these future individuals could vote on financial policy, public debt would be significantly lower than today. This fundamental dilemma of democracy leads

> to a preference for the present and to oblivion with regard to the future. (Tremmel 2006, p. 189)[4]

Democratic systems are supposed to be inclusive and responsive to affected interests, and the unavoidable exclusion of future others violates this ideal (e.g., Goodin 2007; Tännsjö 2007). In other situations, previously excluded others, such as poor people, women, and racial or religious minorities, have been enfranchised to ensure that their interests are not ignored or misrepresented in collective decision-making processes. But future others, who do not yet exist, cannot be enfranchised. The exclusion of future others is a violation of the democratic ideal of empowered inclusion, but it is also an ontological problem that cannot be fixed. If empowered inclusion is the *only* means we have for ensuring that political actors do not ignore the interests of those who would otherwise be excluded, it is hard to imagine how we might make our democratic systems—or any political system for that matter—more responsive to the potential interests and concerns of future others. Those who favour authoritarian responses to the democratic myopia thesis have argued that we will have to train an elite class of rulers to more carefully consider the interests of future others and empower those rulers to impose unpopular policies on current publics (e.g., Bell 2016; Ophuls 2011; Ophuls and Boyan 1992; Shearman and Smith 2007). To my knowledge, no one has yet proposed a democratic solution to the *exclusion of future others* problem.

1.2.4. Democratic Capture

The fourth component of the democratic myopia thesis is different from the others. According to the first two arguments, democracies will be short-sighted when they are working well: when they are sufficiently responsive to the expressed preferences of voters, and when there is a real possibility that rulers will be replaced in elections. The third component of the democratic myopia thesis—the exclusion of future others—is an acknowledgment that democracy cannot approximate its own ideals in practice. The fourth

[4] Dennis Thompson (2005) has expressed similar concerns: "Democracies are systematically biased in favor of the present. In giving greater weight to the present, they neglect the future. From the perspective of the future, their neglect appears as the dead hand of the past. The claims of future popular sovereigns are thus systematically undervalued because future citizens do not have a voice in the present decisions that will affect them" (p. 246).

component of the democratic myopia thesis—the problem of democratic capture—is different because it is predicated on a practical problem: in practice most democracies have been captured by stable, persistent minorities (e.g., Schweickart 2011). This problem is relevant to the democratic myopia thesis if stable, persistent minorities (such as economic elites) have dominant short-term interests that they wish to pursue against the longer-term interests of society more generally.

There are at least two versions of the *democratic capture* argument. One has to do with the unequal influence that older generations, as a group, typically possess in democratic systems when compared to younger generations. The concern is that older people will favour the near term over the long term because they know that they will not be personally affected in 30 or 40 years by the collective decisions (or non-decisions) that we make today. In practice, older generations do have more influence in democratic systems: they tend to vote in higher proportions than younger voters, they occupy more positions of power, and as a group they control more resources than younger cohorts. Older generations also tend to know their interests well and often better than younger people who are still finding their way in the world and working to establish themselves. Given these dynamics, there is, as Dennis Thompson (2010) argues, "a tendency in most modern democracies today to favor the older age group. Because this age group are more numerous, and also able to exercise greater political influence than younger groups, they are privileged in law and public policy" (p. 19).[5]

Young people do, in fact, occupy fewer positions of power in our societies, and they are underrepresented in our elected legislatures (e.g., Bidadanure 2016), but this version of the *democratic capture* argument depends on an empirical claim that is not easy to establish: that older generations, as a group, are likely to pursue their own short-term interests at the expense of the longer-term interests of society. Van Parijs (1998) has argued that there is "at least some *prima facie* evidence showing that age-related self-interest affects voting behaviour" (p. 298). But Van Parijs does not provide substantive evidence to support this claim. Older people will not be personally affected by the long-term costs of our collective actions (or inactions), but this does not mean that they do not have future-regarding preferences or lifetime transcending interests (e.g., Thompson 2009).[6]

[5] Van Parjis (1998) and Tremmel (2006) make similar arguments.

[6] The available evidence on this point is mixed and nuanced. Button (1992), for example, found that districts in Florida with higher concentrations of older voters were more likely to oppose education-funding tax increases in referendum votes. In contrast, Berkman and Plutzer (2004)

Another version of the *democratic capture* argument has to do with the influence of economic elites. Wealthy actors and corporations have considerably more influence on democratic systems when compared to non-elites (e.g., Winters and Page 2009). The wealthy routinely convert their economic resources into political influence through lobbying, philanthropy, campaign contributions, media ownership, and support for political action committees (PACs). Wealthy actors support political candidates who will advance their interests, or they become elected officials themselves (e.g., Dahl 1998; Mansbridge 2012; Mayer 2016; Schweickart 2011). Democratic systems that have been captured by economic elites will be rendered short-sighted if those elites have dominant short-term interests that they wish to pursue over the longer-term interests of society more generally. Consider, for example, this statement from John Feffer, who is the director of *Foreign Policy in Focus*:

> Our political and economic institutions have proven singularly incapable of dealing with such long-term problems as climate change, income inequality, and the proliferation of dangerous weapons. Politicians are subject to the short-term interests of lobbying interests (coal companies, for instance). And market actors have helped to exacerbate these problems through unsustainable economic growth, increased salaries for CEOs, and ramped up markets for profitable arms transfers. (Feffer 2013)[7]

found that higher concentrations of older voters represent a potential source of support for education funding, except in areas with higher concentrations of new (or transient) older voters with fewer ties of loyalty to their local communities. In laboratory experiments, Read and Read (2004) found that "older people discount [the future] more than younger ones, and that middle aged people discount less than either group" (p. 24). Others have found that individuals tend to become more future-regarding, not less, as they grow older (Aspinwall 2005; Steinberg et al. 2009). Krosnick et al. (2006) found that older people are less likely to think that global warming is a problem, and younger people are more likely to support specific government efforts to mitigate the effects of climate change (pp. 25–26). Nevertheless, people of different generations appear to have similar policy preferences on a range of other issues that have differential effects on generations, including Medicare, education spending, and public pension plans (e.g., Fisher 2008; Jacobs and Matthews 2012; Rhodebeck 1993). In short, although there is plenty of evidence that older people have more power in democratic (and non-democratic) systems, it is not clear that older people are more myopic than those in younger generations.

[7] Shearman and Smith (2007) make a similar argument: "In the United States, intense lobbying by dedicated people with ready access to government because of financial contributions to election campaigns has thwarted the implementation of new environmental laws, neutered existing laws, and sabotaged international agreements. . . . Indeed, most so-called Western societies are not democracies as such but plutocracies, societies ruled by the wealthy" (p. 91).

Unlike the "older voter" version of the *democratic capture* argument—which is, at best, predicated on conjectures about how some older people *might* think about the future—the "powerful economic actors" argument rests on firmer foundations. As Jørgen Randers points out, there are good reasons to think that economic elites and market actors will have powerful incentives to favour the near term over the long term.

> The market uses a discount rate of 10% per year (or more) when comparing costs now with benefits in the future. This means that a benefit that lies twenty years ahead will be valued at one-tenth of its real value. In other words, a problem twenty years in the future will be worth solving only if the cost of the solution is less than one-tenth of the value saved. It comes as no surprise to those who know economics that it is "cost efficient" to allow the world to collapse from climate damage, as long as the collapse is more than forty years into the future. The net present value of reducing emissions and saving the world is lower than the net present value of business as usual. It is cheaper to push the world over the cliff than to try to save it. (Randers 2012, p. 165)

Randers goes on to argue that long-term problems such as climate change and poverty reduction cannot be solved by the market itself or by market regulations in democratic systems.

> The reason is obvious: the benefits of climate stabilization and poverty alleviation are too far in the future for businesses to find it profitable to invest in the project today. Little will happen unless someone—and this is most likely the state—enters the picture and changes the conditions under which the market works. The most obvious state intervention would be to introduce new legislation or pricing of externalities as necessary. . . . But new legislation requires a majority in the legislature, at least in democratic society. And since broad-scoped legislation is certain to bother some stakeholder group in the short term, it often fails to be passed, even though it would benefit the majority in the long term. (Randers 2012, p. 166)

It is not necessary to assume that economic elites, or profit-seeking businesses, are *always* short-sighted in order to find this version of the democratic myopia thesis persuasive. As Randers (2012) points out: "Many progressive firms would welcome government initiatives that create even and profitable playing fields in new arenas, for example, in the form of all-encompassing carbon taxes or compulsory water fees" (p. 165). It is also the case that certain types of businesses might favour public policies that produce benefits for them over the long term while distributing costs more widely (MacKenzie 2016a). The introduction of a publicly funded healthcare system in the United States, for example, would threaten the interests of private insurance providers, but it would also relieve other businesses of many of the long-term costs of providing health insurance for their employees.

Nevertheless, profit-seeking businesses are, by definition, interested in making money over the near term. Entrepreneurs often strategize about the long-term futures of their businesses, but money has to be made along the way if a business is to survive. If government regulations threaten to reduce profits over the near term, economic elites can actively, and often successfully, oppose those regulations by lobbying elected officials, depriving them of campaign funds, and funding opposition candidates. And certain types of businesses—those that are potentially mobile but employ a lot of people—can threaten to move jobs elsewhere if governments adopt regulations that would cost them money in the near term (Lindblom 1982). These "investment strikes," as Schweickart (2011) calls them, can put considerable pressure on governments to refrain from aggressive regulation because elected officials typically do not want to be responsible for economic downturns and job losses. It is well-established in political science that incumbents who preside over job losses and faltering economies are more likely to lose power (e.g., Lewis-Beck and Stegmaier 2019).

This version of the democratic myopia thesis raises larger questions about the interdependency of democracy, capitalism, and short-termism. Some scholars have argued that we can make capitalism more sustainable over the long term by more aggressively taxing actions that have negative externalities, such as the extraction and use of fossil fuels, while subsidizing actions that have positive externalities, such as investments in renewable energies (e.g., Hawken et al. 1999; Speth 2008). But these arguments typically fail to account for at least two problems that may be inherent to capitalism. First, it is not clear that we can have capitalist-democracies without democracy being captured by economic elites. Capitalism creates conditions for democratic capture because it generates economic inequality through capital accumulation. There are mechanisms, such as progressive taxation and unionization, that can help mitigate economic inequality, but inequalities are nevertheless inherent in capitalist systems because economic actors must be free—or as free as possible—to make as much money as they can. If economic inequality is a feature of capitalism, capitalist-democracies will be in danger of being captured by economic elites. If this is the case, it is not clear that we will be able to regulate capitalist markets in the ways that proponents of sustainable capitalism think we should (as Randers points out in the earlier quote). In practice, although some democracies have better environmental regulations than others, none have managed to create truly sustainable market economies (e.g., Fiorino 2018).

Second, capitalism may be fundamentally unsustainable because it requires perpetual economic growth: the system—and all the publicly traded companies within it—must either grow or die. If publicly traded companies do not make more money each year, their shareholders will sell their stock and invest in other companies that are growing. This is a problem for two reasons. First, many of our most pressing long-term problems—the destruction of ecosystems, mass extinctions, the depletion of non-renewable resources, ever-increasing carbon emissions, the production of plastic waste, and growth in the human population—track the exponential growth of the global economy over the last 200 years. In 1820 global GDP was worth about $0.7 billion in today's dollars. By 2018 it was worth $78 billion. During the same period, the world's human population grew from 1 billion to 7.6 billion, and energy use increased "from 250 million metric tons of oil equivalent in 1820 to 800 million in 1990 and to 10,000 million metric tons in 2000" (Gamble 2019, p. 99). Second, the very idea of perpetual economic growth is unsustainable. As Kenneth Boulding famously said: "Only a madman or an economist could believe that exponential growth can go on forever in a finite world."[8]

If democracy and capitalism are inherently intertwined, and capitalism is unsustainable over the long term, there may be little that we can do within a democratic framework to fix the most pressing long-term problems that we face, many of which have their root in the market imperatives of capitalism. It is on these grounds that scholars such as Bell (2016), Shearman and Smith (2007), and Randers (2012) have argued that democracy is inherently short-sighted. But perhaps they have the wrong target in mind: they identify long-term problems, such as climate change, that are not being addressed, and they blame the partnership between democracy and capitalism instead of questioning the inevitability of that partnership. It is true that modern

[8] Quoted in Schweickart (2011, p. 3).

democracy has thrived only in capitalist systems, but many scholars—including Marx—have argued that democracy is limited and constrained by capitalism rather than enhanced by or dependent upon it.[9]

Capitalism and democracy are, in fact, conceptually distinct. The former is an economic system predicated on the private ownership of productive resources, competitive markets, and wage labour. The latter is a political system in which power, or at least some forms of power, are distributed as widely and equally as possible within a particular polity. In principle, democratic processes may be used to give whole societies some control over both political decisions and economic ones, such as how the productive resources of society should be used and distributed. Schweickart (2011) has argued that in a "true" democracy—which he defines as "a system in which a universal electorate is reasonably well informed, active, and unobstructed by a privileged minority class" (p. 153)[10]—the electorate would be empowered to challenge the basic institutions of capitalism.

In summary, the *democratic capture* argument identifies a practical problem, not a fundamental one: democratic systems have, in practice, often been captured by stable, persistent minorities with dominant short-term interests and the power to pursue those interests against the longer-term interest of society (or the world) more generally. Unlike the other versions of the democratic myopia thesis, this is not a story about why democracies are short-sighted when they are working well; it is a story about why they are short-sighted when they are working poorly—which is to say, when they are captured by stable, persist minorities (such as economic elites) with dominant short-term interests.

1.2.5. Putting the Democratic Myopia Thesis Together

In practice, each of the four components of the democratic myopia thesis—myopic voters, short electoral cycles, the exclusion of future others, and democratic capture—work in conjunction with each other to render democratic systems functionally short-sighted. Any effort to address one aspect of the

[9] See, for example, Harrington (1981) on Marx's view of democracy.

[10] Edward Bernstein (1899/1988) provides a similar definition of democracy. "We shall come much nearer to the definition if we express ourselves negatively, and define democracy as an absence of class government, as the indication of a social condition where a political privilege belongs to no one class as opposed to the whole community" (p. 80).

problem (such as democratic capture) will do little to solve the problem if other causes of short-termism (such as myopic voters) are not simultaneously addressed. And it is not clear how, or whether, each part of the problem can be addressed. It may be possible to encourage some voters or political leaders to more seriously consider the future, or at least *their* futures, some of the time, but it is probably not possible to encourage all voters to become more future-regarding. Likewise, it is not clear how we can prevent policy disjunctures within a democratic framework. Any political system or institution that does not regularly exchange one set of rulers for another—or at least support the possibility of doing so—should not be considered democratic. And the problem of the exclusion of future others is an ontological one: it is not a normative problem that can be fixed through practical solutions like the extension of the franchise.

When presented in these terms, the democratic myopia thesis is unsettlingly persuasive. There are good reasons to think that democratic systems are both fundamentally and functionally short-sighted, but this conclusion challenges deeply held convictions that many of us have about the normative desirability and political legitimacy of democracy, especially compared to any authoritarian alternatives that might be available. For many of us, the democratic myopia thesis is hard to accept because it would appear to force us to choose between our normative commitments to democracy and the long-term prospects for humanity. When faced with this choice we might prefer to ignore the problem, which is an option—at least for the time being—because the worst consequences of democratic myopia will not affect us until some unspecified time in the future. Others have argued that we must acknowledge that democratic systems cannot deal with pressing—or existential—problems with long-term consequences, and we should therefore consider alternative political systems if we care about the future.

The idea that we will need authoritarian governments to solve temporally complex problems such as climate change is surprisingly common. James Lovelock, for example, has argued that the climate crisis should be likened to a war. "Even the best democracies agree that when a major war approaches, democracy must be put on hold for the time being. I have a feeling that climate change may be an issue as severe as a war. It may be necessary to put democracy on hold for a while" (quoted in Fiorino 2018, p. 1). Randers (2012) is even more categorical in his rejection of democracy: "I do not believe it will be possible to convince people to forgo potential consumption growth. Democratic society will pursue short-term satisfaction and choose their leaders accordingly. Thus success in limiting consumption will require an element of benevolent authoritarianism" (p. 27). Shearman and Smith (2007) do not think that "an element" of authoritarianism will be sufficient. On their account, unless the environmental crisis can be "resolved to preserve a sustainable world there is no case for the continuation of liberal democracy or nation states. There should be one government, and our argument [in this book] would make this government authoritarian" (p. 83).

Others look to specific examples of authoritarian governments such as China or Singapore. Daniel A. Bell (2016) is skeptical about China's environmental record, but he argues that China is better positioned to deal with climate change than most democratic governments. As he explains: "I do not know if China will be able to develop an environmentally sustainable way of life, but so long as it does not adopt a democratic system that privileges the interest of the voting community at the cost of future generations, that's where I'd place my bet" (p. 54).[11]

Others have argued that the climate crisis—or other crises such as overpopulation—will create circumstances that are favourable to the development of authoritarianism. As Heilbroner argues:

> It is customary to recognize, but to deplore, the authoritarian tendencies within civil society, especially on the part of those who, like myself, are the beneficiaries of the freedoms of minimally authority-ridden rule. Yet, candor compels me to suggest that the passage through the gantlet ahead may be possible only under governments capable of rallying obedience far more effectively than would be possible in a democratic setting. (Heilbroner 1991, p. 134)

In Heilbroner's view, authoritarianism is not desirable, per se, but it may be forced upon us as the only viable option in a crisis situation. Mark Beeson (2010) and Wainwright and Mann (2013) have made similar arguments.[12]

[11] In unguarded moments, elected politicians have sometimes expressed similar sentiments. Consider this statement made by Vancouver's mayor Gregor Robertson after he returned from a trip to China in 2010: "You can be critical of a lot of regimes around the world, and you can question how worthwhile democracy is in a lot of countries right now which are, frankly, ignoring the biggest crisis in the history of our species which is climate change. That's where you see the Chinese government taking radical dramatic action in investing in turning the ship around. And you do not see that in Western governments right now, democratically elected, and that's because they're afraid. And that's not serving the greater interests of society" (quoted in Bula, September 13, 2010).

[12] As Wainwright and Mann (2013) argue: "If climate science is even half-right in its forecasts, the liberal mode of democracy—even in its idealized Rawlsian or Habermasian formulations—is at best too slow, at worst a devastating distraction" (p. 9). But like Heilbroner (1991), Wainwright and

Likewise, Ophuls and Boyan (1992) argue that extreme resource scarcities will require restrictions on consumption that are more severe than would be appropriate during times of comparative abundance. They worry that democracies will not be capable of imposing sufficiently strict restrictions on themselves, primarily because voters are not well-positioned to recognize and understand the severity and complexity of problems like climate change or the consequences of resource depletion. The solution that Ophuls and Boyan propose is Platonic: they envision a society controlled and directed by wise, and ideally well-meaning, experts or technocrats who are insulated from the ill-informed opinions, wishes, whims, and short-term concerns of ordinary people. As they explain, an ecologically sustainable "steady-state" society may

> require, if not a class of ecological guardians, then at least a class of ecological mandarins who possess the esoteric knowledge needed to run it well. Whatever its level of material affluence, the steady-state society will not only be ostensibly more authoritarian and less democratic than the industrial society of today . . . but it may also be more oligarchic as well, with full participation in the political process restricted to those who possess the ecological and other competencies necessary to make prudent decisions. (Ophuls and Boyan 1992, p. 215)[13]

In more general terms, authoritarian responses to the democratic myopia thesis proceed in four steps: (1) there is a normative claim that we should not disregard or dismiss the potential interests of the future; (2) there is a set of empirical observations that democratic systems are short-sighted in practice and biased against the potential interests of the future; (3) there is an inferential claim that, given the evidence that democracies are often bad at making long-term decisions, they are, in fact, incapable of acting in future-regarding

Mann (2013) do not favour authoritarian regimes. Instead, they argue that authoritarianism is what we might get as the climate crisis advances and as powerful interests try to protect themselves. They also argue that it is possible to imagine non-hegemonic, anti-state forms of democracy emerging in response to the climate crisis, although they do not see that as the most likely scenario.

[13] Indeed, Ophuls and Boyan (1992) draw explicit connections between their ideas and Plato's, arguing that the "emerging large, highly developed, complex technological civilization operating at or very near the ecological margin, appears to fit Plato's premises more and more closely, foreshadowing the necessity of rule by a class of Platonic guardians, the 'priesthood of responsible technologists' who alone know how to run the spaceship" (p. 210). This theme is continued in Ophuls's (2011) book *Plato's Revenge: Politics in the Age of Ecology* and in Shearman and Smith (2007, see, esp., Chap. 9: "Plato's Revenge").

ways; and (4) there is a normative conclusion that we need less democracy if we care about the future. I accept the first two steps of this argument: we should not disregard or dismiss the potential interests of the future, and, empirically speaking, the democracies we have are often short-sighted. My intervention is to challenge the last two steps of the argument: democracies are incapable of acting in future-regarding ways, and we therefore need less democracy if we care about the future.

Before summarizing the arguments that I make in this book, it is important to acknowledge that there are a number of scholars who, like me, accept certain components of the democratic myopia thesis but reject the idea that authoritarian alternatives would be better. These scholars have argued that democratic systems might be reformed in various ways that would help mitigate harmful short-termism (e.g., Boston 2017; Caney 2016; Dator 1981; Ekeli 2005, 2009; Jones et al. 2018; Smith 2019; Tremmel 2015; Thompson 2005, 2010, 2016; Tonn 1991, 1996).

It is also important to acknowledge that despite the empirical evidence that democracies have poorly managed temporally complex problems such as a climate change, existing democracies have, in fact, done marginally better than authoritarian regimes in responding to the climate crisis (e.g., Hanusch 2018). Fiorino, for example, argues that there is, on balance,

> a compelling case to be made on behalf of democracies. They hold too many advantages in terms of being able to make the required choices and supply the needed qualities of governance. They are less corrupt, foster more innovation, respond better to public needs, engage globally, are better at learning across different levels of government and internationally, and encourage longer-term thinking than occurs in authoritarian regimes. Democracies are preferable on so many normative and practical grounds that establishing a case against them is all but impossible. (Fiorino 2018, p. 113)

At the same time, Fiorino readily admits that no democracies have done enough to address climate change.

In this book, I move beyond debates about democracy and climate change to focus on the challenges of future-regarding collective action more generally. Climate change is one of the most pressing problems we face, but there are many other temporally complex issues, such as disaster preparedness, budget deficits, plastics waste, transportation planning, nuclear proliferation, the storage of nuclear waste, income and wealth inequality, and the generational reproductions of racism and other prejudices, which have not been particularly well managed in authoritarian or democratic regimes. I argue that in addition to being less corrupt (or corruptible), potentially more innovative, more responsive to public needs, and more willing to engage globally, democracies—or, rather, inclusive and deliberative democratic processes—have a number of other features that can help support rather than hinder future-regarding collective action. Effective democratic systems aim to distribute influence as widely as possible, thus giving whole societies the power to make their shared worlds together. But if democracy is a world-making activity, it is also a future-making activity—a point that has been largely neglected by both proponents and critics of the democratic myopia thesis.[14]

I also argue that there are democratic mechanisms that can (or might) help us navigate the short-term dynamics associated with each component of the democratic myopia thesis—even those that have to do with ontological limits such as the exclusion of future others. My primary claim is the following: despite the short-term dynamics associated with electoral democracy, inclusive, deliberative democratic processes are, in fact, the only means we have for making our shared futures together in collectively intentional, mutually accommodating ways. I am not convinced that we *will* make our futures together in sufficiently deliberative ways, but I am convinced that it is what we need to do to get the futures that we think we might want for ourselves and future others.

1.3. Overview of the Book

The book is organized into three parts. Part I—which includes this chapter—lays the conceptual groundwork for the arguments that I make in the rest of the book. In Chapter 2, I discuss and define the terms and concepts that form the basis of a deliberative theory of future-regarding collective action. In Chapter 3, I challenge the idea that we should think about intergenerational relations in primarily justice-based terms. I do not think it is possible—or normatively desirable—to find a "correct" theory of intergenerational justice

[14] It should be acknowledged that theorists of "anticipatory democracy" were interested the future-making potentialities of democracy, even though most of the projects they developed did not empower democratic publics to make future-regarding collective choices or policy decisions (see, Bezold 1978; Toffler 1970; and Section 2.2.6).

that would be applicable to *all* people at *all* times. What we should do (now) for the future is not a question that can be answered definitively—or in purely abstract or philosophical terms—because answers to this question will depend on the particular circumstances that individuals and collectivities find themselves in, and on what past political actors have or have not done. Instead of searching for a "correct" theory of intergenerational justice, we should, as a matter of principle and practice, seek to strike a balance between the legitimate concerns of the present and the potential interests of the future as we understand them. But judgments about how to strike this balance should be made in inclusive deliberative arenas and not formulated (or "discovered") by philosophers working in isolation from affected publics. This normative claim—that we should try to strike a balance between our own concerns and those of the future—is predicated only on the assumption that we should care about how our actions might affect the future. Those who do not share this normative commitment—that we should care about the future—may be unmoved by the arguments in this book. Those who do share this commitment, however, do not need to share any deeper convictions about what intergenerational justice requires.

Part II—which includes Chapters 4, 5, and 6—outlines a deliberative theory of future-regarding action. These chapters form the core of my critique of the democratic myopia thesis. In Chapter 4, I argue that the thesis is predicated on an overly narrow account of democracy, according to which existing, probably myopic, preferences are largely unproblematically aggregated to produce collective outcomes. When democracy works that way, collective decisions *are* often short-sighted—dismissing or ignoring the potential interests of the future. In theory, however, democratic processes should involve both shaping and registering preferences, opinions, expectations, and interests. Where this is the case, democratic processes—such as deliberation—might be used to encourage or incentivize political actors to more seriously consider the future when making decisions. In Chapter 4, I develop two sets of arguments along these lines: one that responds to the *myopic voter* version of the democratic myopia thesis, and another that responds to the exclusion (or non-presence) of future others problem.

In Chapter 5, I make three sets of arguments to support my claim that we need inclusive deliberative processes to shape the future in collectively intentional, mutually accommodative ways. In the first section of the chapter, I argue that we need inclusive democratic processes to avoid futures that favour the interests of some groups of people over others. In the second section, I argue that we need deliberative processes to shape our shared futures in collectively intentional ways: we need to be able to talk to ourselves about what we are doing and where we want to get to in the future. In the third section, I argue that effective deliberative practices can help collectivities strike the right balance between steadfastness and flexibility, a balance needed to reach future goals. When political actors are required to publicly explain and justify their decisions to other empowered actors who might disagree, it will be difficult for them to change course without good reasons for doing so—or, at least, without reasons that are plausibly acceptable to others who might oppose change. At the same time, it will be difficult for political actors in effective deliberative environments to defend and maintain outmoded means or collective objectives that are no longer viable or normatively desirable. This argument addresses the *short electoral cycles* component of the democratic myopia thesis by identifying a democratic mechanism (i.e., reciprocal reason-giving) that can help maintain policy continuity over the long term, *when* continuity is justified, even as governments and generations change.

Chapter 6 explores conceptual territory that has been largely neglected by modern political theorists: the challenges associated with coordinating the actions of non-contemporaries over long periods of time. I argue that we cannot use authoritarian or undemocratic political tools, such as force or coercion, to coordinate the actions of non-contemporaries because current and future publics are free and equal entities with respect to each other. The decisions that we make today will structure the choices that future publics make, but there is nothing that we can do to force future political actors to do what we think they should do after we are dead. As such, the present is both politically dominant *and* impotent when it comes to our relations with future publics: we can do what we want to future others without explanation or justification, but we cannot force them to act according to our wills. Given these circumstances—which are the circumstances we are in—the best we can do is try to encourage future others to act *with* us through communication and persuasion.

Part III—which includes Chapters 7 and 8—deals with institutional design. In Chapter 7, I argue that we need inclusive deliberative processes at all levels of governance—in political *and* economic spheres, and at the local, subnational, national, transnational, and global levels—if we are going to shape our shared futures in collectively intentional ways. I do not presume to know *how* we might create future-regarding democratic institutions within all of

2
Future-Making
Politics, Democracy, and Deliberation

2.1. Introduction

Political theorists tend to focus their attention on political relations between contemporaries. From one perspective, this makes sense. The present is the only arena in which political actions take place. If politics is about dividing scarce resources; negotiating with others; forming associations; claiming rights; and, in general, gaining, maintaining, and losing power; it is, by definition, about relations between contemporaries. We cannot negotiate with the past, and we cannot form associations with those who do not yet exist. We might make long-term contracts or treaties that we hope will last into the future, but future political actors cannot be signatories to our contractual arrangements today. Political relations, like personal relations, are constrained by time.

From another perspective, political theories that do not take the past or the future into account are clearly inadequate. What happened in the past structures our politics and our choices today. We cannot, for example, understand race relations—and racism—in the United States and elsewhere without thinking about the social, political, and economic legacies of slavery or colonialism (e.g., Coates 2014; Vernon 2016). And what we do today will have an impact on future people. We cannot exist in the world without having some impact on it. The resources we use or abuse, the way we build our cities, the social norms we advance or challenge, the principles we adopt to guide our actions, the economic systems we use and support, the money we borrow as collectivities, the technologies we develop, the weapons we use, the social biases and stereotypes we maintain, the migration patterns we allow or prohibit will not only affect future people, they will, in some profound sense, also determine who those future people will be (Parfit 1984). The fact that our presence in the world—"the present"—will have an impact on the future,

Future Publics. Michael K. MacKenzie, Oxford University Press. © Oxford University Press 2021.
DOI: 10.1093/oso/9780197557150.003.0002

renders any political theories that do not take into consideration intergenerational relations radically incomplete.

In this chapter I define and discuss the terms, concepts, and distinctions that are used throughout the rest of the book. I begin with a discussion of several terms and concepts that can help us think more clearly about the future. I then discuss the concept of future-making and argue that politics, or the exercise of public power, is the only means we have for directing other future-making forces toward collectively desirable goals. In the last section of the chapter, I explain what I mean by politics, democracy, and deliberation.

2.2. Thinking About the Future: Concepts, Terms, and Distinctions

2.2.1. The Future Versus "Futures"

Many of us think about "the future" in the singular, as if it is or will be one thing or one eventuality. The implication is that the future is a thing that will exist, and it is our task to either discover what it will be or wait for it to happen. Those who work in the field of futures studies have argued that both terms—"futures" and "studies"—should be pluralized. As Jennifer Gidley (2017) explains, this "move to pluralize the terms may seem minor but it reflected a deeper philosophical and political manoeuvre to democratize and pluralize the future" (p. 8). This approach emphasizes that our futures are not yet determined: we are empowered to make or unmake them, and we have to figure out how to act well to get the futures we think we might want. As James Dator (2019) explains "while it is not possible to predict the future, it is possible and necessary to forecast alternative futures. A forecast is not intended to be a prediction. A forecast is not necessarily a true statement. It is a logical statement; a contingent statement; an 'if . . . then' statement" (p. 402).

The pluralization of the terms "studies" and "futures" also reflects the idea that there are different ways of studying the future, and that the future itself is diverse: there are near and far futures, more and less desirable futures, and each possible future will benefit or harm different groups or types of people in different ways. As Dator continues

> there is not a single future waiting out there to be predicted or even forecasted. Rather there are numerous alternative futures that we can and

should anticipate by various ways and means. But the most important thing about the future is that while it cannot be predicted, it can, in many significant ways, be imagined and invented. New forms of governance should be, among other things, ways by which humanity collectively imagines, invents, and constantly re-imagines and re-invents preferred futures. (Dator 2019, p. 402)

I embrace the idea that the future is both open and diverse, and I use the term "futures" whenever possible, but I have found it difficult to refrain from the more familiar term "the future" in the singular. As such, I alternate between these two terms—"futures" and "the future"—for stylistic reasons and for purposes of clarity. It should nevertheless be understood that when I use the term "the future" I am thinking about diverse possible futures in the pluralistic sense.

2.2.2. Long-Term and Short-Term Issues

We often talk about "short-term" and "long-term" issues or problems in political affairs without subjecting these terms to critical scrutiny. These concepts—like the idea of the future itself—are often left unspecified because the relevant timeframes of issues are implied but not determined by the issues themselves. Government programs that aim to produce benefits—such as improved public transit services—in 5 or 10 years may be considered long-term initiatives, but many issues—such as education reform or public pension plans—have timeframes of 30, 40, or 50 years. Other issues or problems, such as climate change and the storage of nuclear waste, have timeframes of hundreds or thousands of years. We often talk about these issues and problems as if they are all one category type: we say that they are "long-term" issues, but we do not specify the unique political challenges associated with these different temporal horizons.

Furthermore, the very idea that there are "long-term" issues implies that there are also "short-term" issues or problems in public affairs—but this is not obviously the case. It is surprisingly difficult to identify any public issues or decisions that are exclusively short- or long-term ones (MacKenzie 2021). Climate change is a "long-term" issue because what we do today—or fail to do—will affect the future for hundreds or thousands of years, but what we decide to do about climate change *now* will affect us over the short term. And many of those issues that appear to be exclusively short-term ones, such as food production or waste removal, also have both short- and long-term dimensions. If our food systems fail, people will starve in the near term. But how we grow food, which foods we grow, whether we use genetically modified foods to increase yields, and how and where we transport foods are decisions that will have long-term consequences. Likewise, if our garbage is not collected regularly, it will pile up in the streets, make everything dirty, and attract rats and other animals that might spread disease. But our decisions about what to do with garbage after it has been collected—or what to consider garbage in the first place—will have long-term consequences.

While we cannot make clear distinctions between short- and long-term issues or problems in public affairs, it is possible to make useful distinctions between those that will affect us continuously over some period of time and those that are unlikely to have significant impacts until some, normally unspecified, future date. Water pollution is an example of a cumulative problem that affects us now, but which may have more significant effects over time as the problem is made worse each year by our actions. By contrast, failing to adequately prepare for natural disasters might have no impact on us until a natural disaster hits. The politics associated with cumulative problems, like water pollution, are likely to be different from those associated with future problems like natural disasters. We may be more willing to address cumulative problems if we feel their initial effects now and we are aware that they are likely to worsen over time.[1] It is easier to ignore problems that are likely to affect the future only at some unspecified point in the future.

The fact of the matter is that every issue is temporally complex. Every political issue or decision will have costs and benefits that are distributed in time in various complex ways. Instead of trying to categorize issues as either short-term or long-term ones, we should think more carefully about the short- and long-term dimensions of *all* the issues and problems we face and *all* the decisions we make as individuals and collectivities.

[1] It is commonly assumed that cumulative and future problems are difficult to deal with because uncertainty increases as we look farther into the future. This is often a reasonable assumption: we can specify in detail what people in the near future might want or need, but as we look farther into the future it becomes more difficult to anticipate anything more than their basic physical needs—and even those may be less easy to identify than we often think. Nevertheless, Meyer (2016) has rightly observed that there are cases in which certainty *increases* as we look farther into the future. "For example, the prediction that some policy will have changed or that certain resources will have been exhausted is more likely to be true in the further future" (p. 6). Likewise we can know with relative certainty that facilities storing nuclear waste are more, not less, likely to leak as time goes by.

2.2.3. Future Selves and Future Others

It is not possible to make clear distinctions between short- and long-term issues, but it is useful to think about how our decisions will affect (1) ourselves now, (2) our future selves, and (3) future others. Whether any particular issue or decision is likely to affect our future selves will, of course, depend our own stage of life. If you are young, most, but not all, collective decisions are likely to have some impact on your future self. If you are elderly, nearly all collective decisions will have consequences that will primarily affect future others. These distinctions are subjective, but they are nevertheless useful and politically relevant because our motivations—and thus the incentives or institutions we might employ to shape political behaviours—will be different in each case. It is possible to motivate individuals and groups to act in other-regarding ways using mechanisms that seek to align self-interested concerns with other-regarding actions. Tax incentives, for example, encourage people to donate money to charity or act in other ways that are thought to be socially beneficial. Similarly, electoral processes are supposed to encourage presumably self-interested politicians to consider the public interest—or at least the interests of those who are likely to vote for them.

It is more difficult to motivate self-interested people to act on the potential interests of future others. We might appeal to their future interests, but the effectiveness of this approach will be limited by two factors. First, while most of us have a relatively consistent sense of identity over time, our past and future selves nevertheless feel different than our present selves because they *are* different from us now (e.g., Hershfield 2011). We are both connected to and separated from our past and future selves: they are not not us, but they are not us either. It is therefore more difficult to motivate or incentivize people to think about their future selves than their present selves, especially when we must make trade-offs between our present and future interests. We face this challenge when we are, for example, trying to motivate people to save for their retirement or to invest in public pension plans (e.g., Jacobs 2011).

Second, it is only possible to appeal to the future interests of individuals when dealing with issues that do not reach too far into the future. Appealing to their future interests might encourage them to save for retirement, but it will not motivate them to care more about future others. This is the challenge we face when trying to motivate people to support climate change mitigation policies or care about the problems associated with the storage of nuclear waste. The perception—if not the reality—is that most people living today will not suffer the worst consequences of climate change: our future selves might suffer a little as we adjust to climate change, but the worst of it will affect humanity only after most of us are dead. Likewise, we might be inclined to support nuclear energy if we think that we can store nuclear waste safely for decades, even if we are not confident that it can be stored safely for millennia.

If we cannot motivate people to care about the far future by appealing to their own self-interests, we might try to educate them instead. We might try to convince people that they *should* act in the interests of future others or that they are required to do so by justice or religious duty. Such efforts may be effective to some extent, but they are unlikely to be sufficient. In most cases, it will be necessary to supplement "internal" constraints, such as convictions or obligations of justice or duty, with "external" or political constraints, such as institutional incentives or penalties. The problem with penalties is that they are unlikely to be adopted or enforced if no one wishes to see them enforced. When the interests of the living are opposed to the potential interests of future others, there may be no one willing or powerful enough to impose penalties on actions that might threaten the wellbeing of future others.[2] What is needed, then, are institutional incentives to encourage decision makers, whomever they may be, to genuinely represent, and act on, the potential interests of future others when making decisions today. In Chapter 4, I argue that effective deliberative environments can incentivize participants who disagree with each other to actively represent the genuine interests of excluded groups, such as future others. It is difficult to identify any mechanism other than deliberation that might encourage otherwise self-interested actors to more seriously consider, and genuinely represent, the potential interests of future others.

[2] It is commonly thought that the interests of current and future publics are diametrically opposed. What is good for us now is bad for the future, and what is bad for the future is good for us now. This is often the case. We benefit from the extraction and use of fossil fuels, and the future will pay the environmental costs of our energy policies. When we borrow money to pay for tax cuts, we transfer wealth from future publics to current publics. But there are several reasons to reconsider the idea that the interests of the present and the future will be opposed. First, the present is diverse, which means that policies that are good for "us" now may be good for some of us and bad for others. Using fossil fuels has been good for many of us in developed industrialized nations, but it has not been good for everyone, especially those in developing nations or low-lying island nations threatened by rising sea levels. Second, the future will be diverse, which means that some people in the future are likely to harmed or helped more than others by our policies today. Tax cuts that transfer public debts to future generations might harm future publics, as a whole, while benefitting the future children and other relatives of today's richest families. The upshot is this: current publics, in all their diversity, and the future publics, in all *their* diversity, do not *always* have shared collective interests that are diametrically opposed to each other.

2.2.4. Future-Regarding

There are many terms to describe those who focus on the present while ignoring or disregarding the future, but we not do have readily available terms to describe those who are not biased against the future. When someone is primarily concerned with the present—or the near term—we call them short-sighted or myopic. Metaphorically, those who are short-sighted fail to adequately consider the future when making decisions for themselves or others. Those who are myopic are shrouded in, or blinded by, the present: they cannot see past it. By contrast, we do not use terms such as "hyperopia," the opposite of myopia, to describe those who are biased against the present in favour of the future—probably because there are so few people who are hyperopic in the metaphorical sense. Most of us are not blind to the present: we are situated in the present, and we have to navigate it effectively to make it to the future. The present is tangible: it can be felt, smelled, touched, and experienced. The future is intangible: it must be imagined rather than experienced. Given the dominance of the present in our everyday experiences, then, the terms "hyperopia" and "far-sighted" do not describe our temporal situation very well. None of us is focused on the future to the exclusion of the present. But this leaves us without a term to describe those who consciously think about both the present and the future when making decisions for themselves and others.

As a corrective to this deficiency in our language, I use the term "future-regarding" to refer to individuals, collectivities, organizations, or institutions that consciously consider the future when making decisions for themselves or others. This term emphasizes a concern for the future, but it does not imply that we are—by looking at the future—somehow blind to the present.[3]

The term future-regarding is useful because it is a relative of other familiar terms, namely "self-regarding" and "other-regarding." At the same time, it cannot be collapsed into either of these other terms because future-regarding behaviour may be self-regarding when it is primarily directed toward the

[3] González-Ricoy and Gosseries (2016) use the term "future-oriented" to describe political institutions—or actions—that do not disregard the potential interests of the future. This term is intuitively attractive, but it is also potentially misleading because it may be understood to imply that institutions or actions should *focus* on the future to the exclusion of the present. The term future-regarding does not have this implication. When we orient ourselves toward something (like the future) we necessarily orient ourselves away from something else (such as the present). By contrast, when we "regard" or take something into consideration we may do so without disregarding other things.

potential interests of our future selves, or it may be primarily other-regarding when it is directed toward the potential interests of future others. The term "future-regarding" also helps captures the normative idea that we *should* as a matter of principle try to strike a balance between the concerns of the present and the potential interests of the future when making individual or collective decisions.

2.2.5. Current and Future Publics

The term "intergenerational" is used to refer to relations between younger and older contemporaries, as well as to relations between past, present, and future generations who are not contemporaries. In this book, I am primarily interested in our relations with the future (our future selves and future others) and not relations between contemporary actors in different age groups. The crucial difference between these two types of intergenerational relations has to do with the possibility of simultaneous exchanges. Political actors in different age groups can interact directly, deliberate, negotiate, and enter agreements with each other, sign contracts, and transfer resources between themselves. Political issues are often complicated by the divergent interests of individuals in different stages of life—especially when it comes to issues such as pension plans or education spending—but relations between contemporary actors who happen to be different ages can be understood using the conceptual frameworks that we use to understand politics more generally.

Political relations between our current and future selves, and those between our current selves and future others, are different. We cannot interact directly with future others (or our future selves). We cannot deliberate with future people, negotiate agreements, or obtain their consent for our future-regarding actions. Political relations between the present and the future are a one-way street: what we do will affect the future, but the future cannot affect us or our decisions. As such, the present is always in a dominant position with respect to future others, and future people cannot be empowered to protect their own interests.

In this book, I use the term intergenerational relations to refer exclusively to relations between past, present, and future generations and not to relations between individuals in different age groups. This clarification is particularly important in my discussion and critique of the intergenerational justice literature (Chapter 3) and in my discussion of the nature of political relations between current and future publics (Chapter 6).

In addition to the term "intergenerational relations," I also use the terms "current publics" and "future publics" to emphasize the political dimensions of my arguments. A "current public" is any collectivity at the present moment. It consists of all living members of that entity regardless of their age. Current publics may be defined territorially (e.g., states) or culturally (e.g., linguistic or religious groups)—or the term may be used to refer to the whole of humanity (i.e., all those living today).

The term "future publics" refers to any collectivities that might come to exist in the future. This includes future iterations of current publics, but it also includes future political entities that do not yet exist. The term "future publics" might also be used to refer to all of humanity in the future. Depending on our own age and the timescales involved, future publics may or may not include our future selves. When very long timescales are involved, current and future publics will be made up of entirely different individuals, even if those publics exist continuously—with continuous collective identities—over long periods of time.

There is, of course, no guarantee that members of current and future publics *will* conceive of themselves as members of the same publics over time or that relations between current and future publics will only involve relations between different iterations of the same political entities over time. Decisions made by current publics, such as nation-states, may affect future iterations of the same entity, future iterations of other political entities, or humanity as a whole—all depending on the geographic and temporal reach of the likely consequences of those decisions.

It is also important to clarify that members of a current or future public do not necessarily need to be "citizens" in the legalistic sense. In general, I try to avoid the term "citizen" because political actors in any polity may or may not be citizens, and our opportunities for action (as elites and non-elites) do not always depend on whether we are legal citizens of a polity. Current publics, as I have conceived them, include *all* those who think of themselves as members of a particular political entity, whether that entity is defined as a nation-state with citizens or a non-state entity or group with shared political interests. Likewise, future publics will include all those who will be affected by current decisions, and not just those who will be future citizens of the political entities who happen to make those decisions.

This book is about political relations between current and future publics broadly conceived. The objective is to think about how we might make current publics more future-regarding, such that those who are living today do not make decisions that ignore, disregard, or trample upon the potential interests of members of future publics, whomever they might turnout to be.

2.2.6. Anticipatory Democracy

Future Publics engages with, and builds upon, work that was done by an earlier generation of scholars on "anticipatory democracy." This concept was first developed by Alvin Toffler (1970) in the last chapter of his book *Future Shock*. Toffler argues that in order to deal with an ever accelerating pace of change in increasingly complex and diverse modern societies, we will need "a revolution in the very way we formulate our social goals" (pp. 470–471). Toffler argues, like I do, that we cannot rely on technocrats, bureaucrats, or authoritarian leaders to "impose a humane future from above" (p. 480). What is needed, instead, are inclusive, democratic processes that provide whole societies with the resources and opportunities needed to formulate shared goals and visions of collectively desirable futures. The concept of anticipatory democracy was further developed by Clement Bezold (1978) and his colleagues in a collection of essays entitled *Anticipatory Democracy: People in the Politics of the Future*. Many of the projects catalogued in that book engaged hundreds, or even thousands of people in formulating visions of alternative futures.

I share the enthusiasm that these scholars have for the future-making potentialities of inclusive democratic processes. Nevertheless, *Future Publics* both builds upon and critiques the concept of anticipatory democracy in at least three ways. First, many scholars working in this area were primarily interested in the practical or pragmatic benefits of anticipatory democracy. Toffler (1970), for example, argues that in complex and diverse modern societies that are changing at increasingly rapid rates "democracy becomes not a political luxury but a primal necessity" (p. 475). Democracy is viewed as a necessity because what is needed to navigate change is flexibility rather than rigidity. We need political systems that are capable of incorporating diverse inputs in coordinated ways while pursuing clear objectives that have been defined and sanctioned by affected publics. But we also need our political systems to be reflective, and reflexive to changing needs, expectations, and circumstances. Toffler argues that inclusive democracies are the only political systems that can provide this combination of goods (see, as well, Dryzek and Pickering 2019). I agree that we need political systems that are both goal oriented and flexible and reflexive if we are going to get the futures we think we might want (see, e.g., Section 5.4). But unlike Toffer, I also emphasize normative arguments about why we *ought* to use inclusive democratic processes to make our shared futures together (see, e.g., Sections 5.2 and 5.3).

Second, theorists of anticipatory democracy have often—but not always—failed to account for the power dynamics between publics and decision makers, and the short term incentives that decision makers typically face.[4] In Toffler's (1970) account, anticipatory democracy processes would be primarily advisory and appended to existing political institutions. The recommendations or visions formulated in those processes would be "temporary direction-indicators, broad objectives good for a limited time only, and intended as advisory to the elected political representatives of the community or nation" (p. 483). Likewise, the visioning projects described by Baker (1978), Gingrich (1978), Bradley (1978), Stigler (1978), Bezold (2006), and others, such as Ramos (2014), engaged large numbers of people, but they did not *empower* democratic publics to make future-regarding decisions or challenge the near term interests or incentives of political and economic elites. As such, most of the projects and processes that have been described as "anticipatory democracy" where not, in fact, very democratic. They gave diverse publics opportunities to formulate future-regarding collective goals and visions, but they did not empower them to act on those collective intentions. Public engagement processes are valuable as visioning and goal-setting exercises, but in order to follow-through on those visions we will need to rethink how institutional structures and incentives affect the judgments and decisions of those with power. As Dator explains

> the fundamental difficulty in enabling our community to think and act more satisfactorily for the future lies less with the politicians and bureaucrats personally than with the roles that they are expected to play and the demands they must satisfy, and that our present political structure generally does not let the demands from or for the long-range alternative futures reach those incumbents the way demands from the past and present do. It is to some significant extent a structural problem, and not an attitudinal or intellectual one. (Dator 1981, p. 65)

[4] Exceptions include James Dator (e.g., 1981) and Robert Theobald (1978). As Theobald notes: "Even if good information has been gathered [by anticipatory democracy groups] and recommendations are provided to the appropriate authorities, there is no guarantee that anything will come of it" (p. 307).

The approach that I adopt in *Future Publics* follows Dator's line of inquiry and builds upon the work of others who are also interested in reforming—rather than informing—our political processes and institutions to make them more future-regarding (e.g., Boston 2017; Caney 2016; Dobson 1996; Dator 1981; Ekeli 2005, 2009; Smith 2019; Tonn 1991, 1996).

Third, *Future Publics* offers a deliberative theory of anticipatory democracy. James Bohman (1998) has argued that deliberative theory and practice "came of age" in the 1980s and 1990s, which is after Toffler and his colleagues started thinking about anticipatory democracy. With hindsight, one can read a theory of deliberation into early accounts of anticipatory democracy. Nevertheless it is clear that the concept—and utility—of deliberation is not adequately developed in those accounts. Toffler (1970), for example, argues that participants in anticipatory democracy processes should have opportunities to "identify their shared goals as well as their unresolved conflicts" (p. 481). Theobald (1978) argues that "we need to develop new structures that will enable people to develop and state their views as clearly as possible" (p. 313). But neither Toffler nor Theobald explain the mechanisms or practices that would, in fact, help people do these things. In *Future Publics* I aim to articulate the normative relevance and practical utility of deliberation as a necessary component of future-regarding collective action.

2.3. The Forces That Shape the Future

The idea that we should think about the future in political terms assumes that current publics have the power to shape the future in meaningful ways. But we often talk about the future in more deterministic ways. We use words like "prediction" and "forecasting," which seem to imply that the future exists already, at least in some sense, and our task is to figure out what it will be like. The concept of "future-making," by contrast, leaves the future open: there are multiple, probably infinite, possible futures, and we can shape those futures as we might within the realm of human possibility. As Montfort (2017) explains, the term "future-making" is "meant to distinguish a potentially productive perspective on the future (let's build a better future) from a less productive one (let's predict what will happen, for instance, so we can react quickly by anticipating it)" (p. 4).

But what agency do we have over the future? What are the forces that shape the future, and how can they be marshalled and directed toward better futures and away from worse ones? There are forces of nature—such as meteorite strikes—that are or *may be* outside the realm of human influence, but there are other future-making forces that are more clearly within the realm of human action.[5] For the purposes of discussion, we might say that humans shape the future in three primary ways: (1) through drift and inadvertence, (2) through the exercise of private power, and (3) through the exercise of public power or politics.[6] Drift and inadvertence are apathetic forces: they have to do with letting things happen either consciously or unconsciously (e.g., Pitkin 1981; see also Section 5.3). We might drift toward better (or worse) futures, but we are unlikely to get what we want in the future if we let ourselves drift through life while paying attention to only our most immediate needs and concerns. In order to shape the future in specific ways—to create the futures that we think we might want for ourselves and future others—we have to act: we have to exercise power in future-regarding ways.

The power to shape the future is invested in both individuals and collectivities. All individuals have the power to shape the future in small or profound ways by virtue of their very presence in the world. We affect the future in more or less intentional ways through our economic decisions, our social interactions, our decisions (or non-decisions) about procreation, and through our creative or inventive endeavours. When billions of individual decisions about what to buy, where to live, and how to act are aggregated, the collective outcomes—or futures—produced may be either collectively beneficial or harmful. Although some individuals have more economic, social, cultural, or political power than others, no one can make the future on their own. Those who control large sums of money can make consequential decisions about how some of the world's productive resources will be used and distributed. Or they might pay others to invent future-making technologies—such as electric, flying, or autonomous cars; delivery drones;

[5] Acts of fate, nature, or the gods are normally thought of as being outside the realm of human action. Nevertheless, it may be possible to bring previously uncontrollable forces into the realm of human action. In the past, people had no access to the heavenly bodies. Today, we send space craft to explore them. In the future it may be possible to bring asteroids, for example, under our control with technologies that will detect them and redirect those that threaten life on earth. Thus the realm of future-making human actions is not static: it changes with our technologies and with the development (or loss) of our capacities for collective (i.e., political) action.

[6] For a different but compatible take on the forces that shape the future see Dator (1978). He identifies three future-making forces, or dynamics: (1) The conflict between those who favour growth and those who favour conservation; (2) The development of new technologies; and (3) The declining influence of the West and the rising influence of the rest of the world. In another article, Dator (2009) discusses the need for governments that are capable and willing to act in ways that will help us "surf the Tsunamis of change" that are coming toward us (p. 34).

passenger rockets; or genetically modified children—but even the wealthiest or most inventive individuals must rely on others to act with them if they want to get the futures they desire. In practice the future will be shaped by billions of decisions, both big and small. It will be shaped by our individual decisions, our collective actions, and our individual and collective inactions.

If we do not exercise public power to shape the future in collectively intentional ways, the future will be shaped by drift and inadvertence and the exercise of (normally uncoordinated) forms of private power. Indeed, technological developments and market forces (which are two forms of private power) often shape our futures in conjunction with each other but without the consent (or knowledge) of affected publics. When plastic, for example, was invented, it was heralded as a miracle substance: it is cheap, durable, and malleable. Given these attributes, market forces tend to favour plastics, and our world has thus been inundated with them—and it continues to be, even though we now know that plastics are harmful to our health, the wellbeing of other species, and the natural environment more generally (e.g., Geyer et al. 2017). What is more, the harmful effects of plastics pollution will persist for thousands of years even if we stopped producing them now.

Similarly, since we have learned to use fossil fuels as energy, we have continued to burn them at ever-increasing rates because of market demands, even though we know they are causing climate change. Many other inventions—such as the automobile and the internet—have similarly profoundly shaped our modern lives. The automobile radically changed our cities, our social lives, and the natural and built environments in which we live. Given existing market demands, it is difficult for many people to imagine futures where cars are no longer the dominant form of human transportation. Likewise, the internet has radically changed commerce, media, politics, and the ways in which we socialize. It is almost as if these inventions were thrust upon us and then picked up and amplified by market forces—and that they will continue to shape our lives and our futures in more or less desirable ways whether we like it or not. It is for these reasons that many people focus on invention and investment (or market forces) when thinking about the forces that shape the future. Although we have the capacity to make our futures, within the realms of human possibility, we often get futures that are not of our own choosing because we fail to act in coordinated ways to produce the futures that we think we might want as individuals and collectivities. But the role of public power in making (or unmaking) the future often goes unacknowledged in histories of our future-making activities (see, e.g., Montfort 2017).

Automobiles, for example, were invented to serve the transportation needs of individuals, but they were not widely adopted because they are *inherently* more convenient than other existing or possible forms of transportation. Instead, the dominance of cars was made possible through government actions and subsidies. Governments build and maintain the public infrastructures—the roads and bridges—needed to make cars useful and convenient, and they subsidize the exploration, extraction, and transportation of the fossil fuels that cars require (e.g., Plumer 2010). Governments also actively encouraged people to drive—and, in fact, often make it difficult for many people *not* to drive—through the development of car-oriented city-planning regimes. The car-dependent future (i.e., *our* car-dependent present) was not created by those who invented the car and invested in the automotive industry, and it was not an inevitability. Our car-dependent present is the result of all three future-making forces working together. The internal combustion engine was invented by creative individuals; and the automotive industry was made possible through private investment; but our modern world has been inundated by cars, pollution, and traffic jams because of both inadvertence and government actions. Our governments acted to promote, support, and subsidize the automotive industry, but we did not think carefully enough about the collective consequences of widespread car ownership.[7]

The important point is that government action, or the exercise of public power, is the means we have for shaping the future in collectively intentional ways. The future *will* be shaped by drift, inadvertence, invention, and investment—it *will* be the product of billions of individual decisions—but we need to exercise public power to marshal these forces and direct them toward potentially desirable futures and away from collectively undesirable ones. It often appears as if technological developments and market forces overpower and outpace our collective capacities to act, thereby forcing futures upon us that we did not choose together, but where political power appears to be the weaker force, it is because political actors have been captured by those with private power and influence, or they have allowed things to happen through

[7] As H. G. Wells said in a British Broadcasting Corporation (BBC) radio interview in 1932: "See how unprepared our world was for the motor car. It was bound to . . . congest our towns with traffic. Did we do anything to work out any of these consequences of the motor car? No, we did not. . . . In the case of the motor car, we have let consequence after consequence take us by surprise" (quoted in Reid 2015, p. 107).

drift and inadvertence, and not because it would have been impossible to act differently.[8]

We cannot, of course, *control* the future through the exercise of public power. Our futures will be shaped by our actions and inactions, but they will forever remain in the realm of potentiality. We cannot know whether our actions will affect the future in the ways that we hope, and we cannot be sure that future others will act with us to achieve long-term objectives. In some instances, we might make the future worse by trying to make it better: we might have too little or inaccurate information about the likely consequences of our collective actions, or we might try to control complex systems, such as markets or ecologies, that are too complicated to understand in their entirety. It would be naive to think that we can control the future, but we can play a more or less active role in making the futures that we think we might want as collectivities *if* we learn how to exercise public power in future-regarding ways. We will, inevitably get some things right and other things wrong, but it is only through collective action or the exercise of public power—which usually, but does not always, involve governmental action—that we can marshal the other future-making forces and direct them toward better futures for ourselves and future others.

2.4. Politics, Democracy, and Deliberation

We will need a theory—and practice—of future-regarding collective action if we are going to act politically to make the futures we think we might want for ourselves and future others. In this book, I argue that democracy, and in particular deliberative democracy, offers the best, most viable means for us to

[8] Although the role of public power is often neglected in histories of future-making (e.g., Montfort 2017), some scholars, such as James Dator (2009) and Andrew Gamble (2019), have emphasized the role that politics must play in shaping our shared futures in collectively intentional ways. As Gamble argues:

> The human species is in a race against itself. The speed with which it has gained new knowledge and wealth in the last two hundred years has unleashed an accelerating wave of technology which has brought with it new perils which are hard to estimate precisely, but which shadow our future. The proliferation of nuclear weapons and the effect of human activity on the environment and the climate are the greatest of these, but there are several others, such as the rise of artificial intelligence with its potential effect in destroying employment, and the new medical technologies which may transform the human life cycle. Many technologies bring great advantages, but there is concern whether human societies, can adjust fast enough, *and in particular whether politics can manage the transition and the conflicts of interest and profound issues of principle likely to arise.* (Emphasis added, pp. 102–103)

make our shared futures together in collectively intentional ways. In this section, I briefly explain what I mean by politics, democracy, and deliberation.

2.4.1. Politics and Democracy

Politics—or the problem of politics—has to do with acting in the context of others. Political situations arise when we must act with others and there are disagreements about what should or should not be done. We often associate politics with local, regional, and national governance or with international affairs, but politics emerges whenever we have to act in the context of others who might disagree.[9] That is why we sometimes talk about schoolyard politics or the politics of family life. We describe these situations as political because friends and families have to make decisions together and they often disagree. The political tools available for navigating the politics of friendship groups and family life are the same as those available in any other political situation, even though there are, of course, differences of complexity and scale. The complications associated with collective action grow exponentially with the size of the group that is involved (Olson 1965), and politics above the level of an intimate friendship group or family almost always requires some system of representation (see, e.g., Manin 1997). Nevertheless, the tools that political actors have at their disposal are the same in any situation where we must act in the context of others—or *with* others—who might disagree.

For the purposes of illustration, we might say that there are two types of political tools: those that are non-democratic and those that are more democratic. Those that fall into the first category are available to actors who have power over others, or more power *than* others. Such tools include coercion, deception, threats, sanctions, or the use of force or violence to compel other actors to do things. Other non-democratic political tools might include expulsion (for example, of those who disagree) or paying people to do things that they would not otherwise wish to do.[10]

[9] For Hannah Arendt (1957) politics involves acting in—and with—a community of others. For Hanna Pitkin (1981) "politics is competitive and conflictual and has consequences for the relative benefits and burdens of different members of the community. The settling of such conflicts is what politics is for and what it is about" (pp. 345–346).

[10] Jeffrey Winters (2011) gives the example of an oligarch in Southeast Asia who considered paying for the costs of assembling a "regime-destabilizing" crowd of protesters. This oligarch estimated that "it would only cost him about $20 million to $30 million to put 100,000 demonstrators on the streets of his capital for a month—a sum he considered cheap" (p. xiv).

Political tools that fall into the second category include voting or aggregation, rotation, negotiation, and persuasion. These democratic tools are substantively different than non-democratic ones because they are predicated on the normative principle that people should be moved as much as possible *by* their own wills instead of *against* them by the coercive actions of others (e.g., Bächtiger et al. 2018). This does not mean that everyone must agree before collective actions can take place or that there are no forms of coercion (or laws) that might be sanctioned in democratically legitimate processes (e.g., Mansbridge 2012); but it does mean that everyone should be in a position to influence collective decisions to some extent, and that they should have reasons to willingly accept collective decisions even if they do not agree with them.

Political actors might employ democratic tools because they think it is the right thing to do or because non-democratic tools are unavailable or inappropriate. The politics of friendship groups tend to be democratic precisely because friends are normally thought of as equals, and non-democratic tools are typically understood as violations of the norms of friendships. When friends are trying to decide where to go for dinner, for example, they might discuss their options, try to persuade each other, identify a limited number of alternative options, and take a vote. Or they might employ a principle of rotation: "I decided where to go last time, why doesn't someone else decide this time?"

In practice, actors often use more than one type of tool to navigate specific political contexts or decisions. They might, for example, use threats or violence to force others into discussions and negotiations. But if democratic tools are to be generally preferred, as many people have argued (e.g., Arendt 1957; Chambers 1996; Crick 1962; Gamble 2019; Warren 2017; Young 2000), then we might say that "good" political processes or institutions are those that make it harder, less attractive, or more costly for actors to use non-democratic political tools.[11] Because it is possible to use coercion and force only in situations where political power or influence is not widely distributed, institutional designs that aim to distribute power as widely as possible

[11] Arendt (1957) and Crick (1962) argue that the term "politics" should be reserved to describe actions that seek to resolve conflicts through democratic as opposed to non-democratic means. I share their normative conviction that democratic political tools are preferable, but it is, I think, conceptually confusing to reserve the term "politics" only for democratic forms of action. If politics involves acting in the context of others who might disagree, violence, threats, coercion, bribery, persuasion, and voting are all different ways of achieving the same thing: getting others to do what you want them to do.

will also incentivize actors to seek out democratic or deliberative solutions to disagreements. It is, of course, not possible to eliminate power imbalances entirely, but it is normally the case that when power (in whatever forms) is more widely distributed between actors, the opportunities for actors to use non-democratic political tools are reduced.

Power, in this context, refers to an actor's capacity to influence collective decisions or shape agendas (Bachrach and Baratz 1962). Empowerments may include, but are not limited to, rights to speak, participate, vote, veto, sanction, exit, or use violence. Actors might also exercise—or be subject to—forms of power that are less obvious. Foucault (1982) and Lukes (2005), for example, have argued that power is often most effective when it is least observable and when actors are generally unaware of its presence. There is a danger that subtle forms of power—such as assumptions about who is owed deference—can shape decisions even when formal empowerments, such as the right to speak, are approximately equally distributed (e.g., Lupia and Norton 2017; Young 2000). At the same time, formal empowerments, such as voting rights, vetoes, and the capacity to sanction or exit, can help mitigate subtler power imbalances, such as assumptions about what is ideologically appropriate. When actors are empowered to speak, vote, demand respect from others, sanction or exit, they will also be empowered to challenge prevailing ideologies or the deference that they are "supposed" to pay to (certain types of) others.

In summary, politics has to do with acting in the context of others who disagree. We use political tools, such as threats, force, violence, voting, and persuasion, to enable collective actions when actors have conflicting interests and different beliefs about what should or should not be done. Democratic politics are a special form of politics in which non-coercive forms of collective action—voting, rotation, negotiation, bargaining, and persuasion—are used to make binding collective decisions as legitimate as possible—binding decisions that may themselves require coercive enforcement (Mansbridge 2012).

Deliberative democracy, in turn, is a special form of democratic politics that emphasizes the normative value of talk and persuasion over other forms of democratic action, such as voting and strategic bargaining. As Chambers (2003) explains: "Voting-centric views see democracy as the arena in which fixed preferences and interests compete via fair mechanisms of aggregation. In contrast, deliberative democracy focuses on the communicative processes of opinion and will-formation that precede voting" (p. 308). Strategic democratic actions—such as voting and bargaining—have to do with conferring consent and getting as much as one can from collective decisions while respecting the fact that others have different or opposing interests and intentions.

Deliberative democracy has to do with providing public justifications for collective actions—justifications that those who would otherwise disagree might plausibly accept. Deliberation is valuable because it can help individuals and groups (a) clarify the terms of their disagreements, (b) gain some measure of mutual understanding, (c) form collective intentions and thus engage in democratically sanctioned collective actions, and (d) seek mutual accommodation or integrative solutions to shared problems. Deliberation can produce these, or other benefits, even though actors with conflicting interests and opinions cannot normally get everything they might want from collective decisions (see, e.g., Bächtiger et al. 2018; Warren and Mansbridge 2015). As Mark Warren (2019) has argued, the intuitive appeal of deliberative democracy is easy to grasp: "When people agree about a course of action, or understand where the disagreements are, the resulting decision will be more acceptable and thus more legitimate" (p. 2). When talk can generate legitimacy, the costs of taking collective actions and monitoring them will be lower, and the effectiveness of those actions will be higher and more highly regarded. The problem, as Warren explains, is that "compared to other kinds of influence and power, the powers of speech are delicate: they're easy to suppress and difficult to scale" (p. 3).

2.4.2. Deliberative Conditions

Because of its relative fragility, deliberative democracy often seems unrealistic—or too idealistic—in a political world characterized by other forms of power and strategic intent. Deliberative democracy also places seemingly unrealistic demands on participants. In effective deliberative environments, participants must be willing to give and respond to reasons: they should listen to others and adjust their positions or opinions in response to persuasive arguments. They should not engage in intimidation or coercion (in their explicit or subtle forms), they should be sincere in their claim making, provide others with opportunities to speak and be heard, leave their partisan or ideological pre-commitments at the door, and consider arguments primarily on their merits. Furthermore, the reasons that participants give to each other should be accessible in the sense that they might be plausibly understood or accepted by others (e.g., Young 2000, Chap. 1).

Deliberative theory is full of "should" and "must" claims. As Gutmann and Thompson (2004) explain, in a deliberative democracy individuals and groups should "try to find fair terms of agreement" and they "should give reasons that appeal to principles others find reasonable" (p. 3). Importantly, participants in a deliberation "should try to find justifications that minimize their differences with opponents" (p. 7). According to Chambers:

> The rules of discourse stipulate that we must treat each other as equal partners in the process of deliberating about and choosing principles that will govern our collective interaction. Thus, each individual must be given the opportunity to speak her piece and stand up and say yes or no to a proposal. In addition to the negative requirement that individuals be given the space and opportunity to speak, moreover, productive discourses contain the positive requirement that individuals listen to each other, respond to each other, and justify their positions to each other. To treat each other as equal dialogue partners means that we must start from the assumption that each participant has something worthwhile to contribute to the discourse. (Chambers 1996, p. 100)

Similarly, O'Flynn (2007) argues that "deliberative democracy assumes that we will behave reasonably in our dealing with one another—that we will listen to one another with an open mind and will be willing to shift position in the light of the arguments we have heard and the principles upon which those arguments have been based. It further assumes that we will comply with whatever is eventually agreed" (p. 740).

It may be acknowledged that people *should* act in these deliberative ways—or that it is desirable for people to do so; indeed, acting deliberatively is consistent with the Kantian principle that we should treat people as ends in themselves—who must be moved by their own wills and not against their wills—and not as objects to be manipulated and used (e.g., Chambers 1996). The problem, as critics of deliberative democracy have pointed out, is that many people are not inclined to act in deliberative ways in political situations where interests diverge and there are differences of opinion (e.g., Mutz 2008). Specifying how people *should* act in order to deliberate effectively has left deliberative theory open to criticism from those who argue that we cannot bracket material interests, group identities, and power, more generally, in realistic accounts of politics (e.g., Achen and Bartels 2016; Lupia and Norton 2017; Sanders 1997). It is all very well that people *should* keep an open mind, be sincere in their claim making, make arguments that are accessible and plausibly acceptable to others, seek fair terms of accommodation, and do all the other things that deliberative theorists says they should do; but what happens when political actors do not do so, do not wish to do so, or can get what they want without doing so? As Warren (2007) points out: "Critics of deliberative democracy commonly note . . . that citizens are rarely as reasonable, self-aware, respectful, and enthusiastic about politics as deliberative ideals might suggest [or require]" (p. 276).

The demands that deliberation places on participants are considerable—that is one of the reasons that talk and persuasion are more fragile than other forms of power—but it is a mistake to think that participants need to be fully committed to deliberative ideals before we might obtain some of the practical and normative benefits of productive deliberations. We do not need to assume that people must be *willing* to listen to others as a matter of principle; instead, we can assume that they *will* listen if doing so is useful to them or necessary. And those who do not respect each other might nevertheless find themselves in situations where they have to act *as if* they respect each other to get some of what they want from collective decisions. The "realist" critics of deliberation argue that political actors will tend to use whatever tools are available to get what they want from others. I agree. But this does not mean that deliberation is politically unrealistic; it means that we have to think about how we might create productive deliberative environments. What are the conditions that make coercive and non-deliberative power less efficacious and deliberative forms of power more efficacious, and thus more attractive to those who are not otherwise committed to deliberative norms?

In what follows, I argue that deliberation will be used when collective decisions have to be made and domination is not possible. I specify three conditions that, taken together, will encourage political actors to engage with each other in deliberative ways, even if they are not committed to deliberative norms such as open-mindedness, intellectual humility, and mutual respect. What is more, these three conditions—although relatively rare—are easier to create or approximate in the real world of politics than many critics of deliberation have assumed.

Condition 1: Collective Decision Making

In order for deliberation to occur among those who are not already committed to deliberative ideals, those who disagree must be in situations where they have to make collective decisions together. This is a restatement of the political condition itself: politics—or the need for politics—emerges whenever we have to make collective decisions in the context of others who disagree. If individuals and groups making decisions together already agree on what is to be done, no persuasion (or coercion for that matter) will be needed. Similarly, if exit is a viable option, political actors may be able to get what they want or need by disassociating themselves from those who disagree. When individuals and groups can simply "part company" with those who disagree, they will have insufficient incentives to engage in persuasion or reciprocal reason giving: they will not have to talk to each other or listen, they will be free to maintain their positions as dogmatically as they wish, or they might agree to disagree and go their separate ways. The situation is different when exit is not a viable option, which is to say when individuals and groups must make collective decisions together. In this case, actors who do not agree with each other will have to try to persuade if they cannot dominate others or get what they want through threats or coercion or numerical dominance.

Condition 2: Approximate Equality

The second condition for productive deliberation has to do with distributions of power and influence. When political actors can get what they want, not by exiting collective relationships, but by forcing their wills upon others, they will have few incentives to engage in deliberation—they will be able to get what they want from others without trying to persuade. But when actors are approximately equally empowered within collective decision-making processes—and no group can force its will upon others through numerical dominance alone—no one will be able to get what they want without engaging in reciprocal claim making, reason giving, negotiation, bargaining, and persuasion. Equality in this case does not mean that each person or group should have equal power to influence collective *outcomes*. Equality in that form, which is what equal votes ideally provide, is problematic from a deliberative perspective because it implies that good and bad arguments are equally valuable and should be equally decisive in collective decision-making processes (e.g., Bächtiger et al. 2018, p. 6). Instead, what is needed is for each individual or group to have approximately equal *opportunities* to influence collective decisions (see, e.g., Knight and Johnson 1997, p. 280). This means that power and influence must be widely distributed such that no individuals or groups can get what they want from collective decisions while ignoring the concerns and interests of others who might disagree. Everyone should be in a position to voice their concerns, justify their positions, and be taken seriously by others, even if their arguments are not decisive in the end. In practice, this means that in order for productive deliberations to occur among people who are not already committed to deliberative norms, participants must be approximately equal with respect to the possibility of (not) using non-deliberative political tools such as threats, coercion, vetoes, and votes.

Condition 3: No Known Majorities

When collective decisions have to be made among (approximate) equals who (might) disagree with each other, political actors will be forced into deliberative postures: they will have to try to persuade even if they would rather not have to do so. But even in those circumstances, those who are in the majority will have few incentives to try to persuade those in the minority, and they will have license or opportunities to ignore or dismiss minority concerns. Veto powers can help address this problem by making it necessary for each set of actors to consent before collective actions can be taken. But veto powers can also inhibit deliberation by creating situations in which actors have insufficient incentives to *be persuaded*. Those who can prevent collective actions from taking place by using veto powers can dogmatically maintain their positions until others are forced to cave to their demands, even if doing so is worse for the group overall. The situation most conducive to productive deliberation is when no one has an absolute veto over collective decisions, everyone is approximately equally empowered within those decision-making processes, but no one can be sure in advance whether their positions are likely to command a majority. In these situations, political actors will have to try to persuade because they will not be able to get what they want through the use of non-deliberative political tools such as threats, coercion, vetoes, or numerical dominance.

It should be acknowledged that these three conditions are not *necessary* for good deliberations to occur. Productive deliberations might take place when actors are not forced to make collective decisions together but are nevertheless committed to deliberative norms and principles—when they respect each other and are willing to listen and be persuaded by good arguments.[12] When participants are committed to deliberative norms, deliberative practices can

[12] Participants in deliberative polls, for example, are formally equal but they are not expected to make collective decisions together. Nevertheless, these events tend to be quite deliberative (e.g.,

empower those who are not otherwise empowered. But these situations, in which those with access to non-deliberative forms of power deliberate with those who are not empowered on equal terms, are relatively rare—precisely because political actors are likely to use whatever tools are available to get what they want or need from others who disagree.

It should also be acknowledged that while these three conditions are sufficient for good deliberations to occur, political actors will not necessarily choose persuasion as their first option. They might, instead, try to stall, delay, and obstruct decision-making processes with the hope that their circumstances will change and they will be able to use non-deliberative tools in the near future. If this does not happen, if power remains approximately equally distributed such that no one can get what they want through coercion or numerical dominance, those who cannot exit but try to obstruct will eventually be forced to engage in deliberations and negotiations to get some of what they want or need from collective decisions.

Importantly, this way of thinking about deliberation addresses the concerns of deliberative democracy's most persuasive critics. It is commonly observed that people do not want to work out their differences through talk and persuasion or by searching for mutually agreeable accommodations. People would rather opt out of politics with their differences intact than laboriously deliberate their disagreements with others (e.g., Hibbing and Theiss-Morse 2002; Mutz 2006). Others have argued that most people are not capable of doing the difficult cognitive work that good deliberations require: they are not interested in doing it, and they have few incentives to learn how to do it well (e.g., Achen and Bartels 2016; Brennan 2016). Ian Shapiro (1999) has argued that we should stop talking about deliberation altogether because politics is about power and interests not mutual cooperation on fair terms of agreement. According to these critics, deliberation is an unrealistic theory that is designed for our better selves; it is not a viable theory of politics for the real world.

The theory of deliberation that I have developed here addresses these concerns in the following ways. First, it does not matter if people are willing

Fishkin 1995, 2009; Siu 2017). Although some have argued that "real" deliberation can only take place where binding decisions have to be made (e.g., Gutmann and Thompson 1996, 2004), others have argued that "everyday talk"—especially among those who disagree—should be considered deliberative in some respects (e.g., Mansbridge 1999). I tend to agree that deliberation—or discussion with some deliberative aspects—can occur even when binding collective decisions are not being made, but this does not challenge my claim that the need to make binding decisions in the context of equality where no one can dominate others will force political actors into deliberative postures.

and eager to deliberate. We can assume, like the "realist" critics, that people will use whatever political tools are available to get what they want from collective decisions. If this is the case, political actors will use deliberation when non-deliberative forms of power are unavailable. Second, it does not matter (that much) if people are initially ill-equipped to deliberate. When forced into deliberative postures by political circumstances, political actors (whomever they might be) will have strong incentives to learn to listen, provide justifications for their claims, and show respect to one another if they hope to get some of what they want from collective decisions. Third, this account of deliberation does not ignore power, and it does not depend on the unrealistic expectation that actors will eschew other forms of non-deliberative power when those are available. Instead, this theory of deliberation explicitly acknowledges the role that power—or balances of power—can play in creating conditions conducive to good deliberation. When balances of power are such that no one can use coercion and threats, actors will channel their strategic intent into democratic forms of power. When democratic forms of power—such as vetoes and numerical dominance—are not available, political actors will channel their strategic intent into deliberative forms of power. As Warren (2007) explains: "Institutionalizing deliberative democracy turns, in part, on structuring incentives in such a way that communicative utterances that are not necessarily deliberative in intention are captured to produce dynamics that are deliberative in function" (p. 278).

In short, this account of deliberation does not start with good intentions. It does not make stipulations about what political actors should be like if good deliberations are to happen. It does not assume that political actors must be willing to listen to their political opponents or that they will be eager to engage with them on mutually respectful terms. It does not assume that political actors will be open-minded and willing to be persuaded by good arguments when they hear them. But nor does it assume that people will never be willing to engage with others in deliberative terms. We should assume that some political actors will be committed to deliberative ideals such as mutual respect and intellectual humility—and some may even favour these ideals over their own strategic interests in some situations. But we cannot rely on people to act in deliberative ways when other options are available. We should, instead, assume that actors will use whatever political tools are available and build our institutions accordingly if we want to get some of the normative goods that productive deliberations can provide.

2.4.3. Real-World Deliberative Examples

At first glance, the account of deliberation outlined here might seem as unrealistic as any other. It is difficult to create and maintain political environments where exit is not a viable option, where political actors are approximately equally empowered, and where no groups or interests have known majorities. Nevertheless, these conditions are not as rare as we might expect. There are, in fact, many situations where actors engage each other on deliberative terms precisely because other political tools are either unavailable or inappropriate. Consider, again, the friendship group. We tend to think of our friends as equals, and it is for this reason that we often use deliberative tools for making decisions among friends. Where there are dominating persons in social groups, the dominant are likely to make group decisions on their own rather than using talk, persuasion, and negotiation.

There are many other circumstances where non-deliberative forms of power are either unavailable or less effective than deliberative ones. Elected legislatures are often less deliberative than they should be, but they nevertheless create—and are designed to create—conditions conducive to good deliberation. The members of legislative chambers have to make collective decisions together (Condition 1). They might stall, delay, and get gridlocked, but exit is not normally an option: legislators either have to make decisions together or pay the practical and political consequences of inaction. In a legislative chamber each member is formally equal with respect to their vote (Condition 2)—even though they are not always equally empowered with respect to voice and the power of initiative. Furthermore, there is evidence that elected politicians are more likely to resort to persuasion, reason giving, and deliberative negotiation when there are no known majorities in legislative chambers (Condition 3). Steiner et al. (2004), for example, show that deliberative quality is higher where there is less party discipline, where the divide between government and opposition is less clear or more fluid, and where no party or parliamentary group can be assured of their majority in advance of votes being taken (see, as well, Steiner 2012). The reason that legislative chambers are often less deliberative than they might be is precisely because the third condition for productive deliberation is often missing: when there are known majorities and rigid party discipline in legislative chambers, majority parties (or voting blocs) can ignore the interests and concerns of minorities with impunity.

Judicial panels, such as those used in many appellate courts, also create conditions that are conducive to good deliberation. Judges on panels—such as those on the US Supreme Court—have to make decisions or rulings together (Condition 1) and power is equally distributed within the court: each judge has approximately equal opportunities to influence the others through persuasion, each has an equal vote when deliberations are complete, and no one has ready access to non-deliberative forms of influence (Condition 2). Where there are no known majorities in favour or against particular decisions, judges have to seek to persuade each other to make rulings consistent with their own interpretations of the law (Condition 3). Where there are known majorities, judges in the majority will have fewer reasons to try to persuade those in the minority. But even in those situations, judges are likely to engage in deliberation with each other when examining the issues, interpreting the law, and trying to come to their own conclusions about what the law requires.[13] Although most judges are well-trained to engage in deliberation, and many are no doubt committed to deliberative norms, they do not *need* to be committed to those norms in order for good deliberations to take place on judicial panels. The members of a court do not need to like or respect each other, and some might be dogmatically committed to particular ways of thinking about the law or their roles as judges. Some judges may be consciously or unconsciously biased against certain types of arguments or people. Nevertheless, once they are on the bench, they will have to listen to each other, respect each other's arguments, and offer reasoned justifications for their views if they hope to get anything done.

Juries are also often quite deliberative (e.g., Bächtiger et al. 2018, p. 10; Gastil et al. 2007; York and Cornwell 2006). Jurors must make collective judgments about guilt or innocence (Condition 1). Each juror has approximately equal opportunities to make arguments and influence the views of others, and every juror has an equal vote in the final decision (Condition 2). Importantly, jurors do not normally know if they are in the majority before deliberations begin (Condition 3).

In recent years many jurisdictions have experimented with minipublics, or small issue-specific, deliberative forums. The members of minipublics may be self-selected, but they are often randomly selected to ensure that

[13] It would be possible, perhaps, to make judicial panels more deliberative by randomly selecting different judges for each ruling from a larger pool of qualified or sitting judges. This would make it more difficult for judges, or anyone else, to know whether there is a majority in favour of any particular decision before deliberations begin (Condition 3).

different types of people, interests, and ideas are represented. In the typical case, the members of a minipublic will sit for a limited period of time; learn about a specific topic, policy issue, or law proposal; and deliberate with each other. In some cases, minipublics may be empowered to make collective decisions or policy recommendations to governments or voters (e.g., Setälä and Smith 2018). Deliberative minipublics can play a number of different roles in democratic systems. They have, for example, been used to design alternative electoral systems in Canada and the Netherlands (e.g., Fournier et al. 2011; Warren and Pearse 2008), guide constitutional reform processes in Iceland (e.g., Landemore 2015) and Ireland (e.g., Farrell et al. 2013), and help inform voters on complex ballot questions (e.g., Gastil et al. 2018).

Minipublics are, in fact, designed to create conditions conducive to good deliberation. They are often, although not always, charged with making collective decisions, recommendations, or public statements about specific policy issues (Condition 1). Each member of a minipublic is formally equal: they participate as individuals not as members of interest groups or parties; they have approximately equal opportunities to voice their concerns, articulate arguments, and respond to claims made by others; and each member has an equal vote when decisions are made (Condition 2). And because minipublics are formally non-partisan, it is not normally possible for members to know if they are in the majority before deliberations and voting have taken place (Condition 3). In practice, minipublics are highly deliberative, especially when compared to partisan legislative chambers (e.g., Fishkin 1995, 2009; Fournier et al. 2011; Ratner 2008; Siu 2017). Importantly, minipublics are deliberative because of the conditions they create, not because participants have prior skills as deliberators and principled commitments to deliberative norms.

Judicial panels, juries, and minipublics are of interest to deliberative theorists because they create deliberative spaces within otherwise non-deliberative political arenas. Nevertheless, it is possible to find effective deliberative practices where the conditions for deliberation are more loosely approximated. Consider, for example, the deliberative aspects of election campaigns. At first glance there does not appear to be much deliberation going on during campaigns. Candidates make public pronouncements, but they do not normally engage in constructive deliberations with each other or with the public more generally. Their aim is to make distinctions between themselves and others to gain an electoral advantage. As Gutmann and Thompson (2018) point out: "Campaigns by their nature are strategic and competitive interactions, not deliberative exchanges. They do not serve their function if opponents are cooperating when they should be competing" (p. 903).

Nevertheless, the very fact that decisions have to be made at election time (Condition 1) and each citizen has a vote (Condition 2), forces candidates to appeal to the public with reasons, justifications, and explanations for what they plan to do. In many cases, it is unclear before an election who is going to win (Condition 3), and this encourages candidates to persuade voters to support them at election time. Indeed, candidates tend to do more campaigning and persuasion in competitive districts and regions than they do in safe seats and areas. Tellingly, politicians rarely attempt to publicly justify themselves or their policies to those who do not have the vote. Those without the vote, such as migrants or non-citizen immigrants, are more likely to be made scapegoats or targets in election campaigns; they are almost never the addressees of justifications and public reason giving.

There are also deliberative moments in the highly strategic world of international relations. As Risse (2018) explains, a number of case studies have demonstrated that international agreements on issues ranging from the establishment of the International Criminal Court, to environmental treaties, to the indefinite extension of the Nuclear Nonproliferation Treaty have been forged through both bargaining and deliberation (p. 521). Although Risse (2018) and others (e.g., Müller 2004) have emphasized the role that norms play in making deliberation possible in international affairs, we should expect states and non-state actors in the international arena to engage in persuasion and deliberative negotiation when the conditions for deliberation are present. Which is to say if (1) they *have* to make decisions together and exit is not an option or it is too costly; (2) they are approximately equally empowered with respect to non-deliberative sources of influence (such as economic power or nuclear weapons); and (3) it is not clear whether they have enough support from allies to force decisions on others through non-democratic means such as military might or numerical dominance. In these circumstances, which do often prevail in the international arena, states and non-state actors who are not necessarily committed to deliberative norms will have incentives to engage with each other in deliberative terms.

These examples help illustrate that productive deliberations can—and often do—occur in the real political world, even though strategic actors are not always committed to deliberative norms. The conditions conducive to deliberation are not common, but they are not absent from our political world either, and they are more common than many critics of deliberation have acknowledged. It is possible to get many of the normative goods of deliberation (e.g., collective will formation, mutual understanding, respect, and integrative solutions to shared problems) without making the assumption that strategic actors will favour communicative action over other forms of action when non-deliberative political tools are available. In order to get deliberative goods, we cannot expect actors to enter the political realm with fully developed deliberative commitments, but we can work to create political conditions and institutions that make persuasion more attractive and efficient than other forms of power and influence. As Warren (2007) explains, "as a theoretical matter, we should expect participants to enter into communication with strategic intent: it is part of what defines an issue as 'political' that participants disagree, and yet have stakes that motivate them to win. Institutions should be designed to channel strategic intent into talk, with the hope that when participants can *only* get their way through talk, they will seek to persuade" (p. 278).

2.5. Conclusion

In this chapter, I have outlined, defined, and discussed the concepts and terms that form the foundation of a deliberative theory of future-regarding collective action. The future is difficult to imagine and more difficult to describe in systematic ways. We often use terms such as "the future" without specifying whether we are talking about the near future or the far future, our future selves or future others, or whether we think we can predict the future or actively choose between different possible futures. We do not have readily available terms to describe people or institutions that are *not* biased against the future, and we often fail to recognize that all public decisions (and non-decisions) will have both short- and long-term consequences. I have also argued that we will need to exercise public power in future-regarding ways if we want to create desirable futures for ourselves and future others. The critical task, then, is to think about how we can encourage otherwise strategic political actors—who may or may not care about the future or be committed to any principles of intergenerational justice—to more seriously consider the future when making collective decisions today.

3
Moving Beyond Theories of Intergenerational Justice

3.1. Introduction

The most common approach to understanding intergenerational relations involves thinking about what justice between generations might require. This approach is attractive because justice and rights claims typically have priority over other types of political agreements. Duties of justice cannot be legitimately ignored for partisan or strategic purposes, nor can they be superseded by competing principles, values, or norms, unless those competing claims are also framed in terms of justice. Theorists of intergenerational justice are concerned that the interests, needs, and rights of future others will not be adequately protected by politics alone, precisely because political agreements are likely to favour the interests of current publics over those of future publics. Future-regarding political commitments or agreements made today can always be changed or abandoned by future political actors.

I understand the desire to find a "correct" theory of justice that would tell us what we *must* do for future others, but I do not think that is a realistic or normatively desirable goal. As Amartya Sen (1999) argues, there is no "wonderful formula" that would tell us what is just in different (and changing) circumstances, because how we should weigh and balance different, and often competing, goods requires "social evaluation" and collective judgment, and not the application of some "impersonal technology," formula, or philosophical reckoning (pp. 78–79).

If justice, itself, is an essentially contested concept, as Gallie (1956) has argued, it seems especially unrealistic to think that we might find a theory of intergenerational justice that is sufficient to both motivate and legitimize future-regarding collective actions. Terence Ball (1986) has argued that the very idea of intergenerational justice is incoherent if concepts of justice are—and should be—mutable, historically grounded, context dependent, and sensitive to changing circumstances. What was considered just in the past is

Future Publics. Michael K. MacKenzie, Oxford University Press. © Oxford University Press 2021.
DOI: 10.1093/oso/9780197557150.003.0003

not what is considered just today; and what will be considered just by future others will depend on their own judgments about what to value—which will, in turn, depend, in part, on the decisions that current publics make today.

In practical terms, we cannot achieve anything like justice between generations—even if we were to have some sense of what intergenerational justice might entail—because we can have no influence over what has been done in the past (that ship has sailed), and because we have only limited influence over the actions of future others (see Chapter 6). This does not mean that we cannot—or should not—act according to what we believe is right, given our present circumstances and what we think we know about the potential interests of future others. On the contrary, theories of justice—or normative claims about what is right or wrong more generally—have a critically important role to play in helping guide our collective decisions. But theories of intergenerational justice that ignore or abstract away from concrete concerns, specificities, and practical or ontological realities can do little—and less than is normally assumed—to help us navigate the challenges associated with future-regarding collective actions. In this chapter, I argue that we need to move beyond theories of intergenerational justice if we are going to act in future-regarding ways that adequately respond to what we do know—or can know—about the past, the present, and the future.

In doing so, I advance an explicitly political—democratic and deliberative—approach to understanding intergenerational relations; an approach that is elaborated upon in subsequent chapters. I argue that we should aim to strike a balance between the concerns of the present and the potential interests of the future (as we understand them), but that judgments about how to strike that balance should, in each case, be made in inclusive, deliberative arenas and not formulated by philosophers or technocrats working in isolation from affected publics. The collective judgments we make might be considered just or fair (in some sense of those terms) if they are made in sufficiently inclusive deliberative processes, such that no individuals and groups can trample upon the interests of others (see, e.g., Sen 1999; Young 2000). But collective judgments about what should be considered just (or right or wrong) must also be recognized as political agreements, or collective commitments, that respond to contemporary exigencies and are reflexive in the sense of being open to revisions in the face of changing circumstances and concerns (see, as well, Dryzek and Pickering 2019). If we have sufficiently inclusive and deliberative democratic processes, we will be in a better position to decide how the diverse and conflicting interests and concerns represented in current publics should be weighed and balanced against the equally diverse (but as-yet-unknown) interests of future publics. But this is likely the best that we can do. Any judgments about what we should do for (or to) the future will have to remain open to revision: they will not have the status of timeless and immutable theories of justice, and they will not give us the peace of mind that such theories aim to provide.

3.2. Theories of Intergenerational Justice

A vast literature on intergenerational justice has flourished since John Rawls's (1971) initial attempt to deal with the subject in *A Theory of Justice*. There are utilitarian (e.g., Sumner 1978), libertarian (e.g., Steiner and Vallentyne 2009), contractural (Barry 1978; Heath 2013; Rawls 1971, 1993, 1999), reciprocal (e.g., Gosseries 2009), and sufficientarian (e.g., Meyer 2016; Meyer and Roser 2009) theories of intergenerational justice. Some scholars have argued that future people have rights (e.g., Gosseries 2008), while others have argued that we cannot give rights to entities that do not exist and might never come to exist (e.g., Beckerman 2006; Beckerman and Pasek 2001). Mazor (2010) has argued that although future people do not have rights themselves, contemporaries have obligations to each other that pertain to the interests of future people.

Parfit (1984) famously argued that we cannot harm future people in any straightforward, person-affecting way because *who* comes to exist in the future will depend on which decisions we make today. If we make better decisions, one group of people will come to exist. If we make worse decisions, a different group of people will exist. In either case, we cannot say that those future individuals were helped or harmed by the decisions we made. Parfit was uncomfortable with this conclusion because it would seem to imply that we do not have any obligations to future others—or at least to future individuals. Thomas H. Thompson (1981), by contrast, embraced the idea that we do not have obligations to those in the far future with whom we cannot interact directly. Jana Thompson (2009) and Richard Vernon (2016) have argued that questions of justice—and obligations—arise when we are thinking both forward and backward in time.[1]

[1] Meyer (2016) provides an introduction to the literature on intergenerational justice. There are also a number of edited volumes on the subject including Sikora and Barry (1978), Partridge (1981), Laslett and Fishkin (1992), Tremmel (2006, 2009), and Gosseries and Meyer (2009).

It is not my intention to provide a full accounting of why various theories of intergenerational justice succeed or fail on their own terms. Instead, in this chapter, I use two examples—Rawls's just savings principle and a reciprocity-based theory of intergenerational justice—to illustrate my critiques of a justice-based approach to understanding intergenerational relations more generally. After that, I outline some of the advantages of thinking about intergenerational relations in explicitly democratic and deliberative terms. In short, a deliberative approach to understanding our relations with future others forces us to respond to—rather than abstract away from—the realities of the past, our contemporary conditions, and future potentialities in reflexive ways; and that is precisely what is needed if we hope to navigate through the present to get to futures that we think we might want (see Chapter 5; Dryzek and Pickering 2019). Adopting a democratic approach also enables us to take collective actions without having to wait for or find a "correct" or agreed upon theory of justice—the search for which can itself be an impediment to action (Goodhart 2018). Lastly, a deliberative approach to understanding intergenerational relations frees us to think and act in ways that go beyond the minimum requirements of justice (whatever we think those might be).

3.2.1. Rawls's Just Savings Principle

Rawls's just savings principle is one of the most influential theories of intergenerational justice. As is well known, Rawls uses the concept of the veil of ignorance to help us think through what justice, in general terms, might require. Those who are behind the veil of ignorance must decide what is just without knowing details about themselves (such as their genders or ethnicities) or their circumstances (such as whether they are rich or poor). When thinking about intergenerational justice, Rawls stipulates that those in the original position (i.e., those behind the veil of ignorance) are contemporaries, but that they do not know where they will find themselves in the chain of generations or what previous generations will have done for them. This stipulation prevents us from having to imagine an intergenerational conference of the dead, the living, and the not yet living. Instead, Rawls asks us to consider what fair terms of association might look like for contemporaries in the original position who are thinking about intergenerational relations. According to Rawls (1993), the "correct principle is that which the members of any generation (and so all generations) would adopt as the one their generation is to follow and as the principle they would want preceding generations to have followed (and later generations to follow), no matter how far back (or forward) in time" (p. 274).

The principle that Rawls identifies is what he calls the just savings principle. "Obviously, if all generations are to gain (except perhaps the earlier ones), the parties must agree to a savings principle that insures that each generation receives its due from its predecessors and does its fair share for those to come" (Rawls 1999, p. 254).[2] But there are two stages to this process. During the "accumulation stage," generations are required to save for the future. Once enough savings have been accumulated and just background institutions have been established, a society will enter the "steady state stage." During this second stage of the process, generations are required to maintain their inheritances, but they are not obligated to contribute any more savings to future generations—although they may wish to do so if they choose. As Rawls (1999) explains: "Eventually, once just background institutions are firmly established and all the basic liberties effectively realized, the net accumulation asked for falls to zero. At this point a society meets its duty of justice by maintaining just institutions and preserving their material base" (p. 255).[3]

It is not my purpose to critique Rawls's theory of intergenerational justice within the scope of the approach he has adopted—there are many others who have done that already (e.g., Attas 2009; Barry 1978; English 1977; Gardiner 2009; Heyd 2009). My purpose is to critique the idea that we should think about intergenerational relations in purely abstract, philosophical terms. It is, of course, important to acknowledge that Rawls does not aim to construct a realistic account of intergenerational relations: he uses a hypothetical thought experiment to identify an ideal theory that might be used to help guide or constrain our actions. Nevertheless, Rawls's conclusions are so far removed from the realities of intergenerational relations that we

[2] Rawls makes several statements of this principle in different texts. But as he explains in *Political Liberalism*, while there are differences between the various statements of the just savings principle, they are broadly consistent with each other (Rawls 1993, p. 274, note 12).

[3] Rawls does not see the just savings principle as being supplementary to the other principles that he defines in *A Theory of Justice*. Indeed, the just savings principle is supposed to constrain the difference principle, which is the idea that any inequalities must be justified by benefitting those who are worst off the most. As he explains: "In any generation their expectations are to be maximized subject to the condition of putting aside the savings that would be acknowledged [according to the just savings principle]. Thus the complete statement of the difference principle includes the savings principle as a constraint. Whereas the first principle of justice and the principle of fair opportunity are prior to the difference principle within generations, the savings principle limits its scope between them" (Rawls 1999, p. 258).

should question both the practical utility and the normative legitimacy of his approach.

Rawls's theory has an air of unreality because he aims, like other theorists of intergenerational justice, to determine, or discover, what justice would entail for *all* generations through *all* time. As philosophers we might imagine what just relations between generations should consist of, from the first generation to the last, but that approach is not, in fact, consistent with our epistemic positions in time or the powers that we might (or might not) have to coordinate the actions of non-contemporaries. There is no perch that we might sit upon that would give us a view of the whole scope of human experience from the earliest times into the farthest reaches of the future, and while we have some power over our contemporaries, we have no power over the past and limited power over the actions of future others who do not yet exist (see, e.g., Chapter 6). Imagining what just relations through all time might (or should) consist of may be an engaging philosophical activity, but if the abstract models we use to try to understand intergenerational relations are too far removed from our reality as political agents who are both embedded and constrained by time, the conclusions we draw from those models may be insufficient to the task at hand: which is to figure out how we should act *now* given our own interests, needs, and ethical principles, and the potential interests of future others as we understand them.

Rawls's approach demands too much from us in epistemic terms, while at the same time excluding information that we do, in fact, possess and which may be relevant to our judgments about what we should do for the future. Those in the original position, for example, do not know whether the past has saved for them. The purpose of this stipulation in Rawls's theory is to encourage us (i.e., the philosophers) to imagine what just relations between generations might consist of without our judgments being tainted by our material interests. But in the real world, whatever we decide we should do for the future will need to *depend* on what the past has, or has not, done. Indeed, we may have to compensate for the actions of the past if we hope to make the future better. We might, for example, be obliged (in some way) to actively address or eliminate, if we can, the injustices and inequalities that are legacies of slavery in the United States and elsewhere—not just for the sake of our contemporaries but also to free future generations from those injustices (e.g., Vernon 2016). The fact that we *should* have to do this is unjust according to an ideal theory of intergenerational justice: if the past had not acted unjustly, we would not have to shoulder the burdens of having to correct the lingering effects of their mistakes. In this case, then, rather than illuminating what intergenerational justice might require, Rawls's theory of justice misdirects us by depriving us of information that is relevant—indeed essential—to our judgments about what we should do for the future.

In practical terms, there is no possibility to make justice prevail for *all* generations through *all* time because there is nothing we can do today to change what happened in the past, and we only have limited influence over future others who do not yet exist. The task we are faced with is not deciding how past, present, and future others ought to act (or ought to have acted); the task we are faced with is deciding what we should do now—for ourselves and future others—given the situations we find ourselves in. There is little doubt that Rawls understands this, but he is, like other theorists of intergenerational justice, largely unconcerned with the mismatch between his model of justice and the realities we find ourselves in as temporally embedded agents with limited views of the past and the future and little influence over the actions of our non-contemporaries.

Rawls's theory is problematic on normative grounds if, by abstracting away from relevant or essential information, his approach makes it more difficult for us to make good judgments about what we should do for the future. But his theory is normatively problematic for another reason as well. He imagines that it is possible for philosophers, working in isolation from affected publics, to identify principles of justice that might be considered "correct" in an objective and timeless way (e.g., Rawls 1993, p. 274). The assumption is that only a "correct" theory of justice can be used to legitimately constrain collective actions or resist those that are unjust according to that theory. But there are, and always will be, reasonable disagreements about what justice might require in any particular context—such as, for example, whether we have saved enough for the future to transition from the "accumulation stage" of development to the "steady state stage." Nevertheless, Rawls argues that his theory of intergenerational justice is "correct," and thus might be used to justifiably constrain democratically made decisions that are—or are thought be—contrary to his principle of justice. As he explains: "Although one believes in the soundness of a democratic constitution and accepts the duty to support it, the duty to comply with particular laws may be overridden in situations where the collective judgment is sufficiently unjust" (p. 261). There is, of course, room in democratic theory and practice for antagonistic opposition and resistance to procedurally legitimate but unjust collective decisions. But Rawls's theory of justice, like any other, is a historically mutable one grounded in a particular way of thinking about the world, and it should be acknowledged as such (e.g., Ball 1985). Once the particularity of Rawls's theory of justice is acknowledged, it no longer looks legitimate for him, or anyone else, to make claims that their "correct" theory of justice should be given priority over collective decisions, especially those that are made in legitimate (i.e., inclusive, empowered, and deliberative) democratic processes.

3.2.2. Reciprocity-Based Theories of Intergenerational Justice

Other theorists have thought about intergenerational relations as being grounded in obligations of reciprocity. As Gosseries (2009) explains, "the idea of reciprocity refers here to an equivalence in respective contributions, in the context of an exchange." He goes on to clarify that "equivalence does not mean that we should give back the very same object, but rather something of equivalent 'value'" (p. 120). As Gosseries himself points out, at first glance, a reciprocity-based approach to understanding intergenerational relations does not seem promising. Contemporaries in different age groups can exchange goods with each other—making contributions to each other and receiving benefits in return—but non-contemporaries cannot engage in mutual exchanges. The past can make contributions to the future, but the future cannot benefit the past in turn. Furthermore, it is not clear that receiving something is sufficient to establish any sort of obligation to give back something of equivalent value.[4]

Although he does not favour a reciprocity-based theory of intergenerational justice himself, Gosseries (2009) has argued that this approach is more credible than many critics have assumed, and he invites us to think about the following principle: no individual or generation should be required to be a net contributor or allowed to be a net beneficiary in the grand scheme of human interactions over time. Gosseries defends different versions of this principle in a number of ways. He argues, for example, that those who allow themselves to benefit from the contributions of the past while failing to make

[4] Brian Barry (1989) has illustrated this objection with the following example: "If someone offers me a toffee apple out of the blue, and I accept it, does my enjoyment of the toffee apple create even the tiniest obligation to distribute toffee apples to others? I do not see that it does" (p. 232). Gosseries (2009), however, explains why this is not, necessarily, a decisive objection against reciprocity-based theories of intergenerational justice.

contributions to the future may be considered free riders (pp. 130–135). On this account, we have to think of human interactions over time as collective enterprises that require contributions from each person in each generation: those who take but do not contribute are not fulfilling their obligations to the intergenerational collectivity. Gosseries also argues that a reciprocity-based theory of intergenerational justice can cope with generational cohorts of different sizes, which is a challenge that Rawls does not address in his theory of intergenerational justice (pp. 137–144).

It is not my intention to critique the arguments that Gosseries (2009) makes, which are carefully constructed and internally consistent within the scope of the approach he adopts. My intention is to subject the approach itself to critique. The idea that no individual or generation should be required to be a net contributor or allowed to be a net beneficiary is intuitively appealing, but it is, like Rawls's just savings principle, so far removed from the realities of intergenerational relations that we should question its practical utility and normative legitimacy.

Consider, for example, Gosseries's decision to focus his discussion on four abstract and adjacent generations (G1, G2, G3, G4).[5] These generations can interact with each other, as well as make mutual exchanges of goods in both directions, from older to younger and from younger to older people. In the real world there are, typically, three or four adjacent generations living at the same time, and these abstract models of generational relations can help us think more clearly about otherwise impossibly complex problems. But this approach is oddly ahistorical for a theory of justice that is concerned with human relations *over time*. The generations in Gosseries's theory, like the persons behind Rawls's veil of ignorance, are conceptually removed from their positions *in time*, and this both creates problems that are not problems in the real world and abstracts away from problems that are.

Consider, for example, two "problems" identified by intergenerational justice theorists working with abstract models: the problem of the initial generation, and the problem of the generation of extinction.[6] If the

[5] It is common for theorists of intergenerational justice to limit their analyses to a small number of abstract generations. Examples include Birnbacher (2009), Gardiner (2009), Mazor (2010), and Parfit (1984).

[6] These two "problems" are discussed by many theorists who adopt abstract models of intergenerational relations. Gardiner (2009), for example, focuses his discussion of Rawls on these two "problems." And Rawls (1999) himself acknowledges the "problem" of the initial generation when he states that "it is immediately obvious that every generation, except possibly the first, gains when a reasonable rate of saving is maintained" (p. 256).

objective is to ensure that no individual or generation is a net contributor or beneficiary, it is unclear how the first generation might be treated fairly given that they cannot receive anything from their predecessors. This "problem" rules out a reciprocity-based theory that would require transfers that run in only one direction, from older to younger generations, as is the case with Rawls's just savings principle. A reciprocity-based theory must include mutual exchanges between generations, such that older people provide something to younger ones (such as education) and younger generations provide something to older people in return (such as pensions) (Gosseries 2009). But this does not explain how just reciprocal intergenerational relations can start. And when we adopt a model with a limited number of generations, this really does look like a problem: the first generation will be a net contributor, and that is unjust. Furthermore, it is not clear what would obligate—or motivate—the "first" generation to contribute to the whole future scheme of human relations over time. (If the first generation *is* motivated to contribute, their contribution would have to be considered supererogatory, and thus outside the theory of justice itself.)

What is more, the final generation—or the "generation of extinction"—would be a net beneficiary: they would benefit from the work of previous generations, but they would not have to contribute anything to the collective enterprise because there would be no future others to transfer resources to. On this account, in a fully just world, the last generation would appear to be in the most desirable position! But that cannot be right. As Scheffler (2013, 2018) has argued, much of the meaning in our own lives depends on the assumption that there will be a future for others who have meaningful lives. The point of the matter is that these "problems" are artifacts of the way the theories have been constructed.[7] They are not

[7] This is illustrated in Gardiner's discussion of the "problem of the generation of extinction." Without going into the details of his argument, it is worth considering the following quote: "Intuitively, it seems that Proposal D has much to recommend it; but the Constraint Principle gives us no reason to favour Proposal D. Indeed, there is some reason to believe that if the situation is modelled as a single generation trying to decide on proposals, it will choose A, B, or C over D, *since it expects to come into existence under any proposal*, and D promises a lower level of resources than all of the others" (p. 113, emphasis added). The idea that a generation of people might make decisions based on whether they expect to come into existence in the future is so far beyond reality that we have to question the utility of the approach. I am sympathetic to the analytical challenges that Gardiner and other theorists of intergenerational justice are facing, and I am impressed by the analytical sophistication and rigor of their theories and models, but when we start talking about generations of people making policy decisions based on whether those policies will allow them to come into existence in the future it seems likely that something has gone wrong.

problems that we face in the real world, where there never was an "initial" generation (at least in any meaningful sense of this term); where we do not know when there will be a "final" generation; and where it seems, on the contrary, most sensible to act as if there will be future others—even though at some point life as we know it will come to an end, possibly on account of our own actions.

This critique is not only an observation about the impossibility of ever fully realizing ideal forms of justice; it is, instead, a challenge to the very idea that supposedly timeless, ideal forms of intergenerational justice can or should guide our actions in the present. As mentioned, what we *should* do for the future might very well depend on what the past has or has not done, and we may be called upon to do more for the future than justice (or fairness) would require in order to correct or compensate for past injustices. As a philosophical exercise, we can stipulate what just relations between *all* generations might consist of in abstract or ideal terms according to our own concepts of justice, but it is unclear what the utility of such an approach might be given that past generations have very probably violated any conceivable theory of intergenerational justice we might construct, and there is nothing we can do to make future others adhere to, or even understand, our own temporally and philosophically parochial theories of justice.

Importantly, as Ball (1985) has argued, acknowledging that our conceptions of justice and fairness are political, parochial, historically mutable, context dependent, and thus relativistic in some sense, does not mean that we cannot, or should not, act well according to our own lights or normative precepts. Rather than thinking about what intergenerational justice might entail in abstract, ideal, and timeless terms, we should start with were we are now: we are temporally embedded agents with histories and beliefs about how the world ought to be. We have no power over the past and only limited (primarily persuasive) influence over how future others will come to act in their own time (see, Chapter 6). We know our actions will have future consequences, but we cannot be sure precisely what those consequences will be. Instead of thinking about intergenerational relations in abstract, ideal terms, we should think about how to make collective decisions that cater to our own needs and interests (in all their diversity) without ignoring, dismissing, or marginalizing the potential interests of future others as we understand them. Ultimately, that is all we *can* do for the future.

3.3. Intergenerational Relations as Political Relations

There are at least three reasons why we should think about intergenerational relations in explicitly political terms. First, theories of justice are not sufficient to support or compel collective actions. Second, theorists of justice are political in ways that their proponents are often reluctant but remiss to acknowledge. Third, we need to move beyond theories of intergenerational justice because much of what we want to do for the future—indeed, much of what we *should* do for the future—may be considered supererogatory.

3.3.1. Theories of Justice Cannot Compel Action

Theories of justice are not just *theories* of justice: they are also intended to compel action by establishing obligations and duties. This is a Kantian way of thinking about the relationship between duty or obligation and action. For Kant, we are, in a strong sense, compelled to act on moral principles if they establish rationally grounded ethical, moral, or justice-based obligations. On this view, collective action problems may be solved through the theorization of justice alone: if our obligations of justice are grounded in rational claims that cannot be reasonably rejected, then action should follow from theorization without the stuff of politics—without the negotiation, bargaining, persuasion or coercion that may be needed when disagreements about what should be done persist. Once a "correct" theory of justice has been identified, the stuff of politics will be largely irrelevant—and possibility counterproductive—to getting things done in the right way. If there is a just thing that should be done, we have an obligation to do it, and any disagreements or failures to act on obligations or duties of justice should be viewed as evidence of either ignorance of what is right or just or willful neglect of the right or just. If people willfully neglect their obligations or duties of justice, they may be legitimately forced to act in ways that are consistent with those obligations, but that is all that we will have to say about politics once we have established a "correct" theory of justice.

In practice, justice theorists often separate the problem of moral action into two sequentially ordered steps. The first step involves identifying what justice would require in ideal terms. This is the realm of ideal theory. The second step involves trying to approximate principles of justice in the nonideal world where there are conflicting interests and beliefs and where people are not necessarily motivated by justice. This is the realm of non-ideal theory. As Michael Goodhart (2018) has argued, the problem with this two-step approach is not just that it is impossible to realize ideal principles in the real world, but rather that the first step cannot be completed. Questions having to do with concepts such as justice, political legitimacy, democracy, and the human condition more generally cannot be "correctly" answered or decided (for all time) because these concepts are irreducibly complex, context dependent, and essentially contested—which means that they are not amenable to resolution through logical argumentation and eventual agreement (Gallie 1956). If this is the case, we will not—indeed cannot—move past the first step to the second. We will continue to search for a theory of justice that is "correct," and when such a theory is not forthcoming, we will theorize some more, labouring under the assumption that we must identify what justice is before legitimate collective actions can be taken. This approach leads to what Goodhart (2018) has called "theoretical paralysis." But it is not the activities of the philosophers that are paralyzed in the process; philosophical debates about what justice requires will continue to flourish. It is collective action that is paralyzed; we will be unable to act if we think that we have to complete the impossible task of identifying "correct"—or even widely agreed upon—principles of justice before we can take *any* actions as collectivities. At the same time, we must acknowledge that both actions and inactions have consequences, and we thus cannot avoid morally objectionable outcomes until such time as we can correctly identify ideal theories of justice. In these circumstances, which *are* our circumstances, the best we can do is to figure out how to act well in the real political world even though we do not have access to universally accepted moral principles or objectively correct—or timeless and immutable—theories of justice.

3.3.2. Theories of Justice Are Political

The theories of justice that we have, which cannot be considered correct or timeless in any objective sense, are political in at least the following three ways. First, abstract theories of justice are by definition incomplete because collective (i.e., political) decisions will always have to be made about their substantive contents. Rawls's just savings principle, for example, tells us only that each generation has to save enough until just background institutions have been established. But how will we determine what resources should be saved, how much savings are enough, and what just background institutions should consist of? Individuals and groups will have divergent views on these questions and their perspectives will be shaped—as they *should* be—by their own positions within society, their ideological or moral commitments, and their material interests. The idea that we should save (something) for the future does not get us very far: we need political—ideally inclusive and deliberative—processes to workout *what* we are going to save, *how* we are going to save, who will bear the costs of those savings, and how much savings is enough. We need political processes to fill in the substantive contents of any theory of justice.

Second, theories of justice are political in the sense that they aim to do *political* work: which is to say that they are valuable or useful primarily as political resources. Justice theorists make claims about the rights, obligations, and duties of individuals and groups on the assumption that those claims can be used to guide or constrain actions when they are accepted or acknowledged as obligations by others. But any rights claims or theories of justice that might plausibly play this role in public affairs, such as property rights, political rights to participation, and even gun rights in the United States, have been given their status as rights in political processes (see, e.g., Ignatieff 2001). They have been identified, forged, and accepted as rights, not because they have been recognized as natural, timeless, and universal by all actors, but because they have been designated as rights with correlative duties in processes of political wrangling—as in, for example, the very politicized processes of constitution making.

Third, theories of justice are political because what is right or proper in particular cases depends on the mixture of concerns, interests, positions, and claims of those who may be affected or subjected to public decisions. There are no pre-political (or non-political) means of determining how fair accommodations should be made, especially when there are, for example, conflicting resource claims. Collective judgments about how resources should be distributed will depend on how many people there are, what their needs are, how resources were distributed in the past, and what those resources may be used for. We might agree to make distinctions between individuals and groups based on some criteria, such as age, socioeconomic status, or national identity, and we may agree that other distinctions such as gender and ethnicity are not legitimate grounds for discrimination. We might also agree to make exceptions to those agreements in order to produce outcomes that are fairer or more just in some other respects. Affirmative action policies, for example, treat people differently based on race and gender for the purposes of acknowledging and mitigating, at least to some extent, the historical and structural disadvantages that people with certain characteristics still face in some circumstances. The point is not that we should, necessarily, support affirmative action policies; the point is that there are no pre-political or ideal theoretical justifications for them. Affirmative action policies can only be justified—when they are justified—as responses to the particular circumstances that certain people find themselves in. On this account, we cannot know what justice entails—or what fair accommodations might look like—without considering the interests, needs, beliefs, and circumstances of those who will be affected by public decisions or collective actions.

As Iris Marion Young (2000) has argued, there is a tight theoretical connection between democracy, deliberation, and inclusion, on the one hand, and just political outcomes, on the other hand. On her account, we will tend to get political outcomes that not only look just but are just, in a certain sense of that term, when all those who are affected by collective decisions have some meaningful influence over those decisions, such that their interests cannot be ignored or violated by others. It is, for example, inconceivable that laws of slavery would be sanctioned in collective decision processes if potential slaves—whomever they might be—were included and empowered in those processes. Political exclusion was not only a consequence of slavery, it was a necessary component of its existence and maintenance. Young's view of justice is, then, explicitly political, but it does not wholly abandon the idea that we might make claims about what is just, unjust, right, or wrong. It is, rather, that we need, on Young's view, political processes—and specifically inclusive, deliberative ones—to discover what justice in any particular context should look like.[8]

The particular challenge with Young's approach—at least when it comes to defining what intergenerational justice might consist of—is that future others who do not yet exist cannot be included and empowered in our decision-making processes today. Unlike slaves who were excluded

[8] This way of thinking about justice is echoed by others. Gutmann and Thompson (2018), for example, argue: "Compared to other forms [of democracy], deliberative democracy is more likely to protect claims of justice. Yet there are many reasonable conceptions of justice and much reasonable disagreement about which is correct. It would be both morally and democratically self-defeating to insist on the legitimacy of only one comprehensive set of principles in a deliberative democracy" (p. 909). Sen (1999) also develops an explicitly political—and democratic—conception of justice that depends on "social evaluations" made in public discussions, or what might be called deliberative processes.

for racist, political, and economic reasons, future others are excluded on ontological grounds. We cannot deliberate with future others in mutual exchanges, and we cannot know if our future-regarding decisions would in fact be acceptable to them. If we need inclusive political processes to determine what justice entails in particular circumstances, as Young has argued, the unavoidable exclusion of future others (and our future selves) makes it impossible for us to determine what intergenerational justice should entail.

In these circumstances, the best we can do is try to make collective judgments that are not biased against the potential interests of future others as we understand them. But inclusion still has a role to play in legitimizing future-regarding collective actions. Future publics, like current publics, will be politically and culturally diverse: we cannot know which political or cultural cleavages will be most relevant in the future, and some of the cleavages that exist now may be irrelevant or incomprehensible to future others. Nevertheless, if our objective is to strike a better balance between the legitimate concerns of the present and the potential interests of the future, we will need inclusive political processes to obtain the richest and most comprehensive accounts of what future others might plausibly need or benefit from. We cannot know what future publics will need or want, but we can do a better job of thinking about what they *might* need or want by drawing on the diversities that exist in current publics. Instead of looking for ideal theories of justice—which, as I have argued, is an impossible task and a potentially misleading enterprise—we should seek to make our political institutions and decision-making process as inclusive as possible to ensure that existing diversities are adequately reflected in our collective decisions about what the future might want or need.

3.3.3. Doing More Than Justice Would Require

Theories of justice are meant to help us determine what is required by justice and what is not. As Brian Barry (1978) explains, there is a difference "between making successors better off, which is a nice thing to do but not required by justice, and not making them worse off, which is required by justice" (p. 244). Barry's point is that we should focus our attention on our obligations of justice, at least in the first instance, because they are more important than all the other things that we might like to do for future others. Rawls (1999) makes a similar argument: "The just savings principle applies to what a society is to save as a matter of justice. If its members wish to save for other purposes, that is another matter" (p. 255). Similarly, De-Shalit (1995) argues that "although future generations are by definition people who will live after our deaths, our obligations to them are a matter of justice rather than charity or supererogation" (p. 11).

We might, indeed, concede the point that our obligations of intergenerational justice (whatever we think they might be in specific circumstances) are more important than all the other things that we might do for future others. It makes no sense to give future publics museums, schools, bridges, and stable political institutions if we deprive them of the air they need to breathe. But even if we concede this point, we might nevertheless acknowledge that supererogatory concerns are not superfluous or marginal ones in the grand scheme of human relations over time. We might, indeed, wish to do more than justice would require, or at least more than what *we* think justice requires, and many societies have done so (often while harming the future in other ways). In their quest to determine what our obligations of intergenerational justice might consist of, justice theorists have often neglected to seriously consider how our relations with the future are understood and defined by concerns and actions that go beyond whatever their theories of justice might plausibly demand.

There are at least three reasons why we should take supererogatory concerns more seriously when thinking about what we should do for the future. First, once we abandon the idea that there might be "correct" theories of justice that are both immutable and comprehensive, we also have to acknowledge that it will be difficult or impossible to identify the boundaries between what is, strictly speaking, "required" by justice and what is "merely" supererogatory. We probably do not owe future publics parks and museums as a matter of justice, but we might agree that they have a right to know nature and the cultural histories of humanity. If this is the case, museums and parks may be one means of fulfilling our justice-based obligations to the future (whatever we think those might be). But in this example, as with most others, the lines between what is required as a matter of justice and what is supererogatory are not clearly defined, even when we have, or think we have, a plausible, or at least defensible, theory of justice. And abstract theories of intergenerational justice, cannot help us make clear distinctions between requirements of justice and all those other things we might like to do for the future. Rawls's just savings principle, for example, tells us that we have to save for the future, but it does not say what sort of savings are required by justice and which are "merely" supererogatory.

Second, as explained earlier, current publics might feel compelled to try to mitigate the lingering effects of past injustices to make the future better. Such actions might be considered requirements of intergenerational justice, as Vernon (2016) has argued, while at the same time being unjust to current publics who should not, ideally, *have* to shoulder the burdens of correcting past injustices. Many of the decisions we face today are of this nature. There is, for example, a persistent wealth gap in the United States between those who are descendants of enslaved people and those who are not. To make the future better—fairer or more just—current publics might decide to pay reparations to the descendants of enslaved people (see, e.g., Coates 2014), even though they should not have to do so in a just world. Most of the other long-term issues that we might care about, such as the destruction of ecosystems, climate change, plastics pollution, traffic jams, or the proliferation of nuclear weapons, can be understood in these terms as well: current publics *should* act to mitigate these problems for the benefit of the future even though we *should not* have to do so, and we would not have to do so if the past had been more just (or thoughtful) and future-regarding.

Third, much of what we might want to do for the future goes well beyond what would be required by even the most comprehensive theories of intergenerational justice. If this is the case, theories of intergenerational justice, if that is all we have, will provide only an impoverished view of intergenerational relations. Consider the following personal example. As parents my wife and I have a legal duty—which is also an obligation of justice—to provide our daughter with food, clothing, and housing until she reaches the age of 18. But like most parents, we are motivated to do more for our daughter than any theory of justice could plausibly demand. We want to make sure that she is happy, and we will do all we can to help her thrive economically, intellectually, and emotionally both before *and after* she turns 18. We will love her and support her unconditionally. We are willing to sacrifice our own opportunities to create better opportunities for her. These are normal human sentiments that cannot be fully accounted for in our theories of justice. At their most successful, theories of justice can only tell us what we must do to fulfill our duties or obligations, but they cannot specify the full scope of what it is we think we should do—or what we might like to do—on behalf of others.

This personal example has some parallels with how we might think about relations between current and future publics. We often think that individuals and groups are fundamentally short-sighted: we care more about our own immediate needs and less about the needs of our future selves or future others. There are good reasons to care more about the present than the future (see, e.g., Chapter 4), but we should not ignore the fact that while we often do things that are likely to harm the future, we also seek to do many beneficial things *for* the future. We build public institutions such as museums or libraries that we think will benefit our contemporaries and future generations. We strive to build social and political systems that we hope will be both stable and normatively desirable in the future. We build useful structures—buildings, bridges, dams, or canals—that are designed to last longer than our own lifetimes. We create parks for the enjoyment of ourselves and future others. We defend and promote principles or ideals (such as freedom, equality, and democracy) that we believe should be maintained and protected in the future. We try to find cures for diseases that most of us will never get. We do all these things not only because they will benefit ourselves and our contemporaries but also because we hope that they will make the future a better place. Some of these actions—as discussed earlier—might be required by some conceptions of justice, but many of them go above and beyond what would be required by any theory of intergenerational justice. What is more, most of us would continue to do—or want to do—these things even if it were "proved" that we have no plausible obligations of intergenerational justice. If we focus only on questions of justice, we will have an impoverished conception of what intergenerational relations might—or should—consist of: we will be like parents who fulfill their legal obligations but do not do all the other things that good parents should do.

3.4. Political Commitments to the Future

Instead of thinking about intergenerational relations in exclusively justice-based terms, we should think more carefully about how we can forge political—or collective—commitments to the future in inclusive deliberative forums or decision-making processes. Theories of justice—which are limited in all of the ways discussed earlier—aim to specify what we owe the future or the past as a matter of duty or obligation. They are normally identified, conceptualized, or "discovered" by philosophers working in isolation from affected publics. Political commitments to the future, by contrast, are forged in processes of deliberation, negotiation, and bargaining among affected publics. They are collective agreements that indicate in specific terms what we (i.e., current publics) will try to do for the future, how our goals or objectives will be achieved, who is meant to benefit, and which actors will pay the costs of future-regarding actions.

Current publics often ignore, dismiss, or marginalize the potential interests of future others, but we also regularly make collective commitments to act in future-regarding ways. Perhaps the most prominent examples of political commitments to the future are international environmental agreements such as the 1987 Montreal Protocol, the 1997 Kyoto Protocol, and the 2015 Paris Accord. These agreements were forged in political processes, and they specify, in detail, future-regarding goals, the means and timelines by which those goals are meant to be achieved, who will be responsible for taking specific actions, and how compliance will be monitored and encouraged or enforced. The signatories to the 1987 Montreal Protocol, for example, agreed to phase out the use of certain types of ozone-depleting chlorofluorocarbons (CFCs) by 2000 in developed countries. In subsequent meetings, they agreed to a more ambitious timeline, pledging to phase out those chemicals by 1996. Developing countries, as defined by Article 5 of the treaty, committed to a similar but slower schedule of reductions. Unlike many other international agreements aimed at achieving substantive environmental outcomes, the Montreal Protocol has been largely successful (Sunstein 2007).

The Kyoto Protocol was the first major international agreement aimed at reducing global carbon emissions. Like the Montreal Protocol, the Kyoto Protocol outlined a detailed schedule of future-regarding actions. The parties agreed to an overall goal of reducing carbon emissions to 5% below 1990 levels by 2012. To achieve that goal, each country identified its own set of commitments. The United States, for example, committed to a 7% reduction and Canada committed to a 6% reduction, while developing countries such as India and China were exempt from making commitments. The future-regarding goals specified in the Kyoto Protocol were not achieved: many countries (such as Canada) failed to meet their own commitments, and the United States, which is the world's most carbon-intensive economy, failed to ratify the agreement. Nevertheless, as Fiorino (2018) explains, even though "global emissions grew by nearly 40% from 1990 to 2009, this was 29% below what would have occurred [in the absence of the Kyoto protocol] under the likely 'business as usual' scenario" (p. 13).

During the Paris Accord negotiations in 2015, 196 parties agreed to make commitments to reduce carbon emissions by specified amounts and dates. The United States pledged to reduce emissions by 26% to 28% below its 2005 level by 2025. China committed to achieving peak carbon emissions by 2030, and thereafter reducing emissions per GDP unit by 60% to 65% below 2005 levels. China has also committed to increasing the share of non-fossil fuel energy consumption to around 20% by 2030 and increasing its forest stock volume by around 4.5 billion cubic meters compared to 2005 levels.[9] The European Union and its member states committed to a reduction of 40% below 1990 levels by 2030. Canada committed to a reduction of 30% below 2005 levels by 2030. Parties to the agreement are expected to submit new, and ideally more ambitious, Nationally Determined Contributions (NDCs) every five years.[10]

It is doubtful that the goals articulated in the Paris Accord will be achieved by all the countries that are signatories. Nevertheless, the Paris Accord agreements may be understood as political commitments to the future. They were forged in relatively inclusive political environments through deliberation, negotiation, bargaining, and self-commitment. They probably do not go far enough to stop climate change, but they are "fair" in the following sense: they acknowledge that parties, or states, have different levels of responsibility for the climate crisis and different capacities to act.

Although some of the most prominent examples of political commitments to the future come from the international realm where there is not (yet) an enforcement regime, jurisdictions around the world routinely make political commitments to the future in various policy areas. Indeed, political commitments to the future can be made at any level of governance—from the local to the global—on any public issue. Many local, regional, national, and transnational jurisdictions have, for example, recently adopted taxes or bans on single-use plastics such as shopping bags, straws, and cutlery. According to the United Nations, 91 countries (as of July 2018) "have some type of ban or restriction on the manufacture or production, importation,

[9] As Fransen et al. (2015) explain, China's forest carbon goal "is particularly aggressive. Increasing forest carbon stocks by 4.5 billion cubic meters implies an increase in forest cover of 50–100 million hectares (124–247 million acres) of forest, or about two to four times the size of the United Kingdom. This amount of forest would create a roughly 1-gigaton carbon sink, equivalent to stopping tropical deforestation for almost a full year, or taking 770 million cars off the road."

[10] As of February 2021, 190 parties had submitted their initial Nationally Determined Contributions (NDCs) and eight parties had submitted a second set of NDCs (UNFCCC 2021, https://www4.unfccc.int/sites/ndcstaging/Pages/Home.aspx).

and retail distribution of plastic bags. The region with the greatest number of countries adopting this approach is Africa, with thirty-four (34) countries, closely followed by Europe with twenty-nine (29) countries" (United Nations 2018, p. 13). Kenya has one of the most aggressive plastic bag bans. Those found producing, selling, or even carrying a plastic bag in Kenya could face up to four years in prison or an almost US$40,000 fine (e.g., Watts 2018). What is more, this ban was introduced quickly: it came into effect six months after the legislation was passed.[11]

In March 2019, the European Union voted to ban 10 single-use plastics by 2021, including plastic cutlery, plates, and straws, as well as oxo-degradable plastics, and styrofoam cups and containers. The legislation also requires member states to recycle 90% of all plastic bottles by 2029 (Rankin 2019). North America lags behind the rest of the world on this issue, but Canada's government has recently moved to ban single-use plastics by the end of 2021. This commitment was framed in future-regarding terms by Prime Minister Justin Trudeau: "We have a responsibility to work with our partners to reduce plastic pollution, protect the environment, and create jobs and grow our economy. We owe it to our kids to keep the environment clean and safe for generations to come" (quoted in Lewis 2019). The United States has done little to control and regulate the production of single-use plastic items at the federal level, but several states, including New York and California, have adopted plastic bag bans.[12]

One of the most successful political commitments to the future is Norway's sovereign wealth fund. The fund, which was originally called the Government Petroleum Fund, was created in 1990 using revenues from the country's oil and gas sector. Money from the fund is used to support current government programs and spending, but it also serves as a long-term public savings account. The fund is now worth more than a trillion dollars (US), which makes it the largest sovereign wealth fund in the world (Reid 2019). Importantly, the fund was consciously created for the benefit of current *and* future generations. As explained in the 2003 Graver Commission Report:

[11] It is worth noting that producers and sellers can apply for exemptions to the ban in Kenya, and this has meant that the regulations are unevenly applied, with smaller businesses being subject to the ban and larger businesses applying for exemptions (Njuguna 2018).

[12] There is some evidence that plastic bag taxes and bans can work. As Parker (2019) explains, in "Denmark, which passed the world's first bag tax in 1993, residents use, on average, four plastic bags per year. By contrast, in the United States, which is the largest generator, per capita, of plastic packaging waste, Americans use almost one bag per person daily."

> The prosperity enjoyed by present generations carries obligations. Our oil and gas reserves are running out. Since these resources are limited, it is not fair that these riches only benefit the few generations that happen to experience their extraction. The wealth generated by these resources must be safeguarded for future generations. This is an important basis for the establishment of the Petroleum Fund. (Norwegian Ministry of Finance 2003)

Norway's sovereign wealth fund now generates more money each year from investment income than from oil and gas revenues (Campbell 2012). If it continues to be well managed, it could provide a perpetual source of revenue for future Norwegians long after all the oil and gas resources are gone.

Political commitments to the future, like the ones outlined here, can help define and support future-regarding goals and collective actions, but justice theorists (and others) will have good reasons to be concerned that those commitments will fall short of the requirements of intergenerational justice (whatever those might be). Political actors will do what is politically manageable instead of what is right, the potential interests of future others might be ignored or marginalized in political processes, and political commitments to the future might be reversed by future governments. The whole point of a theory of justice is to find order in the disorderliness, incompleteness, and unpredictability of politics: to identify what is right or just as a means of both critiquing and constraining political decisions.

The problem with this approach is that the search for order and predictability requires an escape from politics, which even the best (or most comprehensive and coherent) theories of justice cannot provide. As argued earlier, theories of justice are both incomplete without politics (i.e., they cannot determine what we should do or how we should do it) and infused with politics: they are defined, as they should be, by the interests, beliefs, ideals, principles, and interests of their proponents. Given this, we have to act politically if we wish to shape the future in collectively intentional ways. We have to embrace, manage, mitigate, and continually navigate the unpredictabilities of politics in order to get to the futures that we think we might want, and we must make political commitments to the future even though we cannot be sure that those commitments will be upheld by future publics.

Despite the fact that political commitments to the future are likely to be imperfect, there are a number of advantages to thinking about intergenerational relations in those terms. First, unlike principles of intergenerational justice, which start with abstractions and conclude with abstractions, political commitments to the future are, and must be, grounded in what we know and do not know about our positions in time, the actions of the past, and our relations to contemporary others who might have divergent interests and different ideas about what the future might need or want. Political commitments to the future—such as international agreements to mitigate climate change or regulations on plastic waste—take what we know about our present circumstances, what we know about the past and our contemporaries, and what we think the future might need or want, as starting points for making decisions about what we should do for the future. We will not achieve justice now or in the future, but we can strive to act well given our current circumstances, the actions (or inactions) of the past, and our beliefs about what the future should be like.

Second, political commitments to the future can be outlined to any degree of specificity, as is evidenced in the extensive documents of the Montreal Protocol and other future-regarding collective agreements. Political commitments to the future can be used to specify what we will do, or try to do, for the future; which specific actions will be taken or avoided; who will pay the costs of taking those actions; who might (or should) benefit from those actions; when future-regarding objectives are meant to be achieved; and how those actions will be monitored, encouraged, or enforced. In contrast, theories of intergenerational justice are radically incomplete in precisely those ways: they tell us in general terms what we should do, but they do not specify which actions should be taken to achieve justice.

Third, political commitments to the future may be used to legitimately compel agents to act in future-regarding ways. When political commitments are made in processes that are recognized as fair by those involved, those who fail to follow through on their commitments may be legitimately forced to do so where there are mechanisms or systems for enforcement. As we have seen, those who produce or sell plastic bags in Kenya (without an exemption) may be jailed for four years or fined US$40,000. And European states that do not recycle at least 90% of all plastic bottles by 2029 will be sanctioned by the European Union. Theories of justice might help inform our political commitments to the future, but they cannot, alone, be used to compel people to act in future-regarding ways. There are no means of enforcing principles of justice, or putting them into practice, other than those that we might use to enforce our political commitments to the future; and enforcing supposedly "correct" theories of justice through political means will be illegitimate unless decisions about what justice should entail have been sanctioned in political processes that are recognized as fair by those who will be subject to those decisions.

Fourth, political commitments to the future can be used to support collective actions that aim to do more for the future than justice would require. Theories of intergenerational justice, by definition, can only specify what we are required to do for the future as a matter of duty or obligation. But, as argued earlier, we often want—or feel compelled—to do more for the future than justice would require. We want to make the future better even at some cost to ourselves; we want to preserve and protect our cultural heritages so that they might be understood and enjoyed by future others; we try to make our cities safe, enjoyable, and clean; we engage in philosophical thought and artistic endeavours; and we try to cure diseases like cancer to benefit ourselves *and* future others. We might feel compelled to correct the injustices of the past to make the future better or more just, even though it may be unfair (or unjust) for us to have to do so. Current publics might spend billions of dollars cleaning up plastic waste for the benefit of the future even though they *should* not have to do so and *would* not have to do so if past others had acted in more future-regarding ways. We do not need analytically rigorous, internally consistent, abstract theories of justice that cannot be reasonably rejected in order to make collective decisions to act in future-regarding ways. We do not need to agree on whether future others, who do not yet exist, can be said to have rights. We do not need to know how many generations there will be in the future or how many people will be in each generation. And we do not need to make distinctions between what is "really" a matter of justice and what is "merely" supererogatory. Political commitments to the future may be used to support collective actions consistent with our own conceptions of what justice requires, but they can also be used to support all those other things that we might wish to build or protect for the future that may or may not be "required" by justice—things like museums; symphonies; libraries; parks; nature reserves; public education systems; walkable urban neighbourhoods; clean lakes, rivers, and oceans; and stable, uncorrupt political systems.

3.5. Conclusion

I have argued that we cannot adequately understand intergenerational relations or act in future-regarding ways if we think about our relations with the future in exclusively justice-based terms. Theories of intergenerational justice have an unreality about them: they specify outcomes that cannot be realized, or even approximated, given our epistemic positions in time, the injustices of the past, and our limited influence over the actions of future others. Indeed, it is not clear what it would mean to say that we should act in ways consistent with the precepts of intergenerational justice if that would require justice for *all* generations for *all* time. The fact that concepts of justice are historically mutable and context dependent does not mean that we cannot act well according to our own principles and beliefs about what we should do for the future, but it does mean that the search for intergenerational justice—as it is normally defined by the justice theorists themselves—is a philosophical puzzle with no solution.

In practice, theories of justice cannot be formulated or understood in isolation from political processes, even though they typically have been conceived as a means of superseding the unpredictabilities of politics. Theories of intergenerational justice are radically incomplete without politics: they cannot tell us, in detail, what we should do for the future, who should benefit from future-regarding actions, who should pay the costs of those actions, or how those actions might be monitored and legitimately enforced. What is more, theories of justice are infused with politics: claims of rights and correlative duties must be forged in political processes of deliberation, negotiation, and bargaining before they will be recognized and legitimized as rights and duties by political actors with diverse beliefs and divergent interests. In most cases, we will not be able to agree on what intergenerational justice entails, but we might nevertheless make binding collective decisions to act in future-regarding ways—decisions that will likely fall short of justice in some respects, but that might go *beyond* whatever we think justice might require. Political commitments to the future have to be continually defended, reframed, and renegotiated in political processes that respond to contemporary circumstances and changing political allegiances and interests. This is unfortunate, perhaps, because it means that we cannot escape from the uncertainties of politics, but that is, nevertheless, the world that we live in. If we want to act in future-regarding ways we have to work with—or through—political processes rather than searching for abstract philosophical principles that might lift us above the political fray. We need to figure out how to strike a better balance between the interests of the present and the potential interests of the future, as we understand them. Rather than thinking about what intergenerational justice might entail in only in philosophical terms, the critical task is to think about how we might design political institutions that are not biased against the potential interests of the future and might, instead, encourage political actors to more seriously consider—and act upon—the interests of future others.

PART II

A DELIBERATIVE THEORY OF FUTURE-REGARDING COLLECTIVE ACTION

4

Deliberative Responses to the Democratic Myopic Problem

4.1. Introduction

In Chapter 1, I outlined four components of the democratic myopia thesis: the myopic voter argument, the short electoral cycles argument, the exclusion of future others problem, and the problem of democratic capture. In this chapter, I illustrate that there are democratic—or rather deliberative—responses to at least two of these arguments: the myopic voter argument and the exclusion of future others problem. (I deal with other aspects of the democratic myopia thesis in subsequent chapters.)

In the first half of this chapter, I argue that the myopic voter argument is persuasive only if we adopt an implausibly narrow conception of democracy, according to which existing (probably myopic) preferences are aggregated to produce collective outcomes. When democracy works like this, collective outcomes are likely to be short-sighted—but that is not how democracy normally works in theory or in practice. Instead, legitimate democratic processes, such as deliberation and leadership, may be, and normally are, leveraged to help shape the preferences and perspectives of individuals and groups. If this is the case, democratic processes might be used to actively encourage people to more carefully consider the potential interests of the future when making long-term decisions. In the second half of the chapter, I explain why I think that deliberation can also help encourage contemporary actors to more seriously consider—and sincerely represent—the potential interests of future others. Indeed, deliberation is the only institutional mechanism that I am aware of that might plausibly play this role in public affairs.

Future Publics. Michael K. MacKenzie, Oxford University Press. © Oxford University Press 2021.
DOI: 10.1093/oso/9780197557150.003.0004

4.2. The Myopic Voter Argument

The myopic voter argument is the most commonly cited reason for why democratic systems are biased against the future. If democratic systems are *supposed* to respond to the expressed preferences of voting publics, they will tend to favour the present over the future if the individuals who comprise those publics have dominant preferences for the short-term over the long-term. Short electoral cycles exacerbate this problem because they make it difficult for politicians to invest in policies that will have benefits *after* the next election but costs *before* it. Given this situation, elected officials often find it difficult to make long-term investments even when they recognize the importance of doing so. As discussed in Chapter 1, many scholars have argued that the myopic voter problem is caused by a "natural human tendency" (e.g., Thompson 2010, p. 17). People tend to focus on their most immediate needs and thereby ignore or dismiss longer-term problems which may affect their future selves or future others. If this tendency is part of the human condition, any system of government that is designed to respond to the expressed preferences of affected publics will be short-sighted.

Although it has a certain plausibility, the myopic voter argument provides an incomplete picture of the human condition. People often favour the near term over the long term, but there are many psychological, behavioural, and institutional factors that help shape our orientations to the future in various ways. If our orientations to the future are shaped and conditioned by various contextual factors, we cannot, at the same time, claim that humans in general—and voters, specifically—will always tend to favour the near term over the long term. If our orientations to the future are malleable, even to some extent, democratic processes will not necessarily favour the near term over the long term, even when they are properly responsive to our expressed preferences. One possibility is that democratic processes or practices could be used to help encourage or incentivize longer-term thinking and future-regarding behaviour. Indeed, once we recognize that democracy, in practice, involves both shaping and registering the preferences and expectations of individuals and groups, we must also recognize the possibility that there may be democratic processes—such as leadership, deliberation, or negotiation—that will shape our views and expectations about both the present and the future.

Just to be clear, the critique that I make here is a theoretical one. Proponents of the myopic voter argument have adopted a theory of democracy in which individual preferences are treated as largely fixed and exogenous to the democratic process itself. The assumption is that the preferences of voters already exist—or are produced elsewhere—before they are fed into aggregative mechanisms to produce collective outcomes. On this model of democracy there are, by implication, no democratic processes that might mitigate or reshape the myopic preferences of voters. But even those who favour minimalist models of aggregative democracy, such as Schumpeter (1942) and Przeworski (1999), recognize that democracy involves more than the aggregation of existing preferences; it also involves shaping the preferences of individuals and groups through campaigning, oration, claim making, reason giving, constituency building, persuasion, and negotiation—or, for that matter, leadership (Beerbohm 2015). There are, of course, more or less democratic ways of shaping the preferences and expectations of individuals and groups—misinformation and deception are, for example, undemocratic political tools—but acting politically and democratically necessarily involves trying to shape the opinions, expectations, goals, or commitments of others.

Once we acknowledge that democracy is about shaping and registering the opinions and expectations of participants, we open up the possibility that democratic processes might be used to challenge rather than encourage myopic thinking. In what follows, I argue that deliberation is particularly well-suited to perform this function, but my larger argument does not rely on the specific claims that I make about deliberation. Deliberation is an example of a democratic mechanism that might be used to encourage longer-term thinking and future-regarding action. Democratic leadership is another. There might be others still. The more general point is that the myopic voter argument is predicated on a narrow conception of democracy that is both empirically false and conceptually inadequate. It is a conception of democracy that leaves no room for the possibility that democratic processes themselves might be used to help make people (voters or political actors more generally) more future-regarding.

4.2.1. Are We Biased Against the Future?

Before discussing how deliberation might help us—or some of us—actively challenge the cognitive biases that we have against the future, it will be useful to think more carefully about what those biases are. The myopic voter argument is predicated on the claim that we have a "natural human tendency" to think more about the present than the future (Thompson 2010, p. 17). There are many good reasons to care more about the present than the future, but the idea that people are simply short-sighted does not do justice to the complex ways in which most of us think about the future.

In practical terms, we *have* to care more about the present than the future: if we do not, we might not make it through the present to meet the future. We must solve existing problems before we can confront future ones, and it makes sense to focus on contemporary problems that we know, with a relatively high degree of certainty, are *actually* problems. Even if the present is subject to some uncertainty, the future is normally subject to more.[1] It is clearly important, for example, to solve problems such as what to do with sewage and other household wastes because if these problems are not solved, they will negatively impact our lives over the near term. It is less clear that we should commit to solving a problem like climate change that might negatively affect us or others in 30, 50, or 100 years—even if it would be easier, cheaper, and more effective to take action now.

The problem with future problems is that we can never be sure that they *will* be problems for ourselves or future others: we might not be alive in 30 years, or technology might advance to solve potential problems before they become manifest. It is irrational to invest scarce resources in solving future problems that might never become problems when there are plenty of other problems to solve now. We can reduce the uncertainty associated with certain future potential problems if we have good information about what the future might be like or if we have some control over it, but we cannot reduce uncertainty about the future to the level of certainty that we have about our currently existing problems. Given this, it will almost always make sense to focus our attention, and our resources, on solving existing problems before grappling with future potential problems.

The problem with this way of thinking is that there are, often, very good reasons to be concerned about future problems. We care about existing problems because we have to, but we also care about whether our longer-term interests and objectives will be realized. Indeed, philosophers have often commented on the fact that humans, as cognitive beings, are capable of planning for the future. For Karl Marx, humans are distinguished from

[1] As mentioned previously (Chapter 2, note 1), although it is generally the case that the future is more uncertain than the present, there are some things—such as the inevitability of our own deaths—that can be predicted with greater certainty as we look farther into the future. See Meyer (2016, p. 6) on this point.

other animals by our capacity to imagine the things that we want to create before we create them. We have the capacity to think about the future, adjust our actions accordingly, and produce a world that reflects those imagined states of being.[2] For Hannah Arendt (1951, 1957), our creative capacity to think and act into the future—to create new things and possibilities out of old conditions—is an essential component of what it means to be human.

Furthermore, although we have cognitive biases against the future, most of us care about our future selves (e.g., Hershfield 2011). We want to save for retirement, for example, even though we often find it difficult to do so. But many of us also care about future others—at least to some extent. We care about the communities we are a part of, and we want them to thrive in the future. We value institutions (such as universities, museums, or churches) and cultural goods (such as art or literature) that we want future others to enjoy. And many of us are committed to ideas or principles (such as democracy or human rights) that we believe should be promoted and protected in the future.

Ernest Partridge (1981) has argued that a desire or capacity to care about things that will only flourish past our own lifetimes is an essential component of normal human psychology (p. 204). Jana Thompson (2009) has argued that "lifetime transcending interests" should be conceived of as individual interests even though they also concern the interests and actions of future others. Similarly, Scheffler (2013, 2018) makes a fascinating and persuasive argument that meaning in our own lives depends to a large extent on the possibility that there will be future others with meaningful lives.

The fact that we have lifetime transcending interests that we value for our own reasons and for the sake of others means that we often do act in future-regarding ways even when doing so is costly in the near term. As Jonathan Boston (2017) has observed, people have "demonstrated a willingness across multiple cultures and millennia to embark upon extraordinary, long-term, cooperative endeavors often in circumstances when those who commenced the task knew that they would not live to witness its completion" (p. 38).

These depictions of humanity look very different from those that are presented by proponents of the myopic voter argument. According to one

[2] As Marx (1867/1906) explains: "A spider conducts operations that resemble those of a weaver, and a bee puts to shame many an architect in the construction of her cells. But what distinguishes the worst architect from the best of bees is this, that the architect raises his structure in imagination before he erects it in reality. At the end of every labour-process, we get a result that already existed in the imagination of the labourer at its commencement" (*Capital*, Vol. 1, Chapter 7).

view, humans tend to focus on the near term to the detriment of their own long-term interests and those of others. According to the other view, the human condition is defined by our capacity to think outside ourselves, to plan for the future, to create new opportunities out of old conditions, and to organize our actions to achieve individually or collectively desirable futures over the course of multiple generations.

My sympathies are aligned with the latter view of the human condition because it strikes me as being a more plausible, and a richer and more interesting, description of what we are like. Nevertheless, it is important to recognize that proponents of the myopic voter argument rarely insist that voters are incapable of thinking and acting in future-regarding ways. Proponents of the argument are, instead, concerned about our typical or default patterns of thinking and acting. They are worried that people will tend to favour the near term over the long term even when we recognize, on some level, that we *should* care about the future. The problem, in their view, has to do with cognitive biases. We have the capacity to think and act in future-regarding ways, but our thinking is often conditioned by biases that make us prefer the near term over the long term, especially when we are thinking and acting intuitively.

There is a large literature on cognitive biases that has been summarized by Daniel Kahneman (2011) in his book *Thinking, Fast and Slow.* Many of these biases affect how we are likely to think about the future. One example is the negativity bias. We tend to place more weight on negative outcomes and costs and less weight on positive outcomes and benefits. This means that we are likely to focus on negative events and remember them for longer than positive ones. If we have a fight with a friend, for example, we are likely to remember the fight more clearly than all the good things we might have got out of the friendship. If solving long-term problems—such as climate change—involves paying near-term costs for future benefits, then we will tend to focus on the negatives (i.e., the near-term costs) more than the potential benefits (Jacobs 2011). The fact that the benefits are in the future, and thus also probably more uncertain, only exacerbates the problem.[3]

People also suffer from positive illusions or overconfidence. We believe that we are smarter or more capable than we really are, that we have more

[3] Importantly, our cognitive biases make us discount the future over and above the discounting associated with uncertainty. Even when we are certain that something is going to be a problem (or a benefit) in the future, we are likely to discount it in comparison to more near-term problems (or benefits) if we allow our thinking to be governed by our intuitive responses to long-term problems.

control over events than we really do, and that we are less vulnerable to risks than is really the case (Kahneman 2011, esp. Part III). Our tendencies to be overconfident have been associated with our failures to act on long-term problems such as climate change (Caney 2016; Johnson and Levin 2009). Many people, for example, believe that we will find technological or political solutions to climate change before it is too late or that only future others will be affected by the worst consequences of climate change.

We also tend to be more concerned about those who are part of our in-group and less concerned about (or openly hostile to) those who have other, possibility opposing, affiliations (Brennan 2016). This bias is, of course, the cause of many political tensions between groups within current publics, but it also affects how we think about the future. We may care about future others, but they are also, always, part of an out-group—they are "others." We have "our" near-term concerns and they (will) have "their" concerns. This is, in part, what Thomas Jefferson (1813) meant when he called the future "a distinct nation" (p. 10).

Relatedly, we are more likely to help others when problems affect identifiable individuals or groups, and we are less likely to act when it is unclear who the victims of harm will be. We prefer helping identifiable victims even when the suffering they are facing is equally bad or equally likely to occur to generalized, abstract others (Jenni and Loewenstien 1997). This bias has a temporal dimension because future others are, by definition, a generalized interest. There *will* be future others who come to exist, but they do not yet exist, and their stories or plights cannot yet be individualized (Caney 2016).

In more general terms, we have a bias against abstract problems. We are more likely to act when problems and their consequences are obvious, apparent, or tangible, and we are less likely to act when problems are abstract or difficult to discern. When garbage collectors go on strike and the trash piles up on our streets, we are likely to be spurred into action. But when problems are abstract or their consequences are subtle or diffuse we are much less likely to act. Many problems, such as lead in our drinking water, are as important in the near term as garbage removal, but they are more abstract. When there is lead in our drinking water, we may be unaware of its likely effects, how much lead is too much, or what the consequences of ingesting it might be. We cannot feel it (initially), see it, smell it, or taste it. It is a real but nevertheless abstract problem. The thing about long-term problems is that they are always abstract. The future is always less tangible than the present. The present can be touched and felt. It can be heard and seen. The future must be imagined.

There are a number of specific temporal biases related to the abstract problem bias. Consider, for example, the "creeping problems" bias. As Caney (2016) explains: "Persons often fail to detect certain problems because they are gradual in nature and creep up on us slowly. We barely notice them on a day-by-day, year-by-year basis, and may only realize that there is a problem when it is too late to address the causes, or when it is possible to do so but only at considerable cost" (p. 144). Michael Glantz (1999) has associated our failures to act on environmental problems like climate change with the "creeping problems" bias.

The "availability bias" is also related to the abstract problem bias. Information about the present is often, although not always, more readily available than information about the future. You know what it is like to lose your job if you have recently lost it. It is less clear what it *would* be like to lose your job in the future. You can imagine it, but the prospect is distant: it is conceptual and abstract until it actually happens. Relatedly, the invisibility, or "out-of-sight, out-of-mind" bias involves downplaying the importance of concerns or problems that are relatively easy to ignore. It is always possible to put future problems (like saving for retirement) out of mind until they become present problems that cannot be ignored (Caney 2016).

Similarly, we tend to respond more actively to problems that relate to our lived experiences and less actively, or not at all, to problems that we are made aware of only through less vivid or tangible means, such as scientific or social analyses. We are more likely to act if we experience the effects of something like climate change and less likely to act when we are merely presented with scientific data about the likely effects of climate change (Caney 2016; Weber 2006).

These cognitive biases—or "drivers of harmful short-termism" as Caney (2016, p. 143) calls them—are biases in the proper sense of the term: they involve treating two things which are equal in relevant ways as unequal because of some irrelevant factor. The consequences of a "creeping problem," for example, may be just as severe as the consequences of a more immediate problem, but we tend to react to these two types of problems differently. We might think that every human, for example, has equal moral worth, but we tend to treat identifiable victims differently than unidentifiable ones. In general terms, future problems are always more abstract and thus less vivid and easier to ignore or dismiss than present problems because they are located in the future. But *when* a problem is likely to occur is, or should be, irrelevant to our assessments of what we ought to do about it. Controlling for other factors—such as uncertainty—it is just as bad to choke on smog in 10 years time as it is to choke on smog today.

The list of cognitive biases outlined in this chapter is not exhaustive. There are other biases that may affect how we tend to think about the future. Nevertheless, this list is sufficiently detailed to illustrate the point I want to make: the cognitive biases that proponents of the democratic myopia thesis are most concerned about are primarily rooted in the intuitive (System 1) parts of our brains and not in the analytical (or System 2) parts of our brains (Kahneman 2011). They affect how we are likely to think about the future when we are thinking quickly, efficiently, and intuitively.

In addition, although our thinking is often conditioned by cognitive biases—and these biases are, in a certain sense, always with us—there are ways to circumvent them or mitigate their effects. One option is to use one set of cognitive biases to help overcome or compensate for problems created by other cognitive biases. This is the insight behind the practice of "nudging" (Thaler and Sunstein 2008). It is possible, for example, to encourage more people to save for retirement by adopting "opt-out" policies instead of "opt-in" policies. Most people want to save for retirement, but it is easier to not save. Opt-out policies make saving a little easier—and less cognitively demanding—and not saving a little harder to do. Nudging shapes the architecture of choice situations to make certain, presumably good choices, more likely and other, presumably bad choices, less likely—but it preserves the autonomy of individuals to make their own choices.

Nudging is one means of mitigating the harmful effects of certain cognitive biases. An alternative approach—which may be necessary in situations where nudging is less effective or more undesirable—is to encourage, enable, or incentivize people to make the switch from their intuitive (System 1) brains to their analytical (System 2) brains.

Kahneman (2011) is skeptical about whether people can be encouraged to more fully engage their analytical brains in everyday settings. Doing so will often take too much effort for too little payoff. But people are capable of thinking differently about the future when they are encouraged to do so. Stephen Sheppard and his colleagues, for example, have shown that it is possible to encourage people think differently about climate change and energy production by using pictures, 3D visualization technologies, and even video games to help people experience alternative futures (e.g., Dulic et al. 2016; Schroth et al. 2014; Sheppard 2012). Visualization helps people overcome the abstract problem bias—or the out-of-sight, out-of-mind bias—by making possible future problems more like everyday, near-term problems: more tangible and less abstract.[4]

The fact that it is possible to mitigate the effects of cognitive biases by encouraging people to think about long-term problems differently should give us pause when we are thinking about the myopic voter argument. Depending on the context in which individual preferences are formed, they may or may not be short-sighted when they are fed into aggregative processes. For our purposes, the most interesting possibility is whether there are democratic processes that might help circumvent the cognitive biases that condition our thinking when we are not thinking carefully enough. In what follows, I argue that deliberation can help encourage participants to make the shift—at least some of the time—from using their intuitive, System 1 brains to using their more analytical, System 2 brains when thinking about their political choices, their long-term interests, and the potential interests of future others. Deliberation is of interest in this context because it requires participants to consciously formulate and defend their preferences and claims with reasons that might be plausibly acceptable to others.

4.2.2. Deliberation and Analytical Thinking

In effective deliberative processes, participants are supposed to offer reasons for their positions or the choices that they wish to make, but they must also be willing to be persuaded by the arguments and claims of others. Of course, participants may or may not be persuaded, but they should, at minimum, consider the arguments of others, and they must be willing to adjust their perspectives or preferences when persuasive arguments are made. These, and other stipulations, are often viewed as the regulative ideals of deliberative democracy (e.g., Bächtiger et al. 2018; Chambers 2003; Cohen 1989; Gutmann and Thompson 1996, 2004, 2018). As explained in Chapter 2, I do not think that participants have to be committed to these ideals in order for good deliberations to take place. Instead, I argue that good deliberations are likely to occur whenever political actors are compelled by matters of

[4] Other studies have produced similar results. In general, it appears as if people tend to discount the future less when potential future benefits or problems are made more vivid, concrete, or tangible than they normally are in our everyday lives (see, e.g., Förster et al. 2004; Kim et al. 2013; Pahl et al. 2014; Schroth et al. 2014).

circumstance—or institutional design—to channel strategic intent into talk and persuasion (see, as well, Warren 2007).

Importantly, participants do not have to be persuaded in order for deliberation to have an effect on their thinking. Deliberation requires participants to consciously consider their positions and to formulate justifications for them that others might plausibly accept, and this task activates the analytical parts of the brain. This is important because, as we have seen, our cognitive biases are located in the intuitive parts of our brains. These biases affect how we think about the future when we are not thinking carefully enough. They are intuitive in the sense that they are preprogrammed: they allow for quick, easy, and not particularly cognitively demanding responses to potentially complex situations or problems (Kahneman 2011). Our intuitions, if they are correct, help keep us safe without the time and effort required for us to engage in conscious, reflective, internal deliberation. Effective processes of public deliberation, by contrast, compel us to more consciously consider our claims and preferences by compelling us to formulate plausible justifications for them, and then defend those justifications against the discursive challenges of others. In other words, deliberative practices lure us into cognitively demanding spaces where we are compelled to use our System 2 brains to think through choices that we might otherwise be content to make using our intuitive System 1 brains. When we think more carefully about both the present and the future, we may be able to identify choices that will be more desirable overall; choices that are attractive, or at least not unattractive, to our present selves and beneficial to our future selves or future others as well.

But it is not enough to do our deliberative thinking by ourselves. As Joseph Heath (2014) argues, we are cognitive misers: we tend to prefer to avoid doing the difficult work of analytical thinking if we can. This means that internal deliberations are less likely to discipline our thinking when compared to public reason-giving processes. As Heath explains:

> Introspection is far, far less powerful than any of us would have imagined. And unfortunately, the limits of introspection cannot be ascertained through introspection. Thus the most powerful check that we have on our own tendency toward biased thinking is the willingness—perhaps even the eagerness—of other people to correct us. (Heath 2014, p. 143)

On this view, public reason giving can help discipline our thinking by exposing our claims to discursive challenges made by others (e.g., Mercier and Landemore 2012). If this is the case, deliberation may be an effective *democratic* response to the myopic voter problem. Effective deliberative processes can create circumstances that compel us to engage our cognitive faculties, which is precisely what we need to do if we are to overcome or circumvent the intuitive biases that we have against the future when we are not thinking carefully enough. If our biases against the future are intuitive, then the very act of thinking in more disciplined and analytical ways about long-term issues might help change the way we understand those issues and the decisions we have to make.[5]

The fact that we might come to re-examine our biases against the future through effective processes of public reason giving does not necessarily mean that we will—or should—come to *favour* the future over the present. As I have argued, we should, as a matter of principle, strive to strike a balance between the legitimate concerns of the present and the potential interests of the future, but this does not mean there are no good or justifiable reasons to focus on existing problems before trying to address future ones. What it does mean is that we should not focus all of our attention on existing problems without adequately considering the potential interests of future others. When we make decisions that focus on existing problems, we cannot say that we are biased against the future if we make those decisions in ways that consciously consider the potential interests of future others. If there are good reasons to favour the present over the future, in some limited way or in particular circumstances, effective deliberative processes should help us identify those reasons. If there are good reasons to favour the future over the present, effective deliberations should help us identify *those* reasons.

A number of scholars have suggested that deliberation can help encourage longer-term thinking among participants. If deliberation can encourage participants to advance or adopt generalized perspectives that take into consideration the interests of others, it might also encourage them to adopt positions that take into account the interests of future others (e.g., Elster 1986; Ekeli 2009; Goodin 2003; Gutmann and Thompson 1996). Others

[5] Some scholars have argued that deliberation is not likely to help us overcome our cognitive biases. There is evidence that talking about political issues can make people's biases worse by hardening their preconceived notions and strengthen their pre-existing (possibility unexamined) political commitments. But the studies that demonstrate these effects typically measure political talk, where no collective decisions have to be made, and not deliberation, where collective decisions have to be made (e.g., Brennan 2016; Mendelberg 2002; Mutz 2006); or they examine deliberation in ideologically homogenous groups instead of in inclusive groups where different perspectives are expressed and represented (e.g., Sunstein 2002).

have argued that participants in deliberations may be exposed to longer-term perspectives that they would not have otherwise considered. If these new perspectives raise persuasive claims about the potential interests of future others, participants may be encouraged to reconsider their own immediate interests or objectives (e.g., Dietz et al. 2009; Gundersun 1995; Smith 2003). I have argued that there is another way that deliberation can encourage longer-term thinking. Effective deliberative processes can compel us to think with our analytical brains and overcome—or at least expose—the biases that we have against the future, which are primarily located in our intuitive brains.

4.3. The Exclusion of Future Others

According to the myopic voter argument, democracies are likely to favour the present over the future because that is what people, in general, tend to do. On this view, democracies will be short-sighted when they are working well; that is, when they are sufficiently responsive to the expressed preferences of voters. I have argued that the myopic voter argument rests on an implausibly narrow conception of democracy, one in which existing preferences are simply *registered* in democratic processes but not *shaped* by those processes.

As explained in Chapter 1, there is another version of the democratic myopic thesis that raises a different type of problem: the exclusion of future others. As Dennis Thompson explains:

> Democracy itself affirms that the citizens bound by laws should have a voice in making them. Yet future citizens who will be bound by the laws cannot have such a voice. Democracy's conventional way of addressing the problem of those who do not have a voice is to grant greater opportunities for participation and to institute more extensive representation. But making democracy more inclusive—expanding citizenship and enhancing representation—would not help future citizens. They do not have a voice because they cannot be citizens now. (Thompson 2010, p. 18)

This is a fundamental, or ontological, problem because there is no way to include future others who do not yet exist in our decision-making processes today. As a result, current publics are—and will always be—free to ignore, dismiss, misrepresent, or trample upon the potential interests of future others with relative impunity, just as the interests of any excluded group may be trampled upon by those who have power.

Robert Goodin (2007) has argued that problems of under-inclusion—or exclusion—can be addressed in one of two ways. Those who are, or will be, affected by collective decisions should be included if possible. If inclusion is not possible, the interests of those who are excluded should be considered when collective decisions are made, and compensation should be paid when the interests of the excluded are negatively affected. From a normative perspective, this second option is clearly inferior to the first. Empowered inclusion is the mechanism that helps ensure that democratic processes produce results that are fair and acceptable to those who are, or will be, affected by collective decisions (Warren 2017; Young 2000). If any individuals or groups are excluded or disempowered, others may impose decisions on them that are unjust or contrary to their fundamental interests. By contrast, when those who are, or may be, affected by collective decisions are included in decision-making processes, it will be comparatively difficult for any particular group to impose unfair or unjust policies on others. Properly speaking, then, democracy is about empowered inclusion; it not about simply having our interests properly considered by others.[6]

But when it comes to future others, the second-best solution—that is, inclusion through consideration rather than empowerment—is the *only* option. As such, we have to ask whether it is possible to incentivize contemporary actors to seriously consider, represent, and defend the potential interests of future others as they understand them. Is there any mechanism, other than empowered inclusion, that can encourage political actors to adequately consider the potential interests of excluded others—such as future others—in collective decision-making processes?

One option is to nurture and empower a class of leaders who have the right moral commitments and the skills required to make good judgments about how to balance the interests of the present with the potential interests of the future. This option is favoured by those who have proposed authoritarian solutions to the democracy myopia thesis (e.g., Bell 2016; Ophuls 2011; Randers 2012; Shearman and Smith 2007).[7] As we have seen, this is also the

[6] As Schumpeter (1942), Pitkin (1967), and others have argued, decision-makers cannot claim to be acting democratically just because they consider the interests of those who will be affected by their decisions. If democracy, or democratic representation, is defined in this way, even the most autocratic regimes which claim to consider the interests of their subjects might be considered democratic.

[7] Even in autocratic regimes where leaders have the "right" moral training, it may be difficult to ensure that they act in the interests of future others in the absence of external incentives to do

approach favoured by theorists of intergenerational justice: they do not make the claim that just leaders should be autocratic, but they do think that justice claims should guide—and in some cases be used to compel—political actors to do the right thing. There is nothing wrong with encouraging people to think about the moral or normative obligations that they have to others, including future others, but this approach is likely to be of only limited effectiveness if we think of politics as a realm of strategic action and conflicting material interests. In a political arena that is not—and cannot—be governed by shared normative or moral commitments, we need institutional mechanisms, or political practices more generally, that incentivize political actors to think about future others, particularly when they are not already committed to doing so.

In what follows, I argue that deliberation is a *democratic* mechanism that can, under certain circumstances, encourage participants to actively consider and represent the potential interests of excluded others, *including* future others. I am not aware of any other mechanisms, institutional arrangements, political tools, or practices that might create incentives of this kind.

4.3.1. Deliberation and the Representation of Future Others

In effective deliberative environments, participants must engage in mutual reason giving: they must make claims and justify those claims in terms that others might plausibly accept. In order for productive deliberations to take place, participants must be willing—or compelled by circumstances or institutional incentives—to listen to others and adjust their positions in response to persuasive arguments (see Section 2.4.2.).

At first glance, it is not obvious how these deliberative practices might encourage participants to consider the potential interests of excluded others. Those who are excluded from deliberative processes cannot make their claims or interests known, they cannot defend their positions in response to the claims made by others, and they cannot persuade others to see things

so—incentives that may not be readily available. As Bell (2016) concedes, he does not argue "that CCP [Chinese Communist Party] leaders have a direct incentive to take into account the interests of the unborn and people living outside the state." His argument is "that they are less constrained than democratically elected leaders who worry about the results of the next election" (p. 267, note 49). In what follows, I argue that deliberation—or effective practices of mutual reason giving—can create "a direct incentive" for decision-makers to actively and genuinely consider excluded others such as future generations.

from their perspectives. If participants in a deliberation are united amongst themselves, they might agree to ignore the interests of future others or trample upon them with impunity—or they might fail to think about the future altogether.

But this idea—that participants in a *political* deliberation might be united in opposition to the potential interests of future publics—is not consistent with the account of politics outlined in Section 2.4.1. On that account, politics involves acting in the context of others who disagree. And in practice, there will always be disagreements about what should be done for the future. There will be disputes about who should pay which near-term costs and which contemporary groups or interests are likely to be helped or harmed by our future-regarding actions or inactions.

In deliberations where there are disagreements among participants, it will be difficult for anyone to successfully advance claims that are self-serving against the interests of included others.[8] Self-serving claims are likely to be opposed by those who would have their interests dismissed, undermined, or violated by their political opponents. It should be equally difficult for anyone to make self-serving claims against the interests of *excluded others* in effective deliberative environments where there are disagreements among participants. Any individuals or groups who make self-serving claims against excluded others are likely to be challenged by their political opponents if their opponents can advance or support their own claims or interests by invoking the potential interests of excluded others.

These deliberative dynamics are also relevant when it comes to making collective decisions on long-term issues. When there are disagreements about what should or should not be done to address long-term issues such as climate change or budget deficits, there will be strong deliberative incentives for opposing groups to frame their claims—or challenge the claims of others—in ways that seek to both defend and represent the potential interests of future others. Claims that disregard or diminish the interests of future others will be vulnerable to discursive challenges and counterclaims, as will any disingenuous or implausible claims about the potential interests of future others. If this is the case, even those who do not otherwise care about

[8] There is a distinction between self-interested claims and self-serving ones. As Mansbridge et al. (2010) have argued, it may be possible to defend self-interested claims in effective deliberative arenas if those claims can be made acceptable to others. In general terms, self-interested claims may be justified if they do not involve making zero-sum trade-offs against the interests of others. Self-serving claims, by contrast, always involve zero-sum trade-offs, according to which some individuals or groups make claims at the expense of others.

the future will have pragmatic incentives to *genuinely* consider the potential interests of future others if doing so can give them a deliberative advantage over their political opponents.

It may be helpful to consider an illustrative example involving three groups. Group A is opposed to government spending and borrowing. Group B, in contrast, favours borrowing money to pay for government spending on social and educational programs. Group F are future others who will be affected by whatever decisions are made by Groups A and B. In this scenario, Groups A and B are contemporaries, and they have to deal with their differences in a deliberative environment because neither can dominate the other in non-deliberative ways.

Imagine Group B makes the following claim: "We support the creation of a universal single-payer healthcare system and increases in education and welfare spending, even if this requires borrowing money to pay for these goods. We have to take care of people who are not doing well in our society. This will make society better, healthier, happier, and more productive overall."

In these circumstances, Group A has a strong incentive to defend the potential interests of Group F (i.e., future others) even though they cannot be included in the deliberations. Group A might challenge the claims of Group B as follows: "Increasing government spending substantially will increase the deficit unless taxes are raised, or the economy grows at a rate that is quicker than anticipated. If it is undesirable to increase taxes and unrealistic to expect the economy to grow rapidly, we should not increase government spending substantially because it would be unfair to saddle future generations with public debts incurred for benefits that they will not enjoy."

Once Group A has invoked the potential interests of future others, Group B will have to defend their own position on grounds that are either neutral or favourable to the potential interests of future others. Group B might claim: "The future *will* benefit from the debts we incur today. If we spend money today to make society healthier, happier, and better educated, the future will also be healthier, happier, and better educated, and it is not unreasonable or unfair to expect future members of our society to share some of the debts associated with those benefits."

In this exchange, where there are disagreements between contemporary actors, and where the long-term consequences of government spending and public debt are recognized and made explicit, it is advantageous for both groups to actively defend the interests of the future, *even though future others are not included in the deliberations.* Furthermore, both groups have to make plausible or defensible claims in favour of the potential interests of future others. If they make implausible claims, their political opponents will have incentives to expose those claims as implausible. In general terms, deliberative exchanges should tend to include the potential interests of excluded but nevertheless affected groups when there are disagreements between those who are included.[9] If this is the case, the tight theoretical connection that Young (2000) identifies between deliberation (or democracy) and justice (or fairness), does not necessarily rely on presence and inclusion as she suggests. This relationship might, instead, be more generally observed whenever included groups have sufficient incentives to make genuine efforts to represent the potential interests of those who are excluded. As I have argued here, effective deliberative environments can create such incentives.

It is also worth noting that the deliberative dynamics described in this chapter's scenario do not require either group to have any genuine concern for the plight of those who are excluded. Members of Group A might favour small governments because they are opposed to taxes and government intervention, and they might have no principled, moral, or justice-based commitments to the wellbeing of future others. Likewise, members of Group B might favour government spending on social programs because they are primarily concerned about their own interests. Nevertheless, deliberative exchanges—like the ones described here—can incentivize members of both of these groups to make plausible, defensible, and thus genuine, representative claims on behalf of excluded others. In deliberative environments where there are disagreements among participants and collective decisions must be made through argumentation, persuasion, and negotiation, at least to some extent, it will be difficult for any group to advance policy options that are explicitly self-serving at the expense of *any* other group, including excluded groups like future others. Any claims that do not adequately consider the potential interests of the excluded can be effectively challenged by others on those grounds.

Importantly, the deliberative dynamics that encourage political actors to make representative claims on behalf of future others can, and often do, emerge in less-than-ideal deliberative contexts. They emerge whenever

[9] There is evidence that supports this theoretical conjecture. In a laboratory experiment, Didier Caluwaerts and I found that those who deliberated with others were more likely to support climate action policies with near-term costs and future potential benefits, but only when there were disagreements among participants about what should be done for the future (see MacKenzie and Caluwaerts 2021).

political actors feel compelled to provide public reasons for the positions that they favour. As in the earlier example, fiscal conservatives often cite the potential interests of future others when they make justifications for reducing public debts. Likewise, those who favour swift action on climate change often cite the interests of future others as justification for those actions. These deliberative moves force those who are in favour of public spending or opposed to swift action on climate change into difficult discursive positions: they must think about the future even if they would rather not have to do so, and they must make credible claims that align their own interests or objectives with the potential interests of the future, even if it is difficult to do so. If they do not make credible claims in defense of the potential interests of future others, they will be challenged by their discursive opponents on those grounds, and they may be forced to adjust their positions to make them more future-regarding if they hope to get some of what they want from collective decisions.

4.4. Conclusion

In this chapter, I have argued that effective deliberative processes can help mitigate problems associated with two components of the democratic myopia thesis: (1) the myopic voter argument and (2) the exclusion of future others problem. With respect to the first problem, deliberative processes can help expose and challenge cognitive biases against the future by forcing, or encouraging, participants to engage their analytical brains rather than simply relying only on their intuitive—and probably myopic—responses to temporal complexity. With respect to the second problem, deliberation can create pragmatic incentives for political actors to more seriously consider, as well as act upon, the potential interests of excluded others, such as future others. These deliberative dynamics can create a sort of virtuous cycle in which otherwise self-serving actors compete with one another to be—or become—more future-regarding than their political opponents.

5

Getting to the Future

Inclusion, Deliberation, and Future-Regarding Collective Action

5.1. Introduction

Proponents of the democratic myopia thesis—as well as many of democracy's defenders—have largely neglected to consider the future-making potentialities of democratic agency.[1] This is surprising because the idea that democracy empowers us to make our shared futures together is implied by the more familiar idea that democracy is about making our shared, contemporary worlds together. The three arguments that I make in this chapter emphasize the future-regarding potentialities of democratic agency.

The first argument is about empowered inclusion. We need inclusive decision-making processes to avoid futures that favour the interests of some individuals and groups while ignoring or dismissing the interests of others. The second argument is about deliberation. Inclusion can help us avoid futures that favour the interests of some over others, but inclusion itself is not enough. In order to get the futures we think we might want, we need to talk to each other about what we are doing and where we want to get to in the future. We need deliberative practices—mutual reason giving, justification, persuasion, and negotiation—to move toward futures that seek to accommodate, at least to some extent, conflicting interests and different visions about what desirable futures might be like. If we cannot deliberate our futures together—and act on those deliberations—our futures will be shaped by drift, unguided aggregation, and the exercise of private rather than public power. In the third argument, I explain how deliberative processes can help mitigate some of the

[1] As discussed in Section 2.2.6, those who have written about "anticipatory democracy" (e.g., Bezold 1978, 2006, 2019; Toffler 1970, 1978) have not neglected the future-making potentialities of democratic agency.

Future Publics. Michael K. MacKenzie, Oxford University Press. © Oxford University Press 2021.
DOI: 10.1093/oso/9780197557150.003.0005

challenges associated with the short electoral-cycles component of the democratic myopia thesis.

5.2. Inclusive Processes, Inclusive Futures

The present is the only realm in which action can take place. The past has acted, the future has not yet acted, and if we wish to act, we must do so in the present. Nevertheless, action, itself, must be seen in a temporal perspective if it is to be properly understood. Emirbayer and Mische (1998) have argued that while any specific action might be focused on the past, the present, or the future, agency—or action—always has three temporal "chordal tones," or dimensions. The dimension of agency that is focused on the past—what Emirbayer and Mische call the "iterative element"—is agentic because it involves actively selecting or rejecting past patterns of thought and action. As they explain, even "relatively unreflective action has its own moment of effort; the typification and routinization of experience are active processes entailing selective reactivation of received structures within expected situations, dynamic transactions between actor and situation" (p. 976). The dimension of agency that is focused on the present involves "the capacity of actors to make practical and normative judgments among alternative possible trajectories of action, in response to the emerging demands, dilemmas, and ambiguities of presently evolving situations" (p. 971). The prospective—or future-oriented—dimension of agency involves "the imaginative generation by actors of possible future trajectories of action, in which received structures of thought and action may be creatively reconfigured in relation to actors' hopes, fears, and desires for the future" (p. 971). On this account, future-regarding action involves thinking past what "is"—or thinking beyond what exists to imagine or construct alternative possible futures.

In this section, I argue that we need inclusive democratic processes to imagine potentially desirable shared futures, navigate disagreements about what the future should be like, and identify mutually accommodating futures, insofar as it might be possible to do so. This way of thinking about democracy emphasizes the temporal dimensions of collective action while drawing on the widely accepted idea that democracy is desirable (if it is desirable) because it empowers whole societies to make their shared worlds together. If democracy empowers us to make our shared worlds together—and action is always temporally situated, as Emirbayer and Mische argue—then democracy should be understood not just as a collective, world-making activity but also as a collective, future-making activity.

To understand the role that democracy might play in shaping our shared futures, it is important to recognize that future-making activities always require collective actions. If we want to create desirable futures for ourselves, we have to act in concert with others because our futures will depend not only on our own actions but also on the social and political contexts in which those actions take place (see Section 2.3). We might strive to get a good education or invest our money wisely, for example, but these strategies will payoff in the long-run only if the rest of the world—or our world—cooperates: if we live in a country that values education and is politically and economically stable enough to keep our long-term investments safe. As individuals we might stop using plastic bags or driving cars, but these actions will make the future better only if others act with us.

Future-making is political in nature because there will be disagreements about what should or should not be done for (or to) the future. Individuals and groups will disagree about what desirable futures might be like, which methods or means should be used to achieve desirable futures, and who, or which groups, should pay the costs of future-regarding actions now and in the future. In order to navigate these conflicts, we will need political tools, such as force, coercion, aggregation, or persuasion, to get the futures that we think we might want as individuals and collectivities. But we are not likely to get mutually acceptable futures if only certain types of people—or small groups of technocratic, economic, philosophical, or political elites—are empowered to make our futures for us. Futures made by unrepresentative groups of elites might be desirable in some ways, and they might be better than any number of alternative futures, but they will be also narrowly conceived: they will reflect the interests, perspectives, and understandings of those who are empowered to make our futures for us. Empowered elites might have legitimate future-regarding concerns, but small unrepresentative groups, even if they are well educated, benevolent, wise, and genuinely concerned about future others, cannot hope to know and account for all of the various, often conflicting, concerns, interests, perspectives, and aspirations of those who will be affected by their decisions in the present and in the future.[2] We may be able to identify mutually acceptable futures—or we may

[2] Consider, for example, the Centre for Strategic Futures (CSF), which is a think-tank that is integrated into the prime minister's office in Singapore. The mandate of the CSF is to encourage long-term strategic thinking in the public sector across government departments. It is supposed to

not—but we can only hope to do so if we have sufficiently inclusive democratic practices that empower as many people as possible to influence the collective decisions that will shape our shared worlds and our futures.

This way of thinking emphasizes an aspect of democracy that is implied by many but not articulated often enough. If we think that we need inclusive decision-making processes to properly accommodate conflicting interests among contemporary groups, we should acknowledge that we will also need them to avoid narrowly conceived futures that favour the interests of some groups or types of people over others. What is surprising is how often this aspect of democracy has been neglected by its critics *and* defenders. When it comes to defining and actively shaping the futures that we might want for ourselves and future others, democracy is desirable precisely because it aims to distribute power and influence as widely as possible; and this inclusiveness makes it possible, at least in principle, for whole societies to act in ways that take into consideration and accommodate, at least to some extent, many different, possibly conflicting, visions of desirable futures.

But there are at least two additional reasons why we need inclusive processes when making our shared futures together. The first has to do with the often-neglected fact that future publics will not be politically homogenous. Different groups within future publics will have conflicting interests and concerns, just as we do today. Future publics may have some shared or general interests, such as a fundamental interest in a healthy natural environment, but whatever we do to advance their interests will benefit some future individuals and groups more than others. When acting in future-regarding ways, we may be able to anticipate some of the political cleavages that will be relevant in the future, but those cleavages are likely to change over time in response to social, political, economic, and technological developments—developments ultimately predicated on our own decisions. (Consider, for example, the declining importance of the political divide between Catholics and Protestants in the United States.) Future publics will contain new political cleavages, some of which we might anticipate, such as a divide between

identify and help the government and the bureaucracy pursue the long-term interests of the country. But what *are* the long-term interests of the country? How can these be identified and defined? Who should make those decisions? In practice, given the autocratic structure of the Singaporean system, the long-term interests of the country have been decided by an exclusive group of political and economic elites. Thus the CSF is mandated to pursue a narrow vision of the future as defined by an unrepresentative group. Certain shared objectives—such as economic growth—may make it possible to identify broadly acceptable plans of action, but as soon as a society's overriding objectives become political (i.e., contested), unrepresentative decision processes may become inadequate (Bell 2016).

those who have technologically enhanced bodies and those who do not, as well as many that we cannot yet imagine.

If future publics will be politically diverse, we cannot simply act in ways that will benefit "the future" because different groups within future publics, whomever they might be, will be differently affected by whatever assumptions and decisions we make today. Given these circumstances—which are the circumstances we are in—the best we can do is make sure that our future-regarding decisions are made in maximally inclusive processes that take into consideration as many different existing interests and perspectives as possible. Ensuring that our collective decisions today are made in maximally inclusive processes is the best means we have for making future-regarding decisions that do not neglect, misrepresent, or trample upon the particular interests of specific types of future others. We cannot *know* how our decisions will affect different types of people and groups in the future, but we can make collective decisions in ways that are *more* sensitive to the political diversities that might exist in the future, and the best way to do so is to draw on and extrapolate from all the diversities we have in our own societies today.

Second, and relatedly, inclusive democratic processes can help us navigate issues of intergenerational justice and fairness. I have argued, in Chapter 3, that we should think about questions of intergenerational justice in explicitly political terms. We cannot identify general, abstract principles of justice that will be valid for all generations for all time, but we can act on what we know about the past and the present to try to make the future better, fairer, or more just according to our own convictions about what is right or just. Inclusive democratic processes cannot guarantee that our actions will be fair to all different types of people in both current and future publics, but inclusive processes will make it more difficult for particular types of actors to ignore, dismiss, or violate the interests of others in the present and in the future. Those who are empowered within collective decision-making processes can articulate and protect their interests against the actions of others who might be willing or eager to violate those interests (e.g., Young 2000). Although it would be possible for current publics to ignore or dismiss the interests of future publics as a whole—simply because future others cannot be included in our decision-making processes—this seemingly plausible scenario seems much less plausible once we recognize that both current and future publics will be politically diverse. Rather than acting as a unified force against the interests of future publics, contemporary actors are more likely to defend their own interests and the potential interests of future others who are like them, or potentially aligned with them, against their political opponents whenever they have opportunities to do so (see Section 4.3.1). If this is the case, the best means of avoiding collective decisions that neglect, misrepresent, or trample upon the interests of certain groups, within both current and future publics, is to ensure that as many different types of people and groups as possible are included and empowered when collective decisions are made.

Rather than undermining our capacities for future-regarding collective action, as proponents of the democratic myopia thesis have argued, inclusive democratic processes make it possible for us to shape our shared futures together. This does not mean that we will, in fact, avoid narrowly defined or unjust futures simply because we use maximally inclusive processes to make our collective decisions today. The argument is, instead, that we can only hope to do so if we draw upon and navigate the diversities that exist in our societies today, rather than trying to avoid or ignore them in pursuit of specific, predefined conceptions of what the future should be like.

5.3. Deliberation and Intentional Collective Action

We will need inclusive decision-making processes to avoid narrowly defined futures that may be desirable for some types of people and undesirable for others, but empowered inclusion, itself, is not enough to enable societies to act in collectively intentional, future-regarding ways. Individuals and groups might be empowered to shape their shared worlds, and their futures, through aggregative processes, such as voting or market mechanisms, but such processes can produce desirable or undesirable—and unintended—collective outcomes. In order to get the futures that we think we might want, we need to act *with* others, not simply alongside them. To act with others, we need to form collective wills and shared intentions within inclusive democratic processes, and we need to act on those intentions to control or influence the other forces that will shape the future in the absence of collective action.

As explained in Chapter 2, the future will be shaped by drift and the uncoordinated actions of individuals and groups, if it is not consciously shaped and directed toward specific shared goals through intentional collective action. Drift happens when we are moved by external forces without actively controlling where we are going. The metaphor is of a stream or an ocean current taking us along to a destination that is not of our choosing. We float with the current, buffered by its forces, going wherever it is going.

The term "drift" was first used in this context by Walter Lippmann (1914) in his book *Drift and Mastery*, and it has been adopted by many others since (e.g., Baumgartner and Jones 2009; Burns 1963; Hacker and Pierson 2010; and Mansbridge 2012). In Lippmann's analysis, the world is full of drift. We let ourselves be pulled along by tradition, authority, economic forces, habit, path dependency, and various forms of fatalism, including both positive and negative visions of supposedly inevitable futures (see, e.g., Polak 1973). For Lippmann (1914) drift involves ceaselessly "revolving in the mere routine of the present" (p. 18). Mastery, in contrast, begins when we recognize the forces of drift and control them through conscious, intentional action. Lippmann's is not an argument that anything is possible: there are destinations that we cannot get to, given the situations that we find ourselves in, the constraints of nature, and the limits of human power. There is a sphere of the possible even if we can never quite be sure where the boundaries between the possible and the impossible are at any moment in time. There will be trends that we cannot arrest or redirect, and there will be constraints that we must work within, but the world, on Lippmann's account, is full of drift that can be mastered and directed only through conscious action.[3]

In practice, we often fail to take control of the forces of drift, but Lippmann and others, such as Pitkin (1981) and Mansbridge (2012), believe that we always possess the power to take control of our shared futures as long as we can learn to act together in the public sphere. As Pitkin (1981) points out, political life "is the activity through which relatively large and permanent groups of people determine what they will collectively do, settle how they will live together, and decide their future, to whatever extent that is within human power" (p. 343). Acting together in the public sphere is the only means we have for taking control of our shared futures, but to do so—to get to the futures that we think we might want—we need to forge collective wills and intentions through deliberation: we need to talk to each other about what we

[3] Lippmann defines drift as "unconscious striving" (p. 148), but this definition is problematic in at least two respects. First, we might drift either consciously or unconsciously. We might be unaware of how the currents of drift—habit, tradition, or path dependency—shape or constrain our lives and the options we think we have. Alternatively, we might drift along while being aware that we are doing so, even knowing approximately where we are going, but nevertheless remain unwilling or unable to do anything about it. We might like the destination we are drifting toward or we might not, but it is possible to drift either consciously or unconsciously. Second, the association of drift with striving is inconsistent with Lippmann's larger discussion of the concept. Drift implies a degree of passivity or a posture of letting things happen. In Mansbridge's (2012) account, drift equals trend plus inaction. Trends will continue until we act to stop or redirect them. Hacker and Pierson (2010) give the example of minimum wage laws. The real value of minimum wages will decrease as inflation increases if governments do not regularly act to increase wages alongside inflation.

are doing and where we want to get to in the future. As Pitkin (1981) explains, we "cannot even begin to direct the drift of social forces unless we see those forces truly and deliberate about them in our public forums" (346).[4]

We need inclusive democratic processes to avoid narrowly defined futures, and we need deliberative processes to forge collective wills and shared intentions, but this does not mean that diverse political societies will, in fact, agree on what the future should be like. Nor does it mean that everyone has to agree with each other before we can act on our collective goals or objectives. There will be divergent views about what our shared futures should be like and what we should do to achieve those futures, and those who disagree with collective decisions might nevertheless be forced to comply with those decisions. The great promise of democracy is not that democratic processes will render collective decisions perfectly legitimate; the promise of democracy is to render collective decisions more legitimate than they would otherwise be (Mansbridge 2012). We will not agree on what the future should be like, but we will need deliberation (dialogue, persuasion, reciprocal reason giving, and negotiation) to forge mutually accommodating visions of the future, insofar as it might be possible to do so. Our visions of desirable futures will not be shared by everyone, but they can be rendered more legitimate and mutually accommodating than they would otherwise be, if they are made in properly inclusive and deliberative democratic processes.

It is, of course, possible to imagine desirable futures that are not the products of intentional collective actions. We might drift toward desirable futures by chance, inadvertence, or the inexorable movement of history. Some people, such as techno-optimists believe that every problem has a technological solution and that human societies will develop technological—rather than political—solutions to our most pressing problems precisely when such solutions are most needed.[5] As we have seen, many proponents of

[4] Emirbayer and Mische (1998) also emphasize the deliberative aspects of collective agency. Drawing on Mead's (1937) *Philosophy of the Present*, Emirbayer and Mische argue that agency, especially in its prospective or future-oriented dimensions, requires both "imaginative distancing"—which involves thinking past what "is" or what exists and is observable— and "communicative evaluation." Their analysis highlights "the importance of intersubjectivity, social interaction and communication as critical components of agentic processes: agency is always a dialogical process by and through which actors immersed in temporal passage engage with others within collectively organized contexts of action" (pp. 973–974).

[5] See Gidley (2017) for a discussion of some of the varieties of techno-optimism. There are also techno-pessimists who believe that we will create technologies that will lead us to undesirable futures, dystopias, or destruction. Dator (1978) identifies 10 "images of the future" that are common among different groups of people but are not necessarily mutually exclusive. These include images of the future as fatalistic, static, cyclical, developmental, revolutionary, pessimistic, technologically aspirational, introspective, naturalistic, and malleable but not-yet-determined (pp. 319–323).

the democratic myopia thesis think that we should delegate political power to small groups of people who have the knowledge and skills to make desirable futures for us (e.g., Bell 2016; Heilbroner 1991; Ophuls 2011; Ophuls and Boyan 1992; Randers 2012; Shearman and Smith 2007). As discussed in Chapter 3, theorists of intergenerational justice think that we should rely on philosophers to both guide and constrain our future-regarding collective actions.

The problem with these three approaches—the optimistic fatalist approach, the techno-autocratic one, and the philosophical one—is not just that the first is unrealistic and the other two are paternalistic or normatively undesirable in some other ways. Those are problems, but the other problem is that none of these approaches will do the job. All three approaches are predicated on the assumption that there is some objectively good future that exists like a needle in a haystack waiting to be found (or not found, as the case may be). But desirable futures, whatever they might consist of, are not tangible or immutable objects; they are, instead, the tentative products of mutual relations and iterative interactions. As such, desirable futures are, and must be, co-created. At a fundamental level, it is the ongoing action of creating our shared futures together that will define what our desirable—or mutually accommodating—futures should be like. We cannot know what collectively desirable futures will be like—what we will care about or value or what we think we should value—unless we act together to discover, define, and create those shared futures. That is what acting in the public sphere is ultimately about: it is about forging shared commitments or accommodations among people who have both a reason or need to live together, as well as conflicting interests, opinions, and beliefs. My vision of a desirable future is likely to be different than yours in some ways, and we can only identify mutually acceptable or desirable futures by working together to define, and continually reconsider and redefine, what those futures might be like. The idea that we should empower small groups of individuals—technocrats, autocrats, or philosophers—to get us to an objectively desirable future is misguided if the very thing that they should be aiming at (i.e., mutually desirable futures) must be forged and created through iterative, inclusive, and deliberative collective actions.

An analogy might help clarify this point. We often think and act as if there might be an ideal spouse or friend who is "out there" waiting to be discovered, and that we would have an ideal marriage or friendship if only that person could be found. But that is not how human relationships work.

Relationships evolve and develop over time through ongoing interactions and shared experiences. True friendships cannot be imposed on one party by another unilaterally; they must be mutually acknowledged and developed through co-creation. There is no ideal spouse or friend "out there" waiting to be discovered, but there are always possibilities for mutually satisfying relationships to be developed and nurtured through continued interactions. Analogously, there is no objectively good or desirable future "out there" waiting to be discovered that might be adopted unilaterally or imposed on one group by the action of others—but there are always possible, desirable shared futures that may be nurtured through interaction or squandered through lack of effort or drift.

The fact that it is difficult to create inclusive democratic arenas where we can forge future-regarding collective intentions through deliberative exchanges does not challenge the central claim that I am making: inclusive, deliberative processes are what we need if we are going to make our shared futures in collectively intentional, mutually acceptable ways. If we empower technocrats, autocrats, or philosophers to make our futures for us, they can do nothing else but act upon their own—necessarily narrow—views of what desirable futures might be like. Those who have expertise in certain issue areas, such as the science of climate change, will have important contributions to make to public discussions on those issues, but the voices of experts should not carry any special weight in democratic decision-making processes on questions that fall outside their areas of expertise (e.g., Moore 2017). Experts cannot define collectively desirable futures for us precisely because those futures—like human relationships more generally—will not exist until they are forged in iterative and ongoing processes of co-creation. If we want to create mutually desirable futures, insofar as that might be possible, we will need inclusive democratic processes to avoid narrowly defined futures that ignore, misrepresent, or dismiss the interests of some individuals and groups while favouring those of others, but we will also need deliberative processes to forge—and continually reforge—future-regarding collective intentions.

5.4. Deliberative Democracy: Steadfast and Flexible

In order to achieve collectively desirable futures, we need inclusive deliberative processes to forge mutually accommodating, collective intentions, but we also need to strike a balance between steadfastness and flexibility. If we are too steadfastly committed to specific actions or goals, our future-regarding intentions may be thwarted by changing circumstances. At the same time, we cannot, and should not, adjust our actions in response to *every* obstacle that we might confront. If we do so, we may fail to achieve our long-term objectives because some of the steps along the way were difficult. In order to successfully create desirable futures for ourselves and others, we must remain committed to our goals—but only to the right extent—and we must be flexible when necessary.

Short electoral cycles create dynamics that make it difficult for societies to strike the right balance between steadfastness and flexibility. The long-term plans of any government or administration may be reversed by the next, and this very possibility can discourage political actors, and the publics they serve, from spending political capital and other resources on long-term initiatives that might never come to fruition—even if they would support those plans in principle. The regular rhythms of electoral democracy make democratic systems susceptible to a sort of frenetic energy of perpetual change.[6] But this frenetic energy is also what makes democratic systems dynamic, responsive, and accountable and thus ultimately more legitimate than other types of political systems.[7]

[6] In addition to the incentives created by short electoral cycles, many commentators worry that democracies are subject to policy disjunctures because they are liable to change direction whenever public opinion moves in one direction or the other or is encouraged to do so by eloquent demagogues (e.g., Achen and Bartels 2016; Brennan 2016; Lippmann 1922; Schumpeter 1942). This worry forms a central part of Plato's critique of democracy. In Plato's account, the person with a democratic character "puts [all] his pleasures on an equal footing. And so he lives, always surrendering rule over himself to whichever desire comes along, as if it were chosen by lot" (Plato, *Republic*, 561a–b). Tocqueville makes similar observations in his analysis of American democracy in the 1830s: the system, on his view, was full of energy but it was the frenetic energy of change without purpose. As Tocqueville (1835) explains, "there exists in democratic societies an agitation without a specific aim; a sort of permanent fever reigns there that turns toward all kinds of innovation, and innovations are nearly always costly" (p. 338). Toffler (1978) is also worried about "the wild swings of political attention, focusing now here, and now elsewhere" that he sees as characteristic of most political systems, especially electoral democracies (p. xiii).

[7] As Spitz (1984) explains, the legitimacy of majority rule is predicated on the possibility that collective decisions made by today's majorities might be reversed by future (different) majorities. Gutmann and Thompson (2004) argue that democratic decisions must adhere to a principle of provisionality. They must be considered final for some period of time so that collective actions can be taken, but collective decisions should not be conceived of as permanent: they must be both open to reconsideration in principle and revisable or reversible in practice. The principle of provisionality is important not only because it gives minorities practical reasons to accept majority decisions, but also because provisionality is an essential component of autonomy or agency. When we say we have agency we mean that we are free to both make decisions in the moment *and* change our decisions (or actions) in the future insofar as that is possible (Emirbayer and Mische 1998). The idea that we might make "permanent" collective decisions today—or decisions that will, in effect, be imposed

In addition to providing the foundations for political legitimacy, the flexibility and capacity for change built into the institutional structures of democracy can provide some practical advantages. As David Runciman (2013) has argued, although democracies are often bad at anticipating crises and acting pre-emptively to avoid them,[8] the dynamism and flexibility of democracy means that democratic systems generally do quite well at getting themselves out of crises. There is, of course, no guarantee that democracies can get themselves out of any crisis—and there are democracies that have failed to survive (e.g., Levitsky and Ziblatt 2018; Runciman 2018). But the iterative and punctuated nature of electoral dynamics means that democracies can, at least in principle, adjust when change becomes desirable or necessary. At the same time, these dynamics mean that democracies may systematically fail to strike the right balance between steadfastness and flexibility that is needed to engage in successful future-regarding action.

Classical thinkers such as Montesquieu (1748/1952), the authors of the *Federalist Papers*, and J. S. Mill (1861), for example, argued that institutional separations of power can help provide stability in democratic systems by checking or inhibiting impulsiveness without making the systems overly rigid or undemocratic.[9] If power is divided between the legislative branch, the executive, and the judiciary, or between units in a federal system, significant policy shifts will have to find support in multiple places before any wholesale changes of direction are adopted, but changes of direction will nevertheless be possible when needed or justified.

Checks and balances are typically conceived of, and justified, as bulwarks against impulsive decision making and policy disjunctures, but there is a danger that democratic systems with too many checks and balances will become stagnant, ossified, and deadlocked, and thus unable to act when

upon future publics—violates the autonomy or sovereignty of our future selves and future publics (see, e.g., Paine 1791/1973; Thompson 2005, 2010).

[8] Healy and Malhotra (2009), for example, show that elected politicians systematically fail to pre-emptively mitigate the worst effects of natural disasters even though pre-emptive action is often more effective and cost efficient than disaster relief.

[9] In the *Federalist Papers*, Madison argued that a geographically large republic would provide a check on impulsive or irrational decision making because communication across distances—and between large populations—takes time and irrational passions are not likely to emerge in many groups or localities simultaneously. But as Scheuerman (2004) has pointed out, "the Madisonian hope that geographically large republics would be free of irrational bouts of quick and unseasoned popular debate seems quaint in an age featuring widespread possibilities for simultaneity and instantaneousness in human communication and interaction" (p. 58).

changes of direction are need or justified (Burns 1963). There is, in other words, a danger of overcorrection. Mansbridge (2012) has argued that the political system in the United States is paralyzed not only by institutional design but also by what she calls the "resistance tradition," which is the belief that governments should be limited and constrained to ensure that they do not act against our interests. But the less governments can do against us, the less they can do *for* us. In Mansbridge's analysis, one of the most dangerous problems facing democracy in the United States is the system's incapacity to act, change, and get things done.

Depending on how they are designed—and on the beliefs of those who operate within them—democracies may be either (1) overly prone to policy disjunctures and the frenetic, unpredictable, energy of perpetual change; or (2) they may be subject to so many checks and balances, veto points, and gridlock that changes of direction cannot occur when needed or desirable.

There is evidence that the democratic systems we have are subject to both of these potential problems: policy disjunctures *and* ossification. With respect to policy disjunctures, there are many examples of governments reversing policies that were adopted by their predecessors. The Trump administration rollbacked or repealed more than100 environmental policies during his time in office (Popvich et al. 2021). President Biden has indicated that he will, in turn, review most and reverse many of the environmental policies adopted by the Trump administration, including those having to do with endangered and threatened species, natural habitat protections, oil and gas pipelines, air pollution and carbon emissions standards, toxic chemical regulations, waterway and drinking water protections, and the enforcement of environmental regulations (Milman and Chang 2021). Biden has halted construction on the Keystone XL pipeline, and he has recommitted the US to the 2015 Paris Accord after the Trump Administration left the agreement in 2017.

Even politicians in the same political party will sometimes seek to reverse policies adopted by their predecessors. Consider, for example, the high-speed rail line that is supposed to link San Francisco and Los Angeles. This project was supported by Democratic governor Jerry Brown, but the new governor, Gavin Newsom, who is also a Democrat, has dramatically scaled back funding for the project. As journalists, Thomas Fuller, Jennifer Medina, and Conor Dougherty (2019) explain, the current plans would have the train "begin and end in the Central Valley" without making "a connection to the coast, where most of the region's people—and opportunities—reside." Even proponents of high-speed rail would have to agree that spending billions of dollars on a half-built project is worse than doing nothing at all.

Despite the ever-present threat of policy disjunctures, there is, in fact, a lot of policy persistence in democratic systems. As Coate and Morris (1999) point out: "Conventional wisdom in political economy warns that once an economic policy is introduced, it is likely to persist. Even when its original rationale is no longer applicable or has been proven invalid, a policy will prove hard to remove" (p. 1327).[10] There are many reasons why policies persist in democratic systems even though governments regularly change and each new government typically promises change. First, the number of policies that a government is responsible for in modern societies is vast, and there is no way a government could consider or reverse even a small minority of existing policies over the course of a single mandate. Second, when policies, such as subsidies for specific industries are introduced, actors will tend to adjust their decisions to benefit from those policies; and that, as Coate and Morris (1999) explain, "will increase [those actors'] willingness to pay for the policy in the future. This extra willingness to pay will be translated into political pressure to retain the policy, and this means that it is more likely to be operative in the future" (p. 1327).[11]

Third, when there is uncertainty about the possible effects of policy changes, political actors—and in particular cautious governments—might be inclined to default to the status quo more often than they will be willing to risk change (e.g., Fernandez and Rodrik 1991). Fourth, change typically requires agreement among actors, but no agreement is required for the status quo to persist. As such, once a policy or institution has been adopted, it is often difficult to change. Indeed, even when a large number of people agree that a policy or institution *should* change, they may not agree on *how* it should change. In such conditions, the status quo will tend to persist.[12]

[10] For example, although Trump reversed many of Obama's environmental regulations, he was unable to repeal Obamacare, although he dismantled essential components of the plan. The policy is sticky—it is hard to repeal—even though Trump was elected with a mandate to repeal it, *and* he controlled both houses of Congress during the first half of his first term in office.

[11] Coate and Morris (1999) also argue that these dynamics can lead to "political failure"—where governments fail to invest in effective temporary relief programs or policies because they (and voters) fear that these policies will be difficult to get rid of after their original rationales are no longer relevant.

[12] Something like this seems to have happened in electoral reform debates in Canada. In 2005 there was widespread support in British Columbia for the idea that the Single Member Plurality (SMP) system should be changed to a proportional representation (PR) system of some kind, but many of those who supported PR, in principle, did not support the Single Transferable Vote (STV) system that was proposed as an alternative to SMP (Warren and Pearce 2008; Fournier et al. 2011).

Baumgartner and Jones (2009)—and Jones and Baumgartner (2005, 2012)—have conducted systematic studies of policy change and stability in democratic systems. They demonstrate that "major change is very rare and most policy making is stable and incremental most of the time" (p. xxi). But they also demonstrate that democratic systems are capable of changing course even in seemingly stagnant or stable policy areas. They describe this as a pattern of punctuated equilibrium, in which long periods of policy stability are followed by rapid—or punctuated—moments of significant change. Interestingly, periods of policy change are not always associated with changing electoral mandates, although they may be. Policy change is more often the result of changing coalitions of interests. Policy stability persists when coalitions of interests have an effective monopoly in a policy area. When new ways of thinking about that policy are introduced, such that new or different interests come to see themselves as having a stake in that policy area, policy monopolies may be disrupted, and this can initiate periods of rapid policy change.

Given the evidence, it is not clear that democracies deserve to have a reputation for unpredictability and change. There are strong incentives for elected politicians to do things differently than their predecessors, and the legitimacy of democratic systems hangs on the ever-present possibility of changing our rulers and policy directions, but democracies are not normally characterized by the frenetic energy of perpetual change that many commentators, such as Plato and Tocqueville, have worried about. Nevertheless, many modern commentators continue to believe that authoritarian governments will be better able to act in future-regarding ways, precisely because they do not have to worry (as much) about new governments replacing them and revising their long-term plans. As Daniel A. Bell argues, although China has not yet reduced its carbon emissions as much as it will have to in order to meet its environmental commitments, there are, in his view, reasons to be optimistic:

> Perhaps the best reason to be optimistic is that the same party will likely still be in power several decades from now. The CCP [Chinese Communist Party] is likely to stick to its long-term commitments. In 2014, both President Xi and President Obama made pledges to curb net greenhouse gas emissions by 26–28 percent below 2005 levels by 2025, and in the case of China, to reach a peak year for its carbon emissions by 2030 and to increase the share of renewable energy to 20 percent by that year. Who is more likely to stick to these pledges? The United States may set aside its pledge if the

Republicans win the presidency. No such worries in China, unless the whole political system collapses. (Bell 2016, p. 53)

This statement reads as rather prescient after the election of Donald Trump, who refused to ratify Obama's Paris Accord commitments, and the election of Joe Biden, who has now recommitted to the Paris Accord. Nevertheless, there is a particular danger inherent in adopting authoritarian solutions to the problem of policy disjunctures. Autocratic rulers who are politically secure (or at least more secure than elected rulers) can maintain their policy commitments over time if they wish, but they can also change direction if they wish, with relative impunity and without penalty or justification.

If we need to strike a balance between steadfastness and flexibility to get to the futures we think we might want, autocracies are likely to create the worst of both worlds. Autocrats have the power to be steadfast when appropriate and flexible when needed, but they also have the power to either (1) arbitrarily change direction without justification or (2) steadfastly maintain discredited, unworkable, or failed policy agendas. History is replete with examples of autocrats who were either too impulsive (e.g., Caligula and Nero) or too rigidly fixed on immovable ideological objectives (e.g., Hitler and Mao).

Given these considerations, it is not clear what the better option is. Electoral democracies incentivize politicians to try to distinguish themselves from their predecessors by changing, challenging, and reversing the signature policy achievements of their predecessors. Although policy disjunctures in democratic systems are relatively rare, the fact that democracies create incentives for perpetual change may be enough to make future-regarding action difficult: if the threat of policy disjunctures is real (which it is), political actors in democratic systems may unwilling to invest resources in long-term plans and initiatives that might never come to fruition.

Alternatively, the authoritarian option raises a different set of concerns, not least of which is that authoritarian leaders are, by definition, empowered to act arbitrarily. They might strike the right balance between steadfastness and flexibility needed to bring their societies to appropriate future goals, but they are also (always) empowered to act impulsively when steadfastness is required, and steadfastly when change is required—and that is not a recipe for long-term success. As Philip Pettit (1997) argues, those with arbitrary power can act as they please—or as they see fit to do—without being sanctioned by others, and without giving reasons or justifications for their actions.

In response to this impasse—where neither electoral democracy nor authoritarianism is likely to do the job we need—we should think more carefully about the role that deliberation, or reason giving and mutual justification, can play in helping us strike the right balance between steadfastness and flexibility. Many scholars have identified deliberation as a means of slowing down decision-making processes, improving their cognitive merits, and preventing impulsive, unjustified, or collectively irrational behaviour (e.g., Gutmann and Thompson 2004; Mercier and Landemore 2012; Mill 1859/1978; Scheuerman 2004). What is less often emphasized is that effective deliberative environments can create conditions that are simultaneously conductive to both change, when justified, and steadfastness, when warranted.

In deliberative environments where participants have to justify their claims to others who are similarly empowered, political actors cannot change their minds or their policies arbitrarily. In effective deliberative environments, political actors cannot change direction or deviate from the status quo unless there are reasons to do so that are compelling to others. These deliberative dynamics will not prevent decision makers, or societies more generally, from making mistakes or changing direction when they would have done well, or better, to stay on course, but the requirement that public decisions need to be justified to others who might disagree should function as an ongoing check against unwarranted or impulsive changes of direction.

The same deliberative dynamics should also make change and flexibility possible in collective decision-making processes. Where there are, in fact, persuasive reasons to change course or reverse policy decisions, political actors will not be able to steadfastly maintain the status quo if their preferences and decisions are subject to—and dependent upon—effective processes of deliberative scrutiny. If this is the case, ongoing deliberative processes may be the best and most effective way for groups of people, and whole societies, to strike that balance between steadfastness and flexibility that is needed for successful future-regarding collective action. If the arbitrary rule of authoritarians would give us the worst of both worlds (i.e., too much steadfastness and too much flexibility), effective deliberative processes promise to give us the best of both worlds: steadfastness when appropriate, and flexibility when justified.[13]

[13] It is possible to imagine autocratic systems in which power is centralized but not exercised arbitrarily. In such systems, political elites who are experts in particular fields might be required to justify their plans to other experts in deliberative processes. This seems to be the sort of thing that Shearman and Smith (2007) have in mind when they argue we will need to give climate scientists autocratic

5.5. Conclusion

In this chapter I have argued that we need inclusive and deliberative democratic processes to make our shared futures together in collectively intentional, mutually accommodating ways. It is widely acknowledged that we need inclusive political processes to make collective decisions that fairly accommodate conflicting claims and interests among contemporary actors. It is less often recognized that we will need the same sort of processes to adequately anticipate how our collective decisions are likely to affect different types of people or groups in the future.

I have also argued that we will need deliberative processes to forge future-regarding collective intentions. We need to talk to each other about our shared futures if we are going to avoid futures made by drift, inadvertence, uncoordinated aggregation processes, or the exercise of private power. But it is equally important to recognize that mutually desirable futures can only be constructed in iterative, ongoing processes of co-creation. There are no objectively desirable, shared futures that can be identified by experts, autocrats, or philosophers working in isolation from affected publics. Desirable futures are like friendships: they must be nurtured and co-created by participants, and they cannot be unilaterally imposed by some on others or simply found by those who look hard enough.

Lastly, I have argued that to achieve future-regarding collective goals and objectives, we will need political systems that provide both stability, when justified, and flexibility, when needed. Short electoral cycles create incentives and opportunities for political actors to reverse the policy decisions of their predecessors, and the mere threat that they might do so may be enough to undermine the prospects for effective future-regarding action in democratic systems. Authoritarian leaders can act decisively and steadfastly if they choose, but they can also change the direction of society whenever they want, even if there are no good, or publicly acceptable, reasons for doing so. By contrast, deliberative processes empower participants to make collectively intentional decisions about their shared futures, for better or for worse, but deliberation also helps prevent political actors from making arbitrary

powers to quickly redirect our societies toward ecologically sustainable futures. A technocratic political system that is also deliberative might strike the right balance between steadfastness and flexibility, but such a system would not make it possible for the members of a society to make their shared futures together in collectively intentional, mutually accommodating ways. No matter how deliberative they are, exclusive, autocratic political systems will produce narrowly defined futures that favour the interests of some groups over others.

decisions and changes of direction without providing justifications that others might plausibly accept. As such, ongoing, iterative, and effective deliberative processes can help societies and groups strike that balance between steadfastness and flexibility that is needed for successful future-regarding action.

It is, of course, difficult to image an inclusive deliberative system that would give everyone meaningful influence over the (many) collective decisions that will shape their shared futures. Nevertheless, it is even more difficult to imagine getting to desirable futures through other less inclusive, less deliberative, and more authoritarian means. We cannot build perfectly inclusive deliberative systems, but we can make our democratic systems more inclusive and deliberative than they are. I will discuss these, and related, issues of institutional design in Chapters 7 and 8. In the next chapter, I argue that deliberation—or communication and public reason giving—has an important role to play in coordinating the actions of non-contemporaries over long periods of time.

6

Acting Through Time

Coordinating the Actions of Current and Future Publics

6.1. Introduction

This chapter explores a topic largely neglected by democratic theorists. Is it possible to coordinate the actions of present and future publics separated by long periods of time? This question is important because many long-term projects, such as climate change mitigation or the storage of nuclear waste, must be sustained over many generations if they are going to do any good. If we cannot be confident that future political actors will maintain the long-term projects we initiate, we may be unwilling to invest our resources in those projects, even if we think that they are worth supporting in principle. There is, in fact, nothing that we (i.e., the living) can do to force future publics to do what we think they should. The decisions that we make today will structure the options that future political actors have—and the situations that they find themselves in—but they will be free to make their own decisions in their own time. Given these circumstances, our relations with future publics create an otherwise unfamiliar, and totally unique, political situation; a situation in which a set of political actors (i.e., present publics) are both dominant *and* impotent in their relations with another set of actors (i.e., future publics). We can do whatever we want to future publics without explanation or justification, and there is nothing that they can do to us. At the same time, there is nothing that we can do to force future others to follow our wills. Given this situation, we must think about past, present, and future publics as independent and substantively equal participants in long-term plans and projects, and we must use political tools that are appropriate for acting together among equals. In this chapter, I argue that if past, present, and future publics are independent entities, and thus equal with respect to each other, political relations between them must be predicated on deliberative or communicative practices such as reason giving, justification, and persuasion.

Future Publics. Michael K. MacKenzie, Oxford University Press. © Oxford University Press 2021.
DOI: 10.1093/oso/9780197557150.003.0006

6.2. Coordinating the Actions of Non-Contemporaries

Coordinating the actions of non-contemporaries is important for several reasons. First, as argued in the previous chapter, we cannot actively shape the future without the cooperation of others. Second, many of us do in fact care about what the future will be like. Third, what we think future others might do will affect our future-regarding decisions today. The arrow of time, the direction of causality, runs forward: the present affects the future, and the future cannot change the past. But our expectations about what might happen in the future—and the degree of influence or agency we think we will have over future others—will affect the future-regarding decisions we make today.

More fundamentally, what happens in the future will, to a large extent, define our present (or the future's past). Our actions and decisions must be judged over the course of time. Wars, for example, that were thought to be legitimate and just may be re-evaluated if they have negative or devastating long-term consequences. Likewise, supposedly great inventions may be re-evaluated when we come to better understand their long-term effects and consequences. Plastic, for example, was heralded as a miracle substance that is cheap, malleable, and strong. It *is* all of those things, but we have now discovered that plastics are polluting our water systems and threatening the health of animals and people—and that they are difficult to get rid of once they have been produced and introduced into the environment (e.g., Geyer et al. 2017). The present must be defined and continually redefined by the future. What we are today, or what we become, will depend on what happens in the future.

Likewise, what we decide to do today will depend, in part, on what we think will happen in the future, or what we think future others are likely to do. And our expectations about what will happen in the future can and *should* affect our judgments about what we might do today. For example, we may be unwilling to pay gas taxes to help mitigate climate change if we think that future political actors will eliminate those taxes before they can achieve their purpose. From this perspective, cooperation between present and future publics is essential to motivate future-regarding action. We might invest our resources in making the future better, but we are unlikely to want to do so if we think that future publics will defect from the cooperative schemes or plans necessary to make *our* investments worthwhile.

This might be called the "Generation N" problem: there is always a danger that some future public—the Nth Generation—will defect from the intergenerational cooperation that is necessary to ensure that long-term objectives are achieved. By defecting, Generation N not only deprives the present (e.g., Generations A and B) of the future goods they had hoped their investments would produce, Generation N also deprives all subsequent generations of those goods. This problem is especially acute when it comes to fungible resources that are built up over many generations but that might, at any point, be exploited by a single set of living generations for their own benefit. Living generations might decide, for example, to spend strategic reserves of gold or oil for their own near-term benefit: this is like getting something for nothing. Public pension plans are also vulnerable to this danger (Heath 2013; Jacobs 2011). Any generation might decide to spend all the money that other generations have contributed to a public pension scheme: this would benefit *them*, but deprive future others of their public pension system.

The challenges of intergenerational cooperation pervade our contemporary politics in ways we often fail to recognize. As I have argued elsewhere, there is no such thing as a short-term issue or problem in public affairs: we might make short-sighted decisions, but all of our decisions (and non-decisions) will have long-term consequences of one sort or another (MacKenzie 2021). In many cases, policy investments have to remain in place for long periods of time to be effective and thus justified in the first place. In other cases, the whole point of making an investment is to create something that will last and benefit future others. When we build libraries or universities, for example, we build them for ourselves and for future others: not a specific future generation but for *all*—or all foreseeable—generations (Baier 1981). Sometimes we create problems, such as nuclear waste, that can be managed safely only if many generations cooperate in the storage or disposal of that waste. The difficulty of coordinating the actions of non-contemporaries might be a good reason to *not* produce nuclear waste in the first place; but now that we have nuclear waste, we have to make sure that a rogue generation (a Generation N) does not forget about it or renege on its unwanted responsibilities to care for it. The problem of intergenerational coordination is a definitional component of political affairs, and it should be recognized as such.

6.3. Intergenerational Relations

The difficulties associated with coordinating the actions of non-contemporaries have received attention from only a small number of political theorists—and very few modern, democratic theorists. Those who have thought about these issues may be organized into three category types. First, there are those, such as Edmund Burke, who emphasize the continuity between generations. Second there are those, such as Thomas Paine and Thomas Jefferson, who emphasize the discontinuity between generations. Third, there are those, such as Karl Marx and Hannah Arendt, who emphasize both the continuity between generations and the ever-present possibility of breaking free from the past. In what follows, I briefly discuss each of these ways of thinking about political relations between non-contemporaries. I then outline why I think that such relations must be navigated using the tools of deliberative democracy.

6.3.1. Theories of Intergenerational Continuity

Edmund Burke makes an argument about strong intergenerational continuity. For Burke, we are deeply embedded in our relations with past and future actors:

> Our political system is placed in a just correspondence and symmetry with the order of the world, and with the mode of existence decreed to a permanent body composed of transitory parts; wherein by the disposition of stupendous wisdom, moulding together the great mysterious incorporation of the human race, the whole, at one time, is never old, or middle-aged, or young, but in a condition of unchangeable consistency, moves on through the varied tenor of perpetual decay, fall, renovation, and progress. (Burke 1790/1973, p. 120)

For Burke this intergenerational partnership is worth more than the sum of its individual parts, and it is both invaluable and mysterious. It is invaluable because it is the source and repository of all human knowledge and capacity. We are, in Burke's view, an intergenerational species. We thrive and advance because we have at our disposal the accumulated knowledge of many past generations. No generation of people can start with nothing, with no knowledge or history or language or culture, and develop into a fully formed society over the course of one generation. As Burke (1790/1973) explains: "Time is required to produce that union of minds which alone can produce all the good we aim at." The work of building a complex, just society "requires the aid of more minds than one generation can furnish" (pp. 281–282).

The intergenerational partnership is mysterious because we cannot—at any one moment in time—understand its full complexity. If we cannot create complex human societies over the course of a lifetime, then no single generation can claim to know how or why complex societies work as they do. In Burke's view, the fact that our societies, with all their problems, work as well as they do should be a source of wonderment and reverence. We can, and must, make small changes and improvements along the way—that is how societies advance—but we should not think that we can tear down everything that exists and build something better in its place in one swift revolutionary action. That is what the French revolutionaries tried to do, and in Burke's view the revolution in France was an exercise in human folly and hubris that, as he predicted, would have terrible consequences. It is hubris for a single generation to think that it can dispense with the "stupendous wisdom" we have inherited from the past and rebuild society into something better over the course of a few short years.

There is, as Burke points out, a sort of symmetry in his view of intergenerational relations (Ball 2000). The present is in the middle between the past and the future, and the living are connected as strongly to the former as to the latter. Although we are free to break from the past—we might ignore or reject the "stupendous wisdom" that human societies have accumulated over many generations—we also arrive on earth to find ourselves embedded in complex intergenerational relationships. As individual parts of a great "mysterious" intergenerational partnership, which is the source of our collective and individual knowledge and opportunities, we are obliged, in Burke's view, to pay our allegiance to it. We are obligated by the decisions that our predecessors have made simply because we are members of an enduring intergenerational partnership. Burke argues, for example, that the English, as a collectivity, forfeited their right to elect their kings in the revolution of 1688. As he explains, if they ever possessed this right, "the English nation did at that time most solemnly renounce and abdicate it, for themselves and for all their posterity for ever" (p. 104). On this account of intergenerational relations, generations, and the individuals who make them up, are simply obliged—or should be understood to be obliged—by decisions that their predecessors made on behalf of the intergenerational collectivity.[1]

This idea that we, as individuals, are obligated by the collective decisions that previous generations have made, may seem objectionable to those who believe that individuals—and publics—should be free to make their own decisions in their own time (e.g., Thompson 2005, 2010). Indeed, Burke's ideas were objectionable to many of his contemporaries, such as Thomas Paine and Thomas Jefferson. But there is some truth in Burke's view of intergenerational relations, whether we like it or not: we are, as individuals and publics, embedded in a complex lattice of intergenerational relationships and obligations, each of which stems from our (normally involuntary) membership in our temporally enduring collective entities. We are, for example, required to pay public debts that our predecessors have incurred, and we are required to do so even if we, as individuals, have not directly benefited from that money (Gosseries 2007). We are also obliged, in some sense, to honour any treaties or agreements that were signed by our predecessors (Vernon 2016). We are embedded in intergenerational relations precisely because, as Burke argues, we cannot make sense of ourselves as atemporal beings. Everyone is born into collectivities—societies, families, linguistic groups, cultural traditions, or religions—that have a past and a future. We can reject our own traditions, religions, and political affiliations, but we cannot leap, as it were, from embeddedness to unembeddedness: we must always remain in at least one sort of temporally enduring collective entity or another, unless we live a completely solitary life relying on others for nothing.

6.3.2. Theories of Intergenerational Discontinuity

Theorists of intergenerational discontinuity reject the idea that we should see individuals as temporally embedded entities. Those who adopt this approach reject the moral collectivism that Burke's theory of intergenerational partnership entails. On Burke's account, individuals and publics are obliged by

[1] Burke is not the only theorist to advance a theory of strong intergenerational continuity. The 16th-century Anglican priest and theologian Richard Hooker also thought of society as an "immortal" collective entity with an enduring essence that could bear responsibility over time. "Wherefore, as any Man's Deed past is good as long as himself continueth: so the Act of a Publick Society of men done Five hundred Years sithence, standeth as theirs, who presently are of the same Societies, because Corporations as Immortal: we were then alive in our Predecessors and they in their Successors live still" (quoted in Laslett and Fishkin 1992, p. 15).

decisions made by previous members of their collectivity, even though they did not have anything to do with those decisions, they did not consent to them, they may be harmed (not helped) by them, and they did not—in many cases—actively consent to being part of the collectivities in which they find themselves.

Theorists of generational discontinuity adopt the individual rather than the collectivity as their unit of analysis. On their account, each generation—or current public—is a collection of morally autonomous individuals, and any relations between them or between past, present, and future publics must be actively forged, and continually reforged or sanctioned, through the consent and agreement of living individuals. From this perspective it is normatively illegitimate for the actions, decisions, or institutional arrangements of the past to be imposed on the present—and it is illegitimate for the present to impose itself on the future (e.g., Thompson 2005, 2010). Generations, or rather groups of contemporaries or current publics, should be conceived of as being morally and politically separate from past and future publics, in the same way—and *because*—individuals are morally distinct and autonomous entities.

Thomas Paine, who is, perhaps, the most famous proponent of generational discontinuity, wrote *The Rights of Man* as a response to Burke's *Reflections on the Revolution in France*. In contrast to Burke, Paine adopted an explicitly individualist—and thus atemporal—account of intergenerational relations, and he rejected the idea that the past might legitimately impose obligations on the present or the future:

> Those who have quitted the world, and those who are not yet arrived at it, are as remote from each other, as the utmost stretch of mortal imagination can conceive: What possible obligation, then, can exist between them; what rule or principle can be laid down, that of two non-entities, the one out of existence, and the other not in, and who never can meet in this world, the one should control the other to the end of time? (Paine 1791/1973, pp. 42–43)

To make the point that past, present, and future publics should be conceived of as separate (and separated) entities, Paine argues that we should think of individuals as unique, free, and equal, rights-bearing *creations* rather than historically situated individuals born from their parents and thus connected to the past. According to Paine (1791/1973), "all men are born equal, and with equal natural right, in the same manner as if posterity had been continued by *creation* instead of *generation*. . . . The world is as new to [each child] as it was to the first man that existed, and his natural right in it is of the same kind" (p. 66). Paine seeks to assert the natural freedom of each individual, and, by extension, the natural and inalienable freedom of each living generation to break from the past, but in doing so he also rejects the idea that we might be part of an intergenerational partnership. If Burke's account of intergenerational relations is symmetrical in that we have connections and obligations to both the past and the future, Paine's account of intergenerational relations is also symmetrical but in a different way. For Paine, "the present generation has obligations neither to the dead nor to the unborn" (Ball 2000, p. 73).

Thomas Jefferson, like Paine, thinks that living generations should be free to break from the past, but he rejects the idea that we do not have obligations to the future. If Burke and Paine give us symmetrical theories of intergenerational relations, Jefferson gives us an asymmetrical account of them (Ball 2000). For Jefferson the past cannot impose legitimate obligations on the present, but the present has obligations to future others because what we do will affect them. This is an asymmetrical theory of intergenerational relations, but it is nevertheless a theory of generational discontinuity because Jefferson believed that the best, and perhaps only, way to protect the future from the present is to compel contemporaries to act entirely *within* the present. This is why Jefferson (1789/1999) was concerned, for example, about the accumulation of public debt. He argued that no generation of politicians should be allowed to borrow public money that they could not repay during their time in office. Just as it would be illegitimate for one nation to borrow money in the name of another nation without their consent and cooperation, we should not be allowed to impose our debts on future publics.

Similarly, Jefferson (1789/1999) argued that all laws and constitutional arrangements should come with expiry dates because "a law of limited duration is much more [politically] manageable than one which needs a repeal" (p. 597). In this respect, Jefferson has a radical theory of generational discontinuity, despite that he gives us an asymmetrical theory of intergenerational relations that recognizes that we might have obligations to the future. In Jefferson's view, the primary obligation that we have to the future is to try as hard as we can to act only within the present.

One problem with Jefferson's view of intergenerational relations is that we cannot, in fact, act *only* within the present. We might make short-sighted decisions that ignore or neglect the needs of future publics, but *any* decisions (or non-decisions) will affect the future. Preventing politicians from accruing public debt would help protect the future from debt burdens, but it would also deprive them of any long-term benefits that public borrowing might make possible.

The fact of the matter is that we *are* embedded in intergenerational relations whether we like it or not. We are free—ontologically speaking—to break from the past; to do things our own way; and to reject the ideas, policies, and institutions that we inherit from the past; but we must start from where we are. We are embedded in our relations with the past, our options will be conditioned by decisions made in the past, and the decisions that we make will affect the future in one way or another, no matter what we do.

6.3.3. Theories of Embedded Freedom

Burke neglects the moral autonomy of individuals and current publics, and thereby gives us a theory of strong intergenerational continuity where much weaker continuity exists in practice. Paine and Jefferson, for their part, try to separate generations from each other in an artificially categorical way. In reality, there is continuity between generations, but there is also discontinuity. Burke emphasizes the continuity between generations and presents it as something natural and inevitable, precisely *because* he recognizes and worries about the ever-present potential for generational ruptures (i.e., the Generation N problem). Burke's view of intergenerational relations is not, strictly speaking, that living generations *cannot* break free from the past; his argument is that they should not be so foolish to do so.

Paine and Jefferson emphasize the discontinuity between generations precisely because they recognize that the past does *indeed* impose upon us, and we impose upon the future—that obligations, debts, power, and inequalities are often passed from generation to generation. The past cannot force us to do anything, but their decisions and institutions will determine which groups are empowered in the present moment and how our decisions are made. Jefferson and Paine were aware that past, present, and future publics are not separate nations or spontaneous creations with no past and no future. They used these metaphors to make claims about the normative desirability of generational discontinuity. Their argument is not that past, present, and future publics are disconnected from each other; they argue, instead, that we should act as if they are disconnected from each other, insofar as that might be possible. If intergenerational relations were characterized by either strong continuity or complete discontinuity, Burke, Paine, and Jefferson would have nothing to argue about. As it is, we are embedded in our connections to the past and the future, but we are also, always, free to do as we please within the circumstances that we inherit from the past.

The idea that the living are free to act within temporally embedded power relations that structure but do not completely constrain our actions has been articulated by others such as Karl Marx and Hannah Arendt. In Marx's sweeping theory of world history, earlier generations play a functional but also active—explicitly political—role in preparing the course of history for the eventual realization of human emancipation. In his account, many generations have to suffer—and then act—before humanity can build societies free from oppression and exploitation. In Marx's theory, power relations are transferred through generations, but there is an ever-present possibility that existing power relations will be displaced by revolutionary actions. This is an asymmetric theory of intergenerational relations where previous generations, normally unknowingly, sacrifice themselves for the benefit of future generations.[2]

Marx gives us an account of the human condition that is, in some respects, surprisingly similar to Burke's theory of intergenerational relations. Both Marx and Burke emphasize the historical and political conditions that structure our contemporary options and decisions. Of course, Marx, unlike Burke, critiques generational reproductions of power imbalances and celebrates the human capacity for disruptive, revolutionary action. Nevertheless, both theorists are critical of the idea that individuals can be conceived of as abstract, free-floating, unattached entities who nevertheless have meaningful, identifiable interests.

In Marx's view we cannot—and should not—treat individuals *as if* they are free-floating abstract entities disconnected from their historical, political, and economic circumstances. But that is precisely what Paine and Jefferson thought we *should* do in order to emancipate the present from the past, and

[2] It is worth noting that Marx's account of intergenerational relations—in which the past sacrifices itself for the benefit of the future—is the opposite of most modern concepts of intergenerational relations—in which the present sacrifices the future in favour of our own short-term interests. Theorists of intergenerational justice tend to be concerned only with the latter problem, but it is also unfair (and may, on some accounts, be considered unjust) to expect the present to sacrifice itself for the future. As I have argued, what we should do, instead, is try to strike a balance between the legitimate interests of the present and the potential interests of the future.

the future from the present. Marx, for his part, emphasized the human capacity for radical, revolutionary, or disruptive action, but he rejected the idea that we need to act *as if* humans are unattached entities or temporally unembedded agents in order to realize that potential. In Marx's view, the idea that humans might be conceived of as unattached—and thus conceptually "free" agents—undermines our capacities for collective action, precisely because it abstracts away from the very real historical and economic conditions that structure, but never wholly constrain, our actions. This idea, which runs through Marx's theory of historical materialism more generally, is most clearly articulated in his famous introduction to *The 18th Brumaire of Louis Bonaparte*:

> Men make their own history, but they do not make it just as they please; they do not make it under circumstances chosen by themselves, but under circumstances directly encountered, given, and transmitted from the past. The tradition of all the dead generations weighs like a nightmare on the brain of the living. And just when they seem engaged in revolutionizing themselves and things, in creating something that has never yet existed, precisely in such periods of revolutionary crisis they anxiously conjure up the spirits of the past to their service and borrow from them names, battle-cries, and costumes in order to present the new scene of world history in this time-honoured disguise and this borrowed language. (Marx 1852/2000, p. 329)

In this quote, Marx recognizes that the living are, in fact, free to make their own decisions within the circumstances that they inherit from the past. The present can be radically reformed, but the past cannot be neglected. At the same time, Marx recognizes that even when we make, or *try* to make, radical changes, we are often reluctant to recognize them for what they are or what they could be. We are free to break from the past, but we are also anxious about this power that we possess. In order to make radical change more palatable, we seek to maintain connections to the past even when they are conceptually tenuous or intellectually dishonest—even when we are, in fact, creating something new. On this account of the human condition, we are both structurally and psychologically embedded in our relations with the past, even though we are empowered to make our own history.

Hannah Arendt (1957) also thinks of humans as temporally situated beings, but while Marx emphasizes the structures of history that condition and shape our actions, as well as generational reproductions of power imbalances, Arendt emphasizes the human capacity to initiate change and newness in the world. For Arendt, every individual—and every generation of individuals—brings something entirely new to the world. The human condition is characterized by our capacity for creation and spontaneity. We are not compelled to act in the same way as others, even when we find ourselves in similar circumstances. We have the power to create new things—new social or political arrangements—that have never been seen in the world before. Arendt uses the term "natality" to refer to this human capacity for agency, creativity, and spontaneity.[3] She is, in this sense, a theorist of generational discontinuity. She shares with Paine and Jefferson a commitment to the idea that the living are—and *should* be—free to do as they please regardless of what might have been done before them. The difference between Arendt and these other thinkers is that she always, also, emphasizes the fact that we are embedded in historical, cultural, political, and economic relations. For Arendt, as for Marx, we make our own history, but we do not make it as we please; we do not make it under circumstances of our own choosing, but in circumstances directly encountered, given, and transmitted from the past.

In my view, Marx and Arendt give us a more accurate description of intergenerational relations than those advanced by Burke, Paine, or Jefferson. We are embedded in our historical, political, cultural, and economic contexts. The past and the future are shrouded in time, but they are not completely obscured. The past structures the conditions in which our decisions must be made, but we are, nevertheless free to act, and what we do *will* affect the future. As such, there is no way to fully retreat into the present, as Jefferson thought we should do, such that we might never affect the future. We are unavoidably embedded in our temporal contexts, but we are nevertheless free to make our own decisions, to break from the past, to act creatively and differently in response to familiar circumstances or traditional practices.

[3] The importance of Arendt's concept of "natality" must be understood in the context of her work on totalitarianism. In Arendt's (1951) analysis, totalitarians seek to control both the present and the future, but they have an ideological vision of the world that does not conform to how the world really is. Instead of adjusting their ideologies to conform with reality, they try to make reality conform with their views of how the world should be. Although totalitarians can control the present through the exercise of power, they cannot control the future because of the uncertainty which is the product of the human capacity for spontaneity. They thus seek to control the future by eliminating the human capacity for spontaneity, creativity, and newness. This is, in Arendt's account, the horrific function of the concentration camps: they were technologies to control the future through the elimination of the human spirit—the human capacity to create change in the world.

The radical—ontological—freedom that living generations have to make their own decisions within the conditions they inherit from the past, is what makes intergenerational coordination so difficult. If intergenerational relations really were as Burke described, it would be possible for us to control the future. It would be possible to force the future—in one way or another—to do what we think they should do. This is, of course, impossible. There is nothing that we can do to solve the "Generation N" problem through the use of force, the exercise of power, or the application of sanctions. Once we have departed the world, we can no longer act in it, we can no longer exercise whatever powers we might have possessed to compel others to obey our demands.

This aspect of intergenerational relations—the freedom that living generations possess to act as they choose within their own time—has often gone unnoticed by political theorists. Constitutions, for example, are often conceived of as tools that might be used to constrain or control the future. Constitutions shape the political and institutional conditions in which future decisions will be made, and this had led some to believe that constitutions can actually prevent "future sovereigns" from being fully sovereign over their own affairs (e.g., Thompson 2005, 2010). Constitutions define the rules that we use to govern our political interactions with each other, but they cannot, in fact, be used to control the future. They can increase or decrease the political or economic costs associated with particular decisions, but they cannot prevent the future from reforming, dismantling, or rejecting the political institutions, policies, or cultural practices that they inherit from us.

Except in situations where we make decisions that will have irreversible consequences, the future will not and cannot be fully constrained by the decisions that we make.[4] With respect to most of our actions, most of the time, there is very little that we can do to control the future. We can impose taxes on carbon emissions to protect the environment, and future publics can reverse them if they choose to do so. We can adopt "binding" agreements with other nations—and future publics can choose to pay whatever political or financial penalties may be incurred by leaving or violating those agreements. We can put moratoriums on drilling for oil and gas in ecologically sensitive environments, and future governments can turn them into oil fields if they

[4] There are some decisions that are irreversible. We might, for example, cause species to go extinct or ruin whole ecosystems, and there may be little or nothing future publics can do to revive them (although, even in those cases, it is difficult to say what future others will or will not be capable of doing). We might destroy the world or bring an end to human life on earth through anthropocentric climate change or nuclear war, but short of these disaster scenarios, what we do cannot prevent the future from doing what they want in their own time and circumstances.

choose to do so. Current publics are both politically dominant *and* impotent in our relations with future publics. We can do whatever we want to future others with impunity and without justification, but we cannot force them to do anything that they do not wish to do. Future publics will be free to make their own decisions in the circumstances that they inherit from us.

On this account of intergenerational relations, past, present, and future publics are free and equal with respect to each other, even though decisions made in the past affect the conditions in which future decisions will be made. If this is the case, we have to look for ways to coordinate the actions of free and equal agents if we hope to act *with* future publics over long periods of time. In the last section of this chapter, I argue that we must rely on communication, justification, reason giving, and persuasion to coordinate actions between present and future publics, precisely because free and equal agents cannot use coercion, threats, violence, or sanctions to control each other. Before developing these arguments, however, I would like to consider a possible objection to my central claim that decisions made in the past will condition but not control present and future political actors.

6.4. Generational Reproductions of Power Imbalances

I have argued that the living are ontologically free from the past and the future. There is nothing that past generations can do to control our actions today once they have left the world, and those who do not yet exist can do nothing, themselves, to shape or influence our actions. We—the living—are free to make our own decisions and to do as we please. On the one hand, this way of thinking about intergenerational relations is both obvious and indisputable. On the other hand, it does not seem quite right. The past always affects the present and shapes our choice options. The present is free to act but only within circumstances inherited from the past. If this is the case, the past *can* control us by shaping the circumstances in which we make our decisions. Decisions that were made in the past create path dependencies, for example, that we follow, not because we have actively decided to do so, but because it is costly or politically difficult to depart from those trajectories (e.g., Dryzek and Pickering 2019; Pierson 1994). Although living generations are ontologically free from the past, decisions that were made in the past continue to affect, shape, and constrain our decisions today. As William Faulkner (1951) famously said: "The past is never dead. It's not even past" (p. 73).

How can we reconcile the claim that the living are always free to act with the equally obvious claim that past decisions shape and thereby control our actions? In this section, I argue that these two seemly contradictory claims can be reconciled once we recognize that the past controls the present, not by acting directly upon us, but by empowering or disempowering contemporaries with respect to each other. In other words, the past appears to be controlling—or acting upon—the present because groups of people within the present have been differentially empowered by the past through generational reproductions of power imbalances and inequalities.

There are many ways that power and inequality may be transferred through time from one set of actors within a generation to future others like them in subsequent generations. Monarchical and aristocratic systems, for example, are based on the idea that political power should be held by a small group of people and pass through generations along family lines. Wealth is also passed from generation to generation, normally along family lines, thus perpetuating existing inequities between groups of people from different socioeconomic backgrounds. These transfers of wealth and influence matter, politically speaking, because wealth and other economic resources can be converted into political power, giving the wealthy (and their children) vastly more political influence than others, even in democratic systems (e.g., Winters and Page 2009).

Ideas and beliefs about which groups of people deserve to be powerful can also perpetuate power imbalances through time. For many generations, and in many different societies, women were denied full political rights based on the idea that men are better suited to act within the political sphere. But even when people are made formally equal, as they are in many democratic systems, power imbalances will tend to persist if corrections are not made to address other sources of inherited inequalities. Women have less power than men in political affairs today, even though women have full political rights in most democratic systems, in large part because the ideas and beliefs of the patriarchy—that men are better equipped to rule—continue to be passed from one generation to the next, either knowingly or unknowingly, among both men and women.

Likewise, African Americans in the United States continue to be disadvantaged economically and politically more than 150 years after slavery was abolished. As Ta-Nehisi Coates (2014) has documented, there are many ways in which African Americans have been discriminated against and disempowered: they have been denied educational opportunities, jobs, and mortgages, for example, and each of these denials has made it more difficult for subsequent generations of African Americans to stand on an equal footing with other Americans. But even if African Americans had not been discriminated against after slavery was ended, they would have been at a disadvantage because they were deprived of the wealth that they had help create while they were indentured. When slavery ended, they were set free and expected to start with nothing or very little, while the children of everyone else continued to benefit from the wealth produced during the antebellum period. The fact that this situation would create and perpetuate generational reproductions of power imbalances and inequalities was clear to people even before slavery was ended. As Yale President Timothy Dwight said in 1810:

> We inherit our ample patrimony with all its incumbrances; and are bound to pay the debts of our ancestors. This debt, particularly, we are bound to discharge: and, when the righteous Judge of the Universe comes to reckon with his servants, he will rigidly exact the payment at our hands. To give them [i.e., enslaved persons] liberty, and stop here, is to entail upon them a curse. (Quoted in Coates 2014)[5]

To give former enslaved people liberty but none of the wealth they helped created was an injustice to the first generations of freed slaves, but it is also an injustice that has been perpetuated through the generations (e.g., Vernon 2016).

Generational reproductions of power imbalances can also be established and sustained by institutional structures. Constitutions, for example, often empower—either intentionally or unintentionally—some groups or regions over others. Such empowerments might be aimed at mitigating power imbalances, but they can also create power imbalances and entrench them over time. In the United States, for example, the National Rifle Association (NRA) has been empowered by the 2nd Amendment—or, at least, current interpretations of that amendment. Unlike those who are fighting for stricter gun laws, the NRA has a constitutional clause that has been used to protect their preferences for lax gun laws. The NRA has been able to leverage this advantage (which they have inherited from the past) against a majority opinion that continues to favour stricter gun laws (e.g., Gilens 2012).

[5] Mary Wollstonecraft (1792/1993) raised the same concern when she asked: "Who can tell how many generations may be necessary to give vigour to the virtue and talents of the freed posterity of abject slaves?" (p. 148).

The point of the matter is this: the dead hand of the past often appears as if it is controlling our actions today, but that is not the case. African Americans continue to be disadvantaged politically, economically, and socially because of the legacies of slavery and the discriminations that have been suffered since slavery was abolished. And it has been difficult for contemporary actors to pass gun control laws in the United States because of the 2nd Amendment, which was ratified in 1791. But these are not examples of the past controlling the present; they are, instead, examples of contemporaries acting upon each other from unequal positions. Whenever the dead hand of the past appears to be controlling our actions today, we must look for the mechanisms that have transferred wealth, power, respect, and opportunities to some groups of contemporaries while depriving others of these goods.

The living are, in fact, always free to act: we can decide to pay the costs of breaking out of the constraints that the past has imposed. We can decide, if we choose, to redistribute wealth in the current period and prevent generational transfers of wealth though estate taxes or other mechanisms (see, e.g., Erreygers and Vandevelde 1997; Haslett 1986; cf. McCaffery 1994). We can pay reparations to African Americans in recognition of the continuing disadvantages that the legacies of slavery and discrimination have created and perpetuated through generations (Coates 2014). We can challenge and change ideas and ideologies that help support generational reproductions of power imbalances, such as those that would support hereditary or patriarchal rule.

We can also try to consciously limit the impact of our actions on future generations. We can strive, for example, to make our political institutions reformable and reflexive in principle and in practice (e.g., Dryzek and Pickering 2019; Thompson 2010). Thomas Jefferson (1789/1999) believed that current publics should be empowered—indeed expected—to revisit, revise, and reform their constitutions, if necessary, every 19 years (p. 595). He argued that this practice would help prevent living generations from imposing their wills, and their political structures and inequalities, upon future generations without the consent of the latter. However impractical and disruptive it might be to hold constitutional conventions every 19 years or so, Jefferson's proposal can be understood as an effort to challenge the generational reproductions of power imbalances that will be otherwise perpetuated by any institutional structures or forms.

In more general terms, the democratic project itself may be understood as an effort to break-up generational reproductions of power imbalances.

Democratic systems aim to distribute political power as widely and equally as possible in order to ensure that collective decisions are not made by privileged minorities in their own interests (e.g., Schweickart 2011). It is only once real equalities have been achieved—once contemporaries have been made equal to each other in political, economic, and sociological terms—that we can imagine current publics, as a whole, making their decisions free from the impositions of the past. If the past controls the present and the future through generational reproductions of power imbalances and inequities, any efforts to distribute power and status more equally among contemporaries will also help free the living from the dead hand of the past.

But democracy also functions as a bulwark against the re-emergence of power imbalances. It will be difficult for any groups to act in ways that favour their own interests at the expense of others—and thereby favour the interests of future people who will be like them—if they must act in democratic contexts where others are empowered to advance and protect their own interests. There is, of course, an ever-present possibility that new power imbalances will develop in democratic systems—but they can only do so as a consequence of those systems failing to distribute power and influence equally and widely enough. Inequalities begat inequalities, and this is precisely the problem. When individuals and groups are unequal with respect to each other—when some have more economic or political power or a higher status in society than others—the powerful can leverage their positions to preserve their power and transfer it to future people like them. The democratic project in its purest forms aims to prevent precisely these sorts of generational transfers of power, and it aims to do so by making political actors as equal as possible within each set of living generations. But democracy is not just about preventing political power from being transferred through generations, as is done in monarchies and aristocracies; it is, more generally, about distributing power as widely and equally as possible so that no individuals or groups can dominate others in the present or hold political power for more than a short—and fixed—period of time.

If future publics really are free to make their own decisions in their own time, current publics must act *with* future publics—and not *on* them—if they hope to engage in successful long-term collective actions. If past, present, and future publics are free to act as they please, we must think about them as independent and equal participants in long-term plans and actions and use political tools appropriate in those circumstances where equals must act together to achieve collective goals.

6.5. Coordinating the Actions of Current and Future Publics

In this section, I argue that the tools of deliberative democracy—communication, reason giving, and justification—are the only means we have for coordinating the actions of non-contemporaries. We need to use democratic mechanisms to coordinate the actions of non-contemporaries precisely because past, present, and future publics are free, independent, and thus equal with respect to each other.

There are only a limited number of coordination mechanisms available. There are those based on power (e.g., force, coercion, law, or authority), aggregation (e.g., markets or voting), and communication or persuasion (e.g., deliberation or negotiation). As Qvortrup (2007) points out: "In human societies collective decisions can be reached as a result of three different mechanisms (or combinations thereof): by talking, by voting, or by fighting" (p. 1). The question we are concerned with here has to do with whether—or how—groups of actors who are separated in time can coordinate their actions to achieve long-term goals and objectives. One option—aggregation—can be dismissed at the outset. Future others, who do not yet exist, cannot have their preferences tallied alongside the preferences of those do exist.

Once aggregation is ruled out, there are only two other options: (1) sanctions, force, and coercion; or (2) communication, reason giving, justification, and persuasion. If future publics will be free to make their own decisions in their own time, and there is nothing that we (i.e., the present) can do to force them to do what we want, we will have to try to persuade them to act *with* us.

Take, for example, Norway's sovereign wealthy fund (see Section 3.4). It was created to ensure that the country's oil and gas wealth would be shared by future generations. For this to work (as it has done, so far), each generation must be honest trustees of this shared source of wealth. But the incentives for defection will be huge. Any generation might decide to spend all the money on their own near-term interests thus depriving future generations of their rightful share. There is, however, nothing that the generations who established the fund can do to force future actors to maintain it in perpetuity. The only option is persuasion: they must try to persuade the future to act with them if they hope to achieve long-term goals and objectives. There is no other way.

6.5.1. Intergenerational Authority?

Some might object that there is a difference between the physical application of force and the exercise of power through authority or tradition. It is possible, perhaps, to coordinate the actions of non-contemporaries by striving to make future people believe that decisions made in the past are authoritative and should, on that basis, be maintained. If the concept of power is conceptually distinct from the physical use of force—as Hannah Arendt (1961), Michel Foucault (e.g., 1977, 1982), and Steven Lukes (2005) have argued—then power might, indeed, be exercised *though* time to coordinate or constrain the actions of future publics. Such forms of authority might support intergenerational coordination as long as future others continue to recognize the past as a source of authority or, alternatively, never recognize, and thus never challenge the power or influence that the past might exercise over the present and the future.

As we have seen, Burke (1790/1973) appealed to something like intergenerational authority when he argued that the pledges or decisions of one generation should be understood as obligations imposed on posterity forever (pp. 103–104). Burke did not think that one generation could literally bind posterity "forever"—but he did think that we should act as if this were the case. For Burke it was difficult to imagine how intergenerational partnerships might be maintained without each generation accepting the authority of previous generations to make decisions on their behalf. What is less often recognized is that this concept of authority requires us to make a distinction between power as the capacity to compel actions through the use of force or the application of sanctions, and power as authority that can be exercised without the use of force. If there is nothing that the present can do to physically compel the future to act with us, any concept of authority that might feasibly operate in intergenerational affairs must be predicated on something other than the use of force.

Hannah Arendt (1961) gives us a concept of authority that meets these criteria. She defines authority as being distinct from both force *and* persuasion. As she explains:

> Since authority always demands obedience it is commonly mistaken for some form of power or violence. Yet authority precludes the use of external means of coercion; where force is used, authority has failed. Authority, on the other hand, is incompatible with persuasion, which presupposes

> equality and works through a process of argumentation. Where arguments are used, authority is left in abeyance. Against the egalitarian order of persuasion stands the authoritarian order, which is always hierarchical. If authority is to be defined at all, then it must be in contradistinction to both coercion by force and persuasion through arguments. (The authoritarian relation between the one who commands and the one who obeys rests neither on common reason nor on the power of the one who commands; what they have in common is the hierarchy itself, whose rightness and legitimacy both recognize and where both have their predetermined stable place). (Arendt 1961, p. 92)

Arendt also recognizes that this concept of authority—as a force distinct from the physical use of force—is relevant in intergenerational affairs. Arendt, like Burke, is worried that we will not be able to act into the future without some source of authority that might be used to compel—but not physically compel—the future to act with us. On Arendt's account, we need a source of authority that is recognized by present and future political actors if we are to have any hope of "building, preserving, and caring for a world that can survive us and remain a place fit to live in for those who come after us" (p. 95). In Arendt's analysis, forms of political or civic authority that might reach into the future are all the more important in a modern, or postmodern, world where other sources of authority and stability, such as religion and tradition, are losing their capacity to coordinate actions in complex, rapidly changing, diverse societies (pp. 93–94).

Following Arendt, Michael Mosher has argued that intergenerational relations must be underpinned by reverential appeals to authority or tradition, and they cannot be supported by reason alone. As he explains:

> Breaking the fall into the future cannot come from rational efforts to anchor politics in contract, since any such efforts are always open to the equally rational reinterpretive claims made in the future. On the historicist view, the future can undo every constitutional present. What is needed is a source of authority that cannot be easily undone, namely a structure for political action that is only quasi-rational, a source for reverence as much as for rational argument. (Mosher 2010, p. 8)

On this account, the problem with using reason and persuasion to coordinate the actions of non-contemporaries is that reasons can always be questioned. Thus Mosher argues that intergenerational coordination can only be achieved if the past comes to be seen by the present and the future in reverential terms:

> If luck holds, the authority of a liberal or constitutional order may be sustained by transforming itself from being simply a logical argument, whose logic will endure forever, into a historical legacy. The latter is less rational, more ritualistic, but more likely to retrain political actors and steer them away from being easy prey to time's power to dissolve. (Mosher 2010, p. 35)

6.5.2. Persuasion and Reason Giving in Intergenerational Relations

According to Arendt and Mosher, the actions of non-contemporaries can be coordinated using forms of authority or reverence that do not rely on either force or reasons. There are many examples that help support their claims. The founders of the United States, for instance, are revered and mythologized as a generation whose skills in institution building cannot—and should not—be questioned by contemporary actors. The authority that they are assumed to have possessed, as well as the reverence with which they are treated today, has helped preserve the constitutional structure of the country over many generations.

At the same time, it seems unlikely that political structures and intergenerational relations more generally can rest on authority and reverence (or luck!) alone. If future publics will be free to make their own decisions in their own time, they will also be free to question whatever constitutional arrangements and policy decisions were made in the past, even those that were made by otherwise revered authorities. If authority is left in abeyance when it is questioned, as Arendt argues, intergenerational relations supported by authority or tradition but not by reasons and justifications, may be especially vulnerable to the power of time to dissolve. Political relations between present and future publics predicated on reverence or authority alone will have nothing to hold them together once they are questioned—as they will be—by members of future publics who cannot be compelled to obey the dictates of the past or continue to treat past actors as revered authorities.

There is, as well, another reason to think that authority cannot be an effective coordination device in relations between present and future publics.

As we have seen, Arendt (1961) argues that authority depends on hierarchical relations between decision makers and subjects. But I have argued that there are no hierarchies in intergenerational relations: past, present, and future publics are free and equal political entities with respect to each other. This is not a normative claim that past, present, and future publics *should* be considered equals; it is, instead, an ontological observation that they are, in fact, free and equal with respect to each other. But in Arendt's account, authority cannot be used in conditions of equality; where equality prevails, political actors must resort to persuasion and reason giving if they hope to act collectively.

This conclusion—that relations between political actors or entities who are separated in time must be predicated on justification, reason giving, and persuasion—often goes unnoticed, even by those who implicitly recognize that past, present, and future publics must be bound together, if they are to be bound together, through communicative means. As we have seen, constitutions are often viewed as constraints on future publics, but they are also communicative devises. They speak to the future. They explain to the future which ideals and principles the writers of those documents valued, and which institutional arrangements are most foundational to the societies that the founding generations sought to create (González-Ricoy 2016).

Likewise, the great intergenerational partnership that Burke talks about is not, in fact, supported by authority alone or reverence for the past. It is, instead, built upon the human capacity for communication, both among contemporaries and between generations. In Burke's account of intergenerational relations, each generation stands on the shoulders of previous generations. Progress occurs when each generation makes their own contributions to the achievements of the past, and when no generation is foolish enough to try to break from the past completely. If we were to lose our communicative connections to the past and the future, we would, in Burke's memorable phrase "become little better than the flies of a summer" (1790/1973, p. 193). Flies exist for a while and then they die. They have no connection to the past or the future other than a biological one that is not enough to support and sustain culture or progress. Human societies have biological connections to the past and the future, but we also have communicative and cultural connections to other generations. These communicative and cultural connections make human progress possible by ensuring that each generation is not left to fend for itself but can, instead, draw on the resources that past generations have developed, used, and transferred to us. It is only through communicative means—using persuasion and reason giving—that we might hope to work with future others to achieve long-term goals, whatever these might be. At the most fundamental level, relations between past, present, and future publics must be forged and maintained by practices of intergenerational communication and reason giving. We must try to persuade future others to act *with* us if we cannot control their actions through force or coercion.

6.6. Conclusion

I have argued that deliberative practices—reason giving, justification, and persuasion—are needed to help coordinate the actions of past, present, and future publics over long periods of time. Intergenerational cooperation is important because whatever we think future others might do will condition our actions and our future-regarding commitments today. If we think that future publics are likely to abandon long-term initiatives or projects, such as climate change mitigation policies or nuclear non-proliferation agreements, we may be less likely to invest our economic and political resources in those initiatives, even if we think that it would be the right thing to do. In more general terms, as Burke argued, societies are built upon intergenerational relationships: the lives we live today have been both constrained and enhanced by the actions of our predecessors, and our actions and inactions will shape the lives of future others whether we like it or not. If we want to act in future-regarding ways—if we want to help make better futures by protecting the natural environment, advancing principles that we care about (such as freedom and equality), or building stable and legitimate political and economic systems—we will need future others to cooperate with us in those endeavours. Although tradition, authority, and reverence might help maintain intergenerational relations, those relations will ultimately depend on communication, persuasion, and reason giving. The forces of tradition, authority, and reverence are not enough to support intergenerational partnerships over long periods of time, precisely because living generations will always be free to make their own decisions in their own time and to break from the past if they are willing to pay the costs of doing so.

PART III
INSTITUTIONAL DESIGN

7
Future-Regarding Democratic Institutions

7.1. Introduction

The democratic myopia thesis is persuasive in many respects, but it is predicated on an implausibly narrow conception of democracy. Proponents of the thesis typically fail to consider democratic possibilities that reach beyond the institutions of our existing electoral democracies. In this chapter, I argue that there are democratic institutions that would enhance—rather than inhibit—our collective capacities to act in future-regarding ways. Indeed, many familiar institutions, such as referendums, distribute power widely and thereby empower whole societies to make their futures together, at least in some respects. Other less familiar institutions, such as randomly selected legislatures, would be representative, deliberative, and capable of acting independently from the political dynamics created by short electoral cycles and market imperatives. I am not confident that we will reform our democratic systems to make them more future-regarding, but I am confident that we will, in fact, need better—more inclusive and deliberative—democratic systems if we hope to create better futures for ourselves and future others.

In the first part of this chapter, I argue that future-regarding democratic institutions must meet three criteria. They must be (1) inclusive, (2) deliberative, and (3) capable of acting independently from short-term political and economic imperatives. These three criteria are necessary but not sufficient to support future-regarding collective action. Indeed, there can be no guarantees in democratic politics. As Saward (1996) has argued, no democratic procedure or institution can guarantee substantive policy outcomes without losing something of its democratic character. We will need inclusive, deliberative, and independent institutions to act in collectively intentional, future-regarding ways, but having such institutions cannot provide assurances that we will, in fact, do so.

In addition to these three design criteria—inclusion, deliberation, and independence—there are three other design considerations that must be taken into account. The first is whether a future-regarding institution is

Future Publics. Michael K. MacKenzie, Oxford University Press. © Oxford University Press 2021.
DOI: 10.1093/oso/9780197557150.003.0007

issue specific or general purpose. The second is whether it is protective or proactive. The third is whether the institution—or the basic components of its design—can be used at different levels of governance from the local to the global. I argue that we will need general-purpose, future-regarding institutions that can help protect the future from harm *and* support policies that proactively aim to make our futures better. We will also need future-regarding democratic institutions at all levels of governance from the local to the global if we are going to make our shared futures in collectively intentional, mutually accommodating ways.

In the second part of the chapter, I critically assess a number of future-regarding institutions using these design criteria and considerations. When taken together, and used judiciously, there are a number of democratic institutions—future-regarding constitutional clauses, referendums, citizens' initiatives, randomly selected assemblies or legislatures, and posterity impact statements—that would help counterbalance the myopic tendencies of electoral democracies. But those institutions are not the only possible options. There may be other future-regarding democratic institutions that would be more effective or likely to be adopted given our current political realities. If there are, those institutions will also have to be inclusive, deliberative, and capable of acting independently from short-term political and economic imperatives.

7.2. Design Criteria and Considerations

7.2.1. Three Design Criteria

The first design criterion is inclusiveness. We will need inclusive democratic processes to ensure that the futures we strive for do not favour the interests of some groups or types of people over others (Section 5.2). In ideal terms, each individual would have real and feasible opportunities to contribute to collective decision-making processes, but inclusiveness can also be understood in representative terms; in which case, every individual or group should have their interests properly represented when collective decisions are made.

But inclusion, itself, cannot support a society's capacity for collective agenda setting and will formation (Warren 2017). In order to make our futures together in collectively intentional ways, we need to talk to ourselves about what we are doing and where we want to get to in the future.

Inclusive democratic processes can help us avoid narrow futures that reflect the interests of some while ignoring others, but deliberation—the second design criterion—is needed if we are going to act in collectively intentional ways (Section 5.3). Deliberative processes can help address the myopic voter problem by encouraging participants to challenge their own temporal biases (Section 4.2), and they may be the only means we have for encouraging otherwise self-interested political actors to seriously consider the potential interests of excluded groups such as future others (Section 4.3). Deliberation can also help mitigate the policy disjunctures associated with short electoral cycles by ensuring that collectivities can change course when there are good reasons for doing so, but only when there are good reasons for doing so (Section 5.3). Lastly, to make our future-regarding actions worthwhile, we will need to coordinate with future publics through deliberative means, using communication and persuasion rather than force or authority (Chapter 6).

The third design criterion is independence. We will need institutions that are both politically legitimate *and* capable of acting independently from short-term political and economic imperatives. The problem is this: it is often difficult to get these two goods within the same institution. Unelected officials may be better able, and more willing, to make costly, and possibly unpopular, investments in long-term public goods, but such actors may be rendered politically impotent in democratic systems if they are seen as illegitimate. And future-regarding institutions—like any political institution—can be properly independent only if they operate with their own sources of legitimacy. A future-regarding institution might have the power to make its own decisions, or challenge, delay, or derail the decisions of other political actors who are not incentivized to care about the future; but it will not be effective if it can be relatively easily ignored, disempowered, or dismantled by other actors who face short-term incentives and enjoy some measure of political legitimacy.[1] And although independence is necessary, it is also important to ensure that future-regarding institutions are effectively integrated into existing political and economic structures so that they do not operate on

[1] Consider, for example, the fate of Israel's Ombudsman for Future Generations and Hungary's Commissioner for Future Generations. The Israeli Ombudsman was established in 2001 by one government and dissolved in 2006 after a new government was elected. Likewise, the Hungarian Commissioner for Future Generations was established in 2008 and given widespread powers to expose and prevent harmful short-termism in other parts of the political and economic system. The Hungarian Commissioner's powers were drastically reduced (and it was demoted from an "independent" office to a subordinate one) when a new government was elected in 2012 (e.g., Göpel and Pearce 2013; Smith 2019).

the sidelines of where real decisions are being made. What is needed, then, is a form of "embedded independence." Future-regarding institutions must be embedded in political and economic systems in order to have some influence over other actors; but they must, at the same time, retain their own sources of legitimacy—and thus independence—from those other actors.

7.2.2. Three Design Considerations

There are three additional questions to consider when thinking about future-regarding political institutions. The first is whether they should be issue specific or general purpose. Issue-specific institutions may be useful in some circumstances, but we cannot design separate institutions to deal with each of the many temporally complex issues that we face. Nor can we make decisions about particular issue areas—such as environmental or fiscal sustainability—in isolation from contingent decisions in other issue areas. Institutions that are designed to mitigate harmful short-termism in specific issue areas, may be rendered impotent or ineffective if successful action in those areas would require complementary actions in other issue areas. What is needed are general-purpose, future-regarding institutions empowered to deal with many different temporally complex issues, as well as the trade-offs between decisions made in different issue areas.

The second consideration has to do with whether an institution is supposed to play a protective or a proactive role. We will need future-regarding institutions empowered to protect the future from harm, but we will also need institutions that are capable of initiating proactive policy agendas aimed at making the future better. Most of those who write about future-regarding institutions are primarily concerned with protecting the future from harmful short-termism (e.g., Caney 2016, 2018; Ekeli 2007, 2009; Stein 1998; Thompson 2010). That is, of course, a critically important objective, but it represents only one aspect of future-regarding collective action. In order to strike a balance between the concerns of the present and the potential interests of the future, current publics must be empowered to act in both protective and proactive ways. We need to ensure that the lives of future others are not made worse by our actions, but we also need to make collective decisions about how—or whether—to make the future better in ways that go beyond the minimum requirements of justice (whatever we think those might be). Protective institutions might help prevent the worst possible futures from happening, but they cannot help make our shared futures better in other substantive ways. For that, we will need proactive, future-regarding democratic institutions.

The third design consideration has to do with jurisdictional scope. In order to get the futures we want, we will need to act democratically—and deliberatively—at local, subnational, national, transnational, and global levels, depending on the geographic reach of the issues that we are dealing with. Many of our future-regarding institutions will have limited capacities to act outside of specific geographic spaces, but we will need future-regarding institutions that are capable of operating at the transnational and global levels if we hope to make desirable futures for ourselves and future others. Many of our most pressing long-term challenges, such as climate change, the threat of nuclear war, and the imperatives of global capitalism, can only be managed or directed through international—probably global—collective action. As such, we must think about how we can build future-regarding institutions that are either empowered to take action at the global level or capable of working with other future-regarding institutions at different levels of jurisdictions.[2]

In what follows, I adopt a systems-level approach to institutional design (e.g., Parkinson and Mansbridge 2012; Smith 2009). From this perspective, it is not necessary for every institution within a political system to provide all the democratic—or future-regarding—goods we might think are desirable. Some institutions may be more inclusive than others but less deliberative. Others may be more independent but less inclusive. It is not necessary for *all* of our political institutions to be future-regarding, however desirable that objective might seem. If the aim is to strike a better balance between the legitimate concerns of the present and the potential interests of the future, we will

[2] A lot of what I say in this chapter assumes that sovereign states will continue to be the most important political organizations in the future. I adopt this approach because it is difficult for most of us to think about a political world where this is not the case. But it is important to recognize that states as we know them today are not likely to exist in their current form in the far future. In the future, we might abandon the idea that states should be sovereign, there might be a global government and local governments but few nation-states in between, there might be a global federation of states that are not sovereign in the modern sense of the term, or we might mange our global concerns with non-territorial governmental entities. Indeed, as we look farther into the future, we have to think in more universalistic or global terms, even when we are thinking about the futures of our own political communities. Finland, for example, is burying nuclear waste in an underground bunker called *Onkalo* that is designed to be secure for 100,000 years (e.g., Vuori 2015, p. 195). They want to protect future Finns from the dangers of nuclear waste, but they also know that Finland in its present form will not exist in tens of thousands of years. *Onkalo* is designed to protect "the future"—whoever or whatever happens to be there in thousands of years—from the dangers of nuclear waste.

want institutions that are representative of, and responsive to, the interests of the present, as long as decisions made in those institutions can be balanced with, and may be challenged by, decisions made in other institutions that are future-regarding.

7.3. Future-Regarding Constitutional Clauses

Although our political systems are often myopic, many jurisdictions have adopted future-regarding constitutional clauses (FRCCs) of one type or another. González-Ricoy (2016) defines FRCCs—or what he calls "Intergenerational Provisions"—as "constitutional provisions aimed at protecting the interests of future generations" (p. 171).[3] He argues that while FRCCs can be either "enshrined as fundamental rights or as statements of public policy," to count as constitutional provisions they must have at least three features. First, they must have a constitutional status that places them above ordinary statutory laws. Second, they must be protected from being amended by temporary majorities. Third, they must be "enforceable by some independent body (typically a constitutional court) with the ability to review statutes that may not comply with them" (p. 172).

Tremmel (2006) identifies three broad types of FRCCs. There are those that aim to protect future generations in general, those that aim to preserve the natural environment, and those that aim to prevent structural budget deficits. According to Tremmel (2015), while approximately 30 countries have FRCCs of one sort or another, only five countries (Bolivia, Iran, Malawi, Norway, and Japan) have constitutional clauses that protect the rights of future generations, and two others (Georgia and Uganda) have clauses that protect the interests or needs of future generations (p. 216). Article 112 in Norway's constitution, for example, states: "Natural resources shall be managed on the basis of comprehensive long-term considerations which will safeguard this right for future generations as well."

FRCCs have some of the features of effective future-regarding institutions. They are, first and foremost, protective devices: they are supposed to help

[3] Scholars have used various names to refer to future-regarding constitutional clauses. Tremmel calls them "clauses for intergenerational justice" (2006) and "posterity protection clauses" (2015). Ekeli (2007) calls them "posterity provisions." González-Ricoy (2016) calls them "Intergenerational Provisions" (IGRs).

protect the future from harmful short-termism.[4] They also empower certain types of political actors (normally judges) to make future-regarding decisions independently, which is to say, without being constrained or unduly influenced by short-term political or economic imperatives. FRCCs have, for example, been used to protect the natural environment against the short-sighted actions of powerful economic actors. As González-Ricoy (2016) explains, "in 1997 the Supreme Court of Chile struck down the government's approval of a $350 million logging project, as it found that it threatened the constitutional right 'to live in an environment free from contamination'—a right which the court interpreted as addressing 'not only current generations but also future ones'" (p. 170). FRCCs might also encourage elected officials and economic actors to think pre-emptively about how their actions are likely to affect the future if they want to avoid constitutional challenges.

FRCCs can also help coordinate the actions of present and future publics over long periods of time because they are communication devices: they help explain our long-term objectives to future others, they justify and explain the institutional arrangements that we will pass on to them, and they (often) articulate the principles of justice or fairness that we aspire to obtain and maintain over the course of many generations.

Lastly, although constitutions are often thought of as "national" documents, they can, in principle, be used at any level of jurisdiction. They can be used by local or subnational governments or by organizations—such as NGOs or businesses—to specify the rules by which collective decisions will be made. As a transnational state, the European Union has a constitution, and it is, at least in principle, possible to imagine a global constitution of one sort or another. Habermas (2006), for example, has argued that it would be possible—and desirable—to have a global constitutional order without a global government (see also Scheuerman 2008). In this context, FRCCs might be used to protect *global* future publics from harmful short-termism in specific issue areas—such as climate change, nuclear waste, or the proliferation of weapons of mass distribution—but states or other transnational actors would be free to make their own futures democratically within the constitutional constraints imposed at the global level. The fact that many

[4] As González-Ricoy (2016) points out, Intergenerational Provisions (IGPs) can create "negative duties (to refrain from action) alone or also positive ones (to provide some good or service)." In practice, however, "most existing IGPs exclusively create *negative* and *vertical* obligations, that is, duties on the state to refrain from acting in a certain way" (p. 173).

jurisdictions have adopted FRCCs is evidence that political processes do not always favour the present over the future.

Despite their many potential benefits, FRCCs are limited capacity tools. They can help protect the future from harm, but they are not inclusive deliberative institutions: they do not directly support our democratic capacities to make our futures together in collectively intentional ways. FRCCs are, instead, designed to empower a very small minority (i.e., judicial panels) to make judgments about how the interests of the present should be balanced against the potential interests of the future. Judicial panels may be highly deliberative, but judges, like anyone else, can do nothing other than make decisions according to their necessarily limited, and personal, perspectives on what the future should be like.

Furthermore, FRCCs may be difficult to enforce in practice.[5] They must be written in ways that are general enough to protect against different types of harm but specific enough to be applicable to particular cases—and getting that balance right can be a challenge. It may be difficult for courts to enforce clauses that aim to protect the general interests of future others because any specific action is likely to be both harmful in some ways and beneficial in others. The exploitation of oil, gas, and minerals, for example, can stimulate economic growth, development, and innovation that might benefit the future, but it can also pollute the earth and deprive future publics of their fair share of those resources. Similarly, profligate public spending can harm future others by saddling them with debts, but borrowing money to invest in public goods might also benefit the future. Furthermore, decisions about how natural resources are used and how public money is spent and invested are *political* decisions that should not necessarily be made by judges. As such, judges might be reluctant to rule in favour of the future except in the clearest of cases. If there are no clear cases, then FRCCs will do little to protect the future from harm.

One response would be to make FRCCs as directive as possible to ensure that judges can use them to protect against specific forms of harmful short-termism. This approach might be effective in some cases—and with respect to specific issues—but it would do nothing to protect against other sorts of

[5] For example, although balanced budget clauses are supposed to limit government borrowing, they are often ineffective because legal proceedings tend to move more slowly than yearly budgetary cycles (Tremmel 2006). On the other hand, Jeffords and Minkler (2016) provide evidence that countries with environmental protection clauses have better environmental outcomes.

harmful short-termism.[6] And societies will have to make decisions on many long-term issues, such as education spending, transportation planning, urban design, disaster preparedness, technological development, population growth or decline, and taxation rates. Future publics will also have to deal with issues or problems that we cannot yet anticipate. It is not possible or desirable to try to address all the long-term issues and problems that we might face in constitutional documents. As such, although FRCCs may protect against specific forms of harmful short-termism, their practical application will be limited. If we want to protect the future from harm—and if we want to empower societies to make their shared futures together—we will need inclusive, deliberative institutions with much broader mandates than constitutional clauses can provide.

7.4. Referendums and Citizens' Initiatives

Democratic theorists have often neglected to consider the future-regarding potentialities of referendums and citizens' initiatives.[7] In contrast, referendums on critical or existential political questions—such as national independence or integration—are often justified by proponents in future-regarding terms: they are desirable, it is argued, precisely because they make it possible for whole societies to make decisions about their shared futures together.[8]

[6] To address some of these concerns, Ekeli (2007) has proposed a constitutional provision with both substantive and procedural features. The substantive elements focus on environmental concerns: the state would have a "duty to avoid and prevent decisions and activities that can cause avoidable damage to critical natural resources that are necessary to provide for the physiological (biological and physical) needs of future generations" (p. 391). But instead of simply empowering the courts to strike down legislation as unconstitutional, Ekeli's proposal would give the courts the following three powers: (1) to initiate environmental impact assessments, (2) to delay legislation until a new election has been held, or (3) to trigger a referendum on the issue at hand. Thus instead of detailing the substantive decisions that judges should make on specific long-term issues, Ekeli's constitutional mechanism is designed to *repoliticize* issues that might otherwise be decided without sufficient concern for the potential interests of the future. This constitutional provision would be used to force otherwise powerful political actors to publicly reconsider, and justify, how their actions are likely to affect future generations. But it would, like most other constitutional clauses, have a relatively limited scope: it would help protect the future from environmental harm, but it would not protect the future from other types of harms, nor would it help empower a society to act proactively in future-regarding ways.

[7] For example, in the book *Institutions for Future Generations* (2016), which includes 18 proposals for future-regarding institutions, only one scholar—Kristian Skagen Ekeli—acknowledges the future-regarding potentialities of referendums. And in Jonathan Boston's (2017) otherwise comprehensive book, *Governing for the Future*, referendums are discussed only in reference to Ekeli's work.

[8] For the purposes of this discussion, I will define referendums as public votes on specific policy options or constitutional decisions. I will reserve the term referendums for votes that governments have initiated (Mendelsohn and Parkin 2001; Smith 2009), and the reader should assume that I am

Likewise, citizens' initiatives are designed to empower non-elites to circumvent ordinary electoral processes in order to place issues on political agendas that political and economic elites might rather ignore, and this makes them potentially important democratic tools for future-regarding action. If the political dynamics of short electoral cycles, or the interests of wealthy campaign donors, make it difficult for elected politicians to act in future-regarding ways, initiatives might be used to force governments to address long-term issues that publics care about. In practice, the financial and organizational resources required for successful initiatives may be out of reach for most non-elites;[9] and initiatives—like any other empowerments—might be used to advance either short-term *or* long-term objectives. Nevertheless, initiatives are an example of a *democratic* tool that can be used, at least in principle, to circumvent short-term electoral or market imperatives. To that extent, initiatives can help support a society's capacity to engage in both protective and proactive future-regarding collective action.

The prospects for using referendums and initiatives to advance future-regarding policy agendas will, of course, depend on whether voting publics can be convinced to act in future-regarding ways, even when doing so may involve paying some near-term costs. If we have reasons to believe that political elites are likely to be *more* future-regarding on specific issues than large segments of a voting public, initiatives are likely to produce policies that are more short-sighted than those that might be made by elected officials. But if this is the case, the opposite must also be true. When there are reasons to think that political and economic elites are likely to favour the near term over the long term (perhaps because of the institutional incentives they face or the demands of other empowered actors with short-term objectives), then initiatives might be used to produce collective decisions that are more future-regarding than those that are likely to be made by elected politicians.

talking about binding referendums and not advisory plebiscites. Citizens' initiatives are referendums that have been initiated by citizens through petitioning processes. Typically, a certain percentage of an electorate is required to sign a petition before an issue is approved for a vote in a citizens' initiative. Initiatives are common in many US states, but they are also used in Switzerland and other jurisdictions, such as British Columbia (e.g., Braunstein 2004; Butler and Ranny 1994; Cronin 1989; Smith 2009).

[9] There are ways that initiatives might be made more accessible to non-elites. Jurisdictions, such as Finland, Scotland, and Wales, have adopted e-petitions that allow advocates to collect signatures online. E-petitions have thus far been used to initiate deliberations and votes in legislative chambers, but they could, in principle, be used to initiate votes on specific topics like other citizen's initiatives (Smith 2009, p. 160). I say more about digital democracy in Chapter 8.

Importantly, referendums and initiatives can be used to address many different types of temporally complex issues, including emerging issues that have not yet caught the attention of political elites and institutional designers. But there is also a danger here: referendums and initiatives may be used on any type of issue, but they require voters to make consequential decisions on specific policies in isolation from other contingent concerns. Voters may be asked to make decisions on political independence, for example, but not on related and contingent long-term issues such as trade policy. If we are going to make our shared futures together in collectively intentional ways, we will have to make collective judgments about how trade-offs should be made between certain issues (such as education funding) and other related or contingent issues (such as tax policy).

Another challenge has to do with the deliberative quality of referendum campaigns. Referendum votes are maximally inclusive, but if referendum campaigns are not sufficiently deliberative, they cannot support collectively intentional, future-regarding actions. Simone Chambers (2001) has argued that referendums create dynamics counterproductive to good deliberation. First, referendums are typically decided by majority votes, and this means that those who know, or think they know, that they are in a majority will have few reasons to listen to the concerns and arguments of others, as well as few incentives to try to persuade those who might disagree with them. Even in circumstances where there are no obvious majorities before a vote is taken, political actors will have incentives "to find arguments that will sway only the needed number of voters" (p. 241).[10]

Second, referendums present voters with a fixed menu of options, but the prospects for productive deliberations are best when actors have the power to adjust the options that they face. People might, for example, be more willing to make concessions on particular issues if they can, at the same time, maintain their core convictions—as may be the case when integrative solutions to conflicts (i.e., solutions acceptable to everyone) can be found (Warren and Mansbridge 2015). Referendum campaigns do not allow for this sort of deliberative negotiation to take place.

[10] These strategic incentives cannot be mitigated by adopting supermajority thresholds. When supermajorities are required for change, those who favour change will need to convince *more* people than they would otherwise have to do, but the strategic incentive to sway only the right, or necessary, number of people would still exist. Importantly, supermajorities actually reduce the deliberative burdens on those who favour the status quo. Those who are opposed to change will have to convince *fewer* people than they would otherwise have to do, and many fewer than their opponents.

Third, collective decisions made in referendums are often supposed to be definitive, but this sense of finality can work against good deliberation. Those who lose elections will have opportunities to persuade their opponents to support them in the future. By contrast, the assumed finality of most referendums forces people into defensive positions: they must either win now or lose forever. In such circumstances, political actors may be unwilling to consider or accept any potentially legitimate claims made by their opponents for fear of weakening their own positions or claims.

When viewed in these terms, referendums create a sort of impasse: they empower whole societies to make consequential decisions about their shared futures together, but they also create incentives counterproductive to the deliberations that will be needed to forge future-regarding collective intentions. This problem cannot be solved, but it may be mitigated to some extent. There is no way to make referendum campaigns fully deliberative, but it is possible to make them more deliberative than they would otherwise be. One option, as Chambers (2001) points out, is to hold multiple referendum votes relating to a single topic or set of decisions. For example, instead of holding one vote to ratify a new constitution, several votes on different components of a constitutional package could be held before a "final" decision is made. This approach would make the decisions that voters face more multifaceted instead of dichotomous, thus creating more room for deliberative negotiation while still empowering voters to make consequential decisions about their shared futures together.

Another option is to combine multiple choice ballots with staged, multistep referendum processes. New Zealand, for example, used a three-step process to reform their electoral system in the 1990s. The first step was a non-binding vote on whether the existing single member plurality (SMP) system should be retained or replaced with an unspecified system. In that vote, nearly 85% voted for change. The second step was a non-binding vote on four possible alternatives using a preferential ballot. In that vote, about 70% voted for a mixed member proportional (MMP) system as their first choice. The third step was a binding referendum on whether the country should retain SMP or switch to MMP. In the end, approximately 73% voted for reform (Vowles 1995, p. 104). This three-step approach helped make the reform process more deliberative by insulating preliminary decisions from majoritarian dynamics, and by presenting voters with several possible alternatives rather than a single dichotomous option. During the second stage of the process, voters were incentivized to deliberate the merits and demerits of alternative systems, knowing that their deliberations at that stage would not result in a decisive decision in favour of, or against, any specific electoral system. Thus even those who might have preferred to keep the existing electoral system could freely consider the possible benefits of alternative systems.

A third option is to use double or multiple thresholds. In this case, referendum proposals would require the support of multiple majorities in different communities within a larger polity.[11] Multiple thresholds can facilitate deliberation by making it less clear which side is likely to win a referendum vote. If those with an overall majority cannot be sure that their preferences will prevail in other political communities or segments of the larger polity, they will have to try to persuade members of those other communities to support their positions—and they will have to do so by appealing to the concerns and interests of those other voters.[12]

Referendums and citizen's initiatives can also be used at any level of governance from the local to the transnational, and even, possibly the global.[13] Referendums, themselves, do not help solve the myopic voter problem, and there is always a danger that they will be tainted by misinformation campaigns or captured by special interests with dominant short-term objectives. Nevertheless, the very fact that referendums can be used to empower whole societies to make their futures together, challenges the claim that there are no *democratic* means of doing so.

7.5. Representing the Future

Referendums empower whole societies to make decisions about their shared futures together, but they require voters to make specific decisions

[11] Double thresholds were adopted in British Columbia (2005, 2009) and Ontario (2007) when those provinces voted on electoral system reform. Proposals for reform had to gain majority support in at least 50% of the electoral districts in those provinces, as well as 60% support among voters overall (Fournier et al. 2011).

[12] The United Kingdom, for example, could have implemented multiple thresholds in the 2016 Brexit vote, whereby any decision to leave the European Union would need to be supported by an overall majority, as well as majorities in England, Scotland, Wales, and Northern Ireland. In this situation proponents of the "Leave" campaign—who were concentrated in England and Wales—would have to make deliberative appeals to voters in Scotland and Northern Ireland if they wanted to be successful. They would have to justify their preferences for leaving in terms that voters in Scotland and Northern Ireland might plausibly accept. This would have made it more difficult for the "Leave" side to prevail, but it would also have made the decision to leave more democratically legitimate and the referendum campaign more deliberative.

[13] There are some proponents of global referendums, even though the practical challenges involved would be massive (e.g., Patomäki and Teivainen 2004).

in isolation from other related concerns or contingent issues. Referendums cannot, in any case, be used to make *all* the long-term decisions that societies face because they are too resource and time intensive. If we are going to make collective judgments about how to balance the concerns of the present with the potential interests of the future, we will need future-regarding representatives who are empowered to make decisions on a diverse range of interconnected long-term issues. But this situation poses a dilemma. If elected representatives are subject to near-term political incentives and strategic concerns, and democratic legitimacy hinges on representatives being elected, then it is unclear whether we *can* have democratically legitimate, future-regarding representatives. Democratic theorists have tried to solve this dilemma in three ways, each of which corresponds to a different means of selecting and empowering representatives: appointment, election, and random selection.

7.5.1. Appointed Representatives of the Future

A number of theorists have argued in favour of appointing special guardians of future generations, who would be empowered to represent and protect the potential interests of future others in our political decision-making processes. These guardians would derive their political legitimacy indirectly: they would be appointed by democratically elected governments, but they would not, themselves, be subject to short-term political and economic imperatives. A number of jurisdictions, such as New Zealand, Israel, Hungary, and Wales, have experimented with this approach (e.g., Göpel and Pearce 2013; Jones et al. 2018; Shoham and Lamay 2006; Smith 2019).

Appointed guardians of the future have several useful features. First, they can function independently from the political dynamics of short electoral cycles and the imperatives of the market. Second, they can publicly reprimand elected officials and market actors who ignore the potential interests of future others. Third, they can gather information about long-term trends while analyzing the consequences of public actions and inactions. Fourth, they can help societies identify emerging issues or problems that might otherwise be overlooked by publics, governments, and businesses. The Israeli Ombudsman for Future Generations, for example, initiated a public conversation about the long-term consequences of rising levels of obesity in that country (Shoham and Lamay 2006). Guardians of the future can also play a deliberative role in the development of public policies. By critiquing specific law proposals or economic decisions, guardians can force political and economic actors to publicly justify their plans in future-regarding terms. Guardians can also, in principle, be appointed at any level of governance from the local to the global. The United Nations, for example, could appoint a guardian of global futures.

While guardians of the future can help make our democratic systems more future-regarding, they do not make them *more* democratic, and this means that they can do little to empower societies to make their shared futures together. In practice, guardians of the future have not been inclusive institutions or representative of the publics they are meant to serve. Jurisdictions that have experimented with this approach have created relatively small offices headed by a single guardian or commissioner. One concern with this approach is that the guardian—as a single person—can do nothing other than make his or her own judgments about what the future should be like. The Israeli commissioner, Shlomo Shoham, for example, was accused of promoting a particular vision of the future that was grounded in liberal or secular values that did not adequately reflect the future potential interests of everyone in the country, such as conservative Jewish communities or Palestinians (Shoham 2010, p. 105; Smith 2019). Shoham's office sought to obtain input from affected publics (Shoham and Lamay 2006; Shoham 2010), but that sort of outreach is not a substitute for empowered inclusion. In response to this concern, Graham Smith (2019) has argued that guardians of the future should be paired with inclusive institutions, such as randomly selected minipublics, to make them more representative of the publics—and future publics—they are meant to serve.

Lastly, although guardians of the future are supposed to operate independently, in practice they have been vulnerable to dissolution when governments change. The most powerful guardians, in Israel and Hungary, existed only as long as the governments that appointed them (Smith 2019). Jones et al. (2018) have argued that the vulnerability of appointed guardians may be directly related to the power and influence they have: the more power they have to challenge, delay, or derail the agendas of elected officials or the decisions of economic actors, the more threatening they will be to those who have the power to dissolve or defang them.[14] To solve this problem, the powers

[14] Other future-regarding advisory bodies have suffered similar fates. Many of the anticipatory democracy processes mentioned by Bezold (1978, 2006) and his colleagues, for example, have been dismantled, ignored, or discontinued by powerful political actors. As Bezold (2019) explains: "While

and responsibilities of the guardians could be entrenched in constitutions, but this approach would not help address the democratic deficiencies of the institution. Guardians of the future may have some role to play in future-regarding democratic systems, but the institution itself would not help make those systems more inclusive, representative, deliberative, or democratically legitimate.

7.5.2. Elected Representatives of the Future

A number of theorists have recommended institutional reforms that would incentivize and empower elected officials to act in future-regarding ways. These proposals aim to use elections to empower certain representatives, while changing or mitigating some of the short-term incentives that elected officials normally face. Timo Järvensivu (2012), for example, has recommended the creation of a second, or supervisory, legislative chamber that would have elected members who sit for 15-year, non-renewable terms. This institution—which might be called a "long legislature"—would have some democratic legitimacy, but its members would not be subject to the political dynamics of short electoral cycles. Members of a long legislature would be comparatively free to challenge other political and economic elites—and myopic voters—because they would not need to seek political or financial support for their re-election campaigns.

A long legislature might help introduce some future-regarding considerations into otherwise myopic policymaking processes, but its members would not be accountable to voters once elected, and this would challenge their claims to democratic legitimacy and potentially reduce their influence or scope for acting in the interests of future others. Furthermore, it is not clear that a long legislature would create sufficient incentives for voters or representatives to think and act in future-regarding ways. Myopic voters would have incentives to elect representatives who they believe will not act too aggressively in the interests of future others. Likewise, political and economic elites would have strong incentives, and the resources needed, to field candidates who would serve their own short-term interests. The long legislature might be especially vulnerable to being captured by elites with

there are government agencies and departments around the world that do foresight all the time, it is also true that governmental foresight waxes and wanes, just as it does in companies. Unfortunately, previous waves of foresight within organizations are often forgotten" (p. 275).

dominant short-term interests because it would be a particularly valuable political asset, giving those who are elected influence over public policy for long periods of time.

Andrew Dobson (1996) has argued that there should be quotas of reserved seats for special representatives of the future in legislative chambers. These representatives would be drawn from, and elected by, individuals who had previously demonstrated a genuine concern for future others, such as members of environmental groups. Those who meet these criteria would have two votes: one for their regular representatives, and another for their special representatives of the future. This proposal raises a number of red flags. It violates the democratic principle of equality by giving some voters more votes than others, and it would rig the democratic system in favour of those with particular policy preferences (such as environmentalists). Furthermore, it is not clear who would, or should, decide who should be entitled to participate in the elections for special representatives of the future. More fundamentally, the proposal would not solve the problem that Dobson seeks to address because it would be difficult to ensure that seats meant for special representatives of the future are not captured by political or economic elites with short-term objectives. Indeed, those with short-term interests to protect would have strong incentives to capture these seats to prevent others from acting against their interests.

In response to Dobson, Kristian Skagen Ekeli (2005) has argued that everyone should be entitled to vote for special representatives of the future. Ekeli's proposal does not violate the democratic principle of equality, and it eliminates the need to make judgments about who should be allowed to participate in elections for representatives of the future, but it does not solve the other problems with Dobson's proposal. In both cases, political and economic elites with dominant short-term interests would have strong incentives to capture seats that are supposed to be reserved for genuine representatives of the future. And it is unclear how this problem could be addressed within the scope of the proposals themselves.

Ekeli's proposal also seems to imply that voters and partisan groups will have split personalities: they will consciously and rationally pursue their short-term objectives when voting for their "regular" representatives, but they will make different, more future-regarding, decisions when voting for special representatives of the future. If the democratic myopia problem is caused by myopic voters, giving voters more votes is not going to solve the problem. Voters would likely favour the same sort of policies and candidates in both elections, and political elites and parties would be incentivized to run the same sort of candidates in both elections.

These three proposals—Järvensivu's, Dobson's, and Ekeli's—are worthy of consideration, not because they provide solutions to the electoral myopia dilemma, but because they illustrate how difficult it is to overcome the dilemma. The more power elected representatives of the future are given, the more likely it is that they will be captured by powerful actors with short-term interests to protect. And any system that would empower independent actors, such as judges, to make decisions about who should or should not be entitled to participate in elections for future representatives would undermine the legitimacy of those elections.

Another option is to incentivize "ordinary" politicians to act as representatives of the future *after* they have been elected. Thinking in these terms, Ekeli (2009), has argued that we should consider using submajority rules to empower and incentivize elected representatives to act in future-regarding ways.[15] According to this proposal, any minority making up one-third of a legislative chamber would be given two procedural powers: (1) the right to delay legislative proposals until after the next election if they would plausibly "inflict serious harms or risks upon posterity," and (2) the power to trigger a referendum if the minority agrees that a law would "have a serious adverse impact on the life-conditions of posterity" (p. 449). These procedural rules would empower duly elected representatives to protect the future even if future-regarding legislative majorities could not be obtained.

Ekeli's (2009) proposal is attractive in a number of ways. Submajority rules would force legislative majorities to publicly justify their law proposals in future-regarding terms; they would incentivize lawmakers to act preemptively to avoid having their otherwise short-sighted law proposals derailed; they could be used to initiate public debates on topics with long-term consequences; and they would empower voters to make certain long-term decisions in referendum votes. Nevertheless, there several practical and normative problems with this approach. The procedures that Ekeli outlines might be used in the ways that he had intended, but they might also be used by legislative minorities to pursue their own short-term political objectives.

[15] Submajority rules may be less common than supermajority rules, but they are not less legitimate. As Ekeli (2009) explains, submajority rules can be used to set other procedural rules or to establish agendas for subsequent decision-making processes (p. 449). Indeed, submajority and supermajority rules are the obverse of each other: in either case, a minority is empowered to prevent a majority from making a collective decision.

To prevent that from happening, Ekeli would require legislative minorities to present a prima facie case that a law proposal poses significant risks to the future. The burden of proof would fall on the majority to defend their law proposal in future-regarding terms, and the courts would be empowered to resolve ongoing disputes. But it is not clear that this approach would prevent abuses of the system. Elected representatives would have incentives to use submajority rules to delay *any* legislative proposals that would threaten their short-term interests, even in cases where they know their claims are likely to be overturned by courts. In this way, the system that Ekeli proposes might backfire: legislative minorities might use submajority rules to delay or prevent governments from taking future-regarding actions.

In short, there are no easy or obvious solutions to the electoral myopia dilemma. Any rules or procedures that would give some elected representatives special powers to pursue long-term objectives—such as longer terms in office, quotas of reserved seats, or submajority rules—can also be used to pursue short-term objectives. What is needed are unelected representatives who nevertheless have some claim to democratic legitimacy. In what follows, I argue that randomly selected legislative assemblies can provide this otherwise-difficult-to-find combination of democratic goods.

7.5.3. Randomly Selected Representatives of the Future

Random selection—or "sortition"—has been used for centuries to fill public offices, but the practice has been largely displaced by elections in modern democratic states (e.g., Dowlen 2008; Manin 1997). In recent decades, however, there has been a renaissance of interest in random selection. Many jurisdictions, for example, have started using small, ad hoc randomly selected assemblies—or "minipublics"—to address a wide range of policy issues (e.g., Setälä and Smith 2018). A number of democratic theorists have argued in favour of permanent legislative bodies with members who are randomly selected—instead of elected—and regularly replaced by new members (e.g., Abizadeh 2020; Barnett and Carty 1998; Burnheim 2014; Callenbach and Phillips 1985; Dator 1981; MacKenzie 2016b; McCormick 2006, 2011; Read 2012; Gastil and Wright 2018; Zakaras 2010). A German-speaking community in Belgium recently became the first jurisdiction in the world to create a permanent, randomly selected assembly charged with providing policy advice to elected officials. The assembly—or Citizens' Council—has 24 randomly selected members, each of whom serve for 18-month terms. The Citizen's Council decides which public issues should be addressed by other ad hoc, randomly selected assemblies, and the advice from those assemblies is provided to the elected government (Van Reybrouck 2019).

In this section, I argue that random selection may be a practical solution to the electoral myopia dilemma.[16] For the purposes of discussion, I focus on a hypothetical institution: a randomly selected second chamber. Members of this chamber would serve relatively short terms (of, say, two years), and half the chamber would be replaced every half term so that veteran members could mentor new members and provide some measure of institutional memory and consistency.

The members of the chamber would be selected using stratified random processes to ensure that individuals from all politically relevant groups are properly represented in each iteration of the assembly. Selection criteria might include gender, age, ethnicity, language, or region, depending on the nature and needs of the polity from which members are drawn.[17] Members would be paid salaries equivalent to those of elected representatives to help ensure that people from all socioeconomic backgrounds would be able to participate, and legal protections would be put in place to ensure that members could return to their jobs after serving in the chamber. The chamber would have two sets of powers. First, it would be empowered to review, delay, and amend any law proposals adopted in the elected legislature. Second, it would be empowered to initiate its own law proposals, which would then need to be reviewed and sanctioned in the elected chamber before they could be passed into law.

[16] Alvin Toffer (1978) briefly mentions "selection by lot" in connection with his theory of anticipatory democracy, but he does not develop the point (p. xx). James Dator (1981) proposes a "fourth branch" of government which would be composed of an assembly with half of its members elected and half selected by lot for a limited period of time. As Dator (2019), explains, the job of this "fourth branch" would be to "evaluate the impact of actions by the other three branches and, if they find those actions to be injurious to the interests of future generations, to declare them 'unfuturistic.' If the two houses of the legislature subsequently vote, by a simple majority, to override that declaration, then an election [would be] held for both houses and for those members of the 'fourth branch' who are subject to election . . ." (p. 346).

[17] Organizers of the Citizens' Assemblies on Electoral Reform in British Columbia (2004) and Ontario (2006)—which were randomly selected assemblies charged with assessing the electoral systems in those provinces and making recommendations that resulted in referendum votes—employed a three-stage, stratified random process to select members. First, names were randomly selected from the provincial voters' lists and invitation letters were sent to those people. Second, those who were invited and interested attended information sessions. Third, those who agreed to serve were selected at the information sessions using stratified random processes (Fournier et al. 2011; Warren and Pearce 2008).

A randomly selected chamber based on this model—or some similar one—would be well positioned to represent the potential interests of the future, particularly if the members of the chamber were given an explicit mandate to do so.[18] The chamber would be democratically legitimate because it would be broadly representative of the public it is meant to serve, and the members would be free to think about the future needs of society, as a whole, without being unduly influenced by electoral considerations or the demands of campaign donors. Indeed, members would be independent in the truest sense of the term: they would not owe positions to their partisan credentials, to well-financed groups with dominant short-term interests, or to their status as economic or political elites. They would not be appointed by or beholden to elected officials, and they would not have to worry about re-election. They would have no political masters except each other, to whom they would be discursively accountable. Those selected to serve would owe their positions to the luck of the draw, and this would provide the foundation for their independence.

A randomly selected chamber would also be inclusive in a representative sense, and much more representative than the average elected legislature. Economic elites, white-collar professionals, males, members of majority groups, and extroverts tend to be overrepresented in elected legislatures. A randomly selected chamber would, by contrast, include people from different socioeconomic backgrounds, ages, genders, cultural or linguistic groups, and personality types; and it would, therefore, be uniquely positioned to make collective judgments about how the concerns of the present, in all its diversity, should be balanced with the potential interests of diverse future publics. A randomly selected chamber would also include people with different perspectives on what should or should not be done for the future, and this would help ensure that legislative decisions do not routinely or systematically favour the long-term interests of some groups while ignoring or dismissing the interests of others.

A randomly selected second chamber would also help make the political system, as a whole, more deliberative. Elected officials are often constrained in their deliberations by their partisan commitments. Members of a randomly

[18] For a similar proposal see MacKenzie (2016b). The chief differences between this proposal and my earlier one are the following: (1) I am now convinced that it would be democratically legitimate to empower a randomly selected chamber to initiate its own law proposals, as long as those proposals must be subsequently adopted by an elected legislature (see, e.g., Gastil and Wright 2018); and (2) I now believe that members of the chamber should be given a specific—and primary—mandate to act as special representatives of the future.

selected chamber would, in contrast, be free to debate public issues and law proposals on their merits without worrying (as much) about strategic political concerns. The members of the chamber would, of course, come with their own political commitments and perspectives, but they would have few incentives to approach issues in purely partisan ways. They would be selected *as individuals* and not as representatives of partisan interests, and they would need to persuade each other to get things done. Members of a randomly selected chamber would also have the power to hold elected officials discursively accountable for their law proposals. Elected officials would have to publicly justify their actions in future-regarding terms to the satisfaction of a representative, non-partisan, deliberative assembly. If they could not do so, they would risk having their legislative agendas disrupted.

As a general-purpose institution, a randomly selected chamber would also have the capacity to consider many different long-term issues and make trade-offs between them. The members could make judgments about specific issues, such as budget deficits, while considering how those decisions might affect other long-term considerations, such as public spending on pensions, education, or infrastructure. The chamber would play a protective role by stopping or delaying legislative proposals that risked harming the future, but it could also play a proactive role by initiating future-regarding policy proposals of its own.

Erik Olin Wright (2018) has argued that a randomly selected second chamber would also be in a position to actively challenge short-term market imperatives and the demands of economic elites (see, also, McCormick 2011). It would help address the democratic capture problem because it would be difficult for powerful groups with short-term interests—or anyone else—to use economic or political resources to gain influence in a randomly selected chamber. This would leave the chamber comparatively free to act in ways that might challenge—or undermine—the short-term interests of otherwise powerful economic actors.

In summary, using random processes to select representatives of the future has a number of advantages over other selection methods. A randomly selected chamber would not be electorally accountable to the public, but it would be democratic in other ways. It would be inclusive, representative, and discursively accountable for its actions. It would be empowered to deal with all different types of long-term issues, including future issues that we do not yet know about, and it would play both a protective and a proactive role in policymaking processes. The members of the chamber would have political influence for limited periods of time, but they would not be (or become) elites themselves, and they would face few institutional incentives to favour the near term over the long term. If what I argued in Chapter 4 has any merit, the deliberative conditions created within a randomly selected chamber should encourage members to more seriously consider the potential interests of excluded others, such as future others, and to challenge any cognitive biases that they might have against the future. The members of a randomly selected chamber would also be in a position to advance unpopular policies with near-term costs if there were compelling, future-regarding reasons for doing so. In short, a randomly selected chamber would help ensure that legislative processes strike a better balance between the concerns of the present and the potential interests of the future. The elected legislature would, as now, actively represent the concerns of the present, the randomly selected chamber would represent and speak for the potential interests of the future, and the two chambers would have to work together to get legislation passed.

7.5.4. Possible Critiques of a Randomly Selected Chamber

A randomly selected chamber would be well positioned to represent the potential interests of future others in legislative processes, but there are a number of possible concerns that should be addressed. The first has to do with whether randomly selected representatives would be capable of making good judgments about complex policies with long-term consequences. As Michael Bartlett (2012) has argued "selection by lot is no more a guarantor of wisdom than is accident of aristocratic birth. Some jurors [or randomly selected representatives] may be wise. Others may be feckless." This is a legitimate concern, but it is important to recognize that *any* legislative chamber, whether elected, appointed, or randomly selected, will have some members who are wiser or more knowledgeable than others, and that each individual will know more about some topics than others. The whole point of a representative chamber is to ensure that people with different experiences and ways of thinking about public issues are included when decisions are made. What matters is not whether any one individual is competent on any particular issue; what matters is whether the chamber as a whole is capable of making well-considered judgments. Like elected representatives, randomly selected ones would have access to research resources, they would be empowered to call on experts for advice, and they would be expected to consult with the public on important issues. There is evidence that other randomly selected assemblies have made competent, well-informed, deliberative judgments about complex public policy issues such as electoral reform (Blais et al. 2008; Fournier et al. 2011), genetically modified foods (MacKenzie and O'Doherty 2011), and environmental pollution (O'Doherty et al. 2013).

Another concern has to do with whether randomly selected representatives would pursue their own short-term interests at the expense of both current and future publics. Indeed, there would be no obvious adverse personal consequences for doing so, except perhaps public censure. Nevertheless, the institution itself would disincentivized self-serving actions. First, the members would be a diverse group, and it is thus unlikely that the chamber as a whole—in any one of its iterations—would sanction policies that favour the near-term interests of any particular individuals or groups. Second, there is evidence that people normally seek to perform the roles they are given in institutional settings (e.g., Biddle 1986; Goodin 1986; Ilgen and Hollenbeck 1991; Strijbos et al. 2004). If members of the chamber are told that they should act as special representatives of the future, they are likely to approach their jobs with this objective in mind, especially if they do not face other incentives to focus on the near term instead of the long term. Members of the chamber would be encouraged to articulate and advance the potential interests of the future, even if doing so would impose some near-term costs on themselves. Third, in an effective deliberative environment—where each participant is formally equal and no one is dependent upon anyone else for their status within the institution—those who make explicitly self-serving claims at the expense of others, including future others, are likely to be challenged by those with different views about what should or should not be done for the future (see Section 4.3.1).

Despite the potential benefits of a randomly selected chamber, the institution could, in practice, make the problem of policy disjunctures worse. Each group of randomly selected representatives would be different from the last and would be empowered to overturn any decisions or policies adopted by their predecessors. In this way, the institution might make it *more* not *less* difficult for a democratic society to pursue long-term collective objectives. There are at least two responses to this concern. First, randomly selected representatives—unlike elected ones—would have no obvious reasons to try to distinguish themselves from their predecessors. Second, deliberative processes can help provide stability by mitigating against unjustified policy changes (Section 5.4). A randomly selected chamber would be empowered to overturn decisions made by their predecessors, but anyone who wished to do so would have to provide reasons that would be acceptable to a diverse group of non-partisan representatives. It is unlikely that any two iterations of a randomly selected chamber would have radically different views about what is—or is not—in the long-term interests of society as a whole.

Another concern has to do with whether elite actors might find ways to influence or control the decisions made by a randomly selected chamber. If the processes used to select members have integrity, economic and political elites would not be able to use their resources to influence *who* is selected to serve in the chamber. (Indeed, one reason random processes are attractive is because they aim to remove human intentionality from selection processes.) Nevertheless, there may be other ways for elite actors to exercise control. Owen and Smith (2018), for example, have argued that randomly selected representatives might be particularly vulnerable to manipulation and the demands of lobbyists because they would not have well-informed views on many complex and unfamiliar policy issues. They might also be more willing to accept bribes compared to other representatives, precisely because they would not have to worry about their public reputations or their prospects for re-election. Lastly, randomly selected representatives might be motivated to obtain as many personal benefits as possible during their time in office, knowing that they might never again be in a comparable position of power. These are legitimate concerns, but there is no reason that they cannot be addressed—more or less effectively—through legal means. It would be possible, for instance, to make both bribes *and* lobbying illegal in the randomly selected chamber. Lobbyists, elected officials, experts, and advocacy groups might be given opportunities to make presentations to the chamber, but they could be legally prevented from lobbying members as individuals. Indeed, those who seek to peddle their influence in a randomly selected chamber might find it particularly difficult to do so: they would not be able to rely on party affiliations to target those who might cast deciding votes, and they would have little prior information about how individual members are likely to vote on specific policy decisions. As a further safeguard against manipulation, it would be possible to use random processes to distribute committee assignments and other empowerments *within* the chamber to make it difficult for lobbyists and other influence peddlers to know who to target before votes are taken (Owen and Smith 2018).

A randomly selected second chamber would be a permanent, general-purpose, future-regarding institution, but random processes could be used in other ways within our political systems to address the electoral myopia problem. Ad hoc assemblies might be used on specific long-term decisions, such as whether to increase taxes on fossil fuels. And randomly selected standing committees might be used to help guide decisions on ongoing issues such as urban planning or economic development. It is possible to imagine political systems in which many randomly selected assemblies—both permanent and ad hoc ones—are used to make future-regarding policy decisions at all levels of governance.

Randomly selected assemblies could also be used to navigate transnational or global issues. In 2007, for example, a randomly selected deliberative poll, called "Tomorrow's Europe," was formed to discuss the future of the European Union. It had more than 300 participants drawn from all 27 EU states, and deliberations were conducted in 23 languages with simultaneous translations (Dryzek et al. 2019, p. 35). Dryzek, Bächtiger, and Milewicz (2011) have argued that it would be possible to create a global citizens' assembly to deliberate, and navigate, public issues of global concern.

In summary, random selection is an attractive option for selecting and empowering representatives of the future, and it is more attractive than the other available options, appointment and election. Appointed guardians of the future—as individuals—cannot adequately represent current and future publics in all their diversity, and they may lack the democratic legitimacy to act decisively. Elected representatives of the future might have democratic legitimacy, but it is, as we have seen, difficult to take the short-termism out of electoral processes. Randomly selected assemblies would not be electorally accountable to the people that they are meant to serve, but they would be discursively accountable, broadly representative, and independent enough to challenge elected officials and economic elites. In short, randomly selected chambers could provide the democratic goods that will be needed—at the global, transnational, national, subnational, and local levels—if we are going to make our futures together in collectively intentional, mutually accommodating ways.

7.6. Posterity Impact Statements

Posterity impact statements are another institution that could help encourage and support future-regarding collective action in democratic systems. This institution would impose legal requirements on political and economic actors to publicly justify their actions in future-regarding terms. Posterity impact statements could help make our political systems more future-regarding, but only if they are effectively scrutinized and challenged by other empowered actors in deliberative processes.

Posterity impact statements might be put into practice in a variety of ways. Thompson (2010) has argued that contemporary political actors—or "current sovereigns"—should be required to issue posterity impact statements whenever they make decisions that will, or might, affect the democratic capacities or freedoms of "future sovereigns." Decisions to adopt, for example, supermajority rules, which would make it difficult for future sovereigns to change laws or constitutions, should be justified in terms that future sovereigns might plausibly accept. If such arguments cannot be found, then those actions should not be taken.

Thompson's approach is, in my view, the right one, but it is focused too narrowly on protecting the democratic freedoms of future publics. Thompson argues that we should not seek to make decisions *for* future others because we cannot know their interests or their needs. Instead, we should seek to preserve the democratic rights and capacities of future publics to make their own collective judgments in their own time. I share these concerns, but Thompson's proposal does not go far enough. It is not good enough to merely seek to preserve the democratic freedoms and capacities of future publics if all our decisions (and non-decisions) will impact them in consequential ways. In my view, political and economic actors should be compelled to think about the likely future consequences of *all* their actions and justify them in future-regarding terms, even though we cannot know what future publics will want or need in their own time.

The basic idea of the posterity impact statement is not unfamiliar. In many countries, businesses such as mining companies, oil producers, and chemical plants are required to issue environmental impact statements before they are granted permits to operate. The idea that *all* our decisions should be publicly justified with respect to their possible impacts on the future is also consistent with the indigenous concept of the Seventh Generation Principle, according to which we should situate all of our decisions in a temporal perspective that includes at least seven generations (O'Sullivan 2011). It is unclear (to me at least) whether the Seventh Generation Principle is an ethical one that is meant to be internalized by community members or a procedural rule that would require leaders to publicly justify their decisions or preferences in future-regarding terms. (Indeed, these two possibilities are not necessarily mutually exclusive.)

It is also worth considering whether the Seventh Generation Principle should require us to think about the impacts of our actions on seven generations into the future, which might be difficult to do, or whether we—the present—should be conceived of as always the fourth generation looking three generations backward and three generations forward. What is clear is that the principle is meant to be applied to *all* the decisions that an individual or community makes (see, e.g., Lyons 1980, p. 174). This is analogous to the idea that we might establish legal or institutional requirements for *all* decision makers to issue posterity impact statements whenever they make decisions likely to affect the future, which is most of the time. Posterity impact statements should seek to clarify the possible impacts that decisions will have on the future, but they should also seek to justify those decisions in future-regarding terms.

Posterity impact statements would serve several useful purposes. Most importantly, they would encourage—or compel—decision makers to think about the potential interests of future others, consider how their actions are likely to affect the future, and justify those actions in future-regarding terms that are potentially acceptable to others, including future others. Posterity impact statements can also help support future-regarding collective action. If we think that our long-term plans and projects are likely to be acceptable to future others—rather than abandoned by them—we may become more willing to invest our own scare resources in those long-term plans and projects. Lastly, although future others who do not yet exist cannot hold us accountable for the claims that we make on their behalf, public statements about how particular actions are likely to affect the future would make it possible for contemporary actors to hold each other accountable for the future-regarding claims that they make.

Posterity impacts statements are unlikely to be effective in these ways unless they are properly scrutinized in robust deliberative processes. Political and economic actors who are compelled to issue posterity impact statements will be free to make disingenuous or implausible claims unless they are held discursively accountable for their claims by other actors who have the power to delay or derail their plans. It would take some effort and resources to ensure that posterity impact statements are subject to proper deliberative scrutiny, but there are institutions that could play this role. A randomly selected chamber, for example, would be well positioned to scrutinize any posterity impact statements issued by elected governments, and lawmakers would have strong incentives to make credible claims about how their actions are likely to affect future publics if they know that any disingenuous, badly researched, or implausible claims would be in danger of being rejected by a randomly selected, deliberative chamber.

It would be too onerous to expect a single randomly selected chamber to review all the posterity impact statements that would have to be issued by other actors, such as corporations, but it would be necessary to ensure that those statements are also subject to deliberative scrutiny. One option would be to convene an ad hoc randomly selected assembly every time a large economic actor—such as a mining company or housing developer—is required to issue a posterity impact statement. The assembly, which might be made up of one or two dozen randomly selected members, would hear testimonies from experts, supporters, and opponents of the company's plans; they would deliberate with each other and make collective judgments about whether to accept or reject the company's future-regarding claims. If the company's claims were rejected, they would be required to adjust their plans and issue a new posterity impact statement that would then be scrutinized by another deliberative assembly. This process would force economic actors to engage with other empowered actors in deliberative ways before any actions are taken that might affect—or harm—future publics. There may be other ways to ensure that posterity impact statements are subject to deliberative scrutiny, but it is difficult to think of institutions other than randomly selected assemblies that would be deliberative, representative, and independent enough to do the job well.

It is important to emphasize that those who are charged with scrutinizing posterity impact statements would not be expected to *favour* the future over the present in their assessments. They would, instead, be expected to balance the concerns and interests of current publics, in all their diversity, with the potential interests of future publics, in all *their* diversity. In an adequately representative deliberative assembly, where members have various material interests and divergent opinions about what should be done for the future, it will be difficult for any actors to defend claims that dismiss or misrepresent the potential interests of different types of future others or futures publics as a whole.

Posterity impact statements are of interest for another reason as well: they can, at least in principle, be used at any level of governance from the local to the global. It is most difficult to imagine effective governance processes—of *any* type—at the global level, but this does not mean that economic actors and governments should not be required to justify their actions (or inactions) to transnational and global publics in future-regarding terms. To be effective, posterity impact statements that address transnational and global issues would have to be scrutinized by other empowered actors in deliberative processes, just like any other posterity impact statements. The institutions that would be required to make this happen have not yet been developed, but we should nevertheless be thinking about how that might be done.

7.7. Conclusion

In this chapter, I have sought to demonstrate that it is possible to redesign our democratic systems to make them more future-regarding. Future-regarding constitutional clauses, carefully designed referendums and initiative processes, randomly selected assemblies, and posterity impact statements would help counterbalance the myopic tendencies of our "ordinary" electoral processes. What is more, these institutions would not make our political systems more future-regarding by making them *less* democratic; they would make our political systems more future-regarding by making them *more* democratic.

I do not wish to imply that these are the only future-regarding institutions that might be available. (I discuss others, such as democratic workplaces and digital democracy platforms in the next chapter.) Nor do I think that these democratic institutions—or any others—can provide any guarantees that we will, in fact, get the futures we think we might want for ourselves and future others. Nevertheless, the institutions that I discuss in this chapter and the next are practical, technically feasible, and democratically legitimate. Whether we are likely to reform our democratic systems to make them more future-regarding is another question entirely—a question that is briefly discussed in the next chapter.

8
Conclusion
Unresolved Themes

8.1. Introduction

The idea that democracies are structurally short-sighted and must be tempered or replaced if we are going to make better futures for ourselves and future others is a sort of conventional wisdom. This idea has been advanced by scholars and others as a truth about democracy, but it has not been subject to sustained critical scrutiny. It is, however, worthy of critique because it challenges some of our most deeply held convictions. If democratic systems are structurally—and irreparably—short-sighted, we may have to choose between democracy and whatever commitments or obligations we have to future others. I have argued that we do not have to make this choice. My aim in this book has been to demonstrate that we will need better, more inclusive, and deliberative democracies if we are going to make better futures for ourselves and future others. There is, in my view, no other option: either we find ways to make our political and economic systems more inclusive and deliberative or our shared futures will be made for us by others in ways not likely to reflect our near-term *or* long-term collective interests, or those of future publics.

In this concluding chapter I briefly discuss a number of topics that have been alluded to but left unresolved in the rest of the book: the relationship between capitalism and democracy; the challenges and the promises of digital democracy; the role of ideas and concepts in shaping our temporal perspectives and understandings; and the prospects for institutional reform. I am not confident that we will make our democratic systems more inclusive and deliberative, but I am convinced that we *could* do so, and that we will need to do so if we want to make our shared futures together in collectively intentional and mutually accommodating ways.

Future Publics. Michael K. MacKenzie, Oxford University Press. © Oxford University Press 2021.
DOI: 10.1093/oso/9780197557150.003.0008

8.2. Capitalism and Democracy

We will need robust democratic and deliberative institutions to get the futures we think we might want for ourselves and future others, but many of the long-term problems that we face today—such as plastics pollution, climate change, and economic inequalities within and between countries—have been created by, and are deeply entrenched in, the logics and imperatives of global capitalism. As with democracy, there are structural incentives that make future-regarding action within capitalist economics difficult.[1] One such incentive is the growth imperative: capitalist economies must grow to remain healthy (e.g., Schweickart 2009). This imperative does not require every enterprise within a capitalist economy to continually grow: there are many privately owned, normally small, businesses that operate profitably without growing much, providing services that people need and incomes for their workers. (Think, for example, of locally owned coffee shops, restaurants, or pubs.) But capitalism as a larger economic system is propelled by publicly traded companies and speculative investments. In publicly traded enterprises growth is an imperative. Investors will seek to put their money wherever the potential for growth is the highest. If an enterprise fails to grow each year—even if it remains profitable—investors will have reasons to put their money elsewhere, unless they can be convinced that the enterprise will grow in subsequent years. There is, then, no steady state for publicly traded companies, they only have two gears: they are either growing or shrinking. And those are, as a result, the only two gears in capitalist economies more generally. The problem with the growth imperative is ontological: nothing on earth can continue to grow *and survive* indefinitely. If we are to make better futures for ourselves and future others, we will have to find ways of constraining capitalism or replacing it with an economic system that can produce goods we need without mortgaging our futures and those of others.

If we could protect our democratic processes from the outsized influence of powerful economic actors facing growth imperatives, we might succeed in regulating capitalism more effectively than we have done, thus

[1] In saying that capitalism is one of the forces that limits our collective capacities for future-regarding action, I do not mean to imply that capitalism is the only system that might be associated with these problems. As Dryzek and Pickering (2019) explain, the "Soviet Union left behind a legacy of widespread environmental destruction (McNeill and Engelke 2016), and it is entirely possible that capitalism as we know it will be superseded by a different economic system—but human impacts on the Earth system will continue unabated" (pp. 13–14).

making it more environmentally or socially sustainable than is currently the case (Hawken et al. 1999). In the previous chapter, I argued that innovative institutions, such as randomly selected legislatures, would help create bulwarks against the influence that powerful economic actors typically have in our legislative systems. Eric Olin Wright (2018) has made a similar argument. We *will* have to make our democratic systems less susceptible to the outsized influence of powerful economic actors if we want to make them more future-regarding, but readers will be forgiven for thinking that next to the juggernaut of global capitalism a few randomly selected chambers—at local, regional, national, or international levels—will hardly be sufficient. If we are going to make our futures together in collectively intentional ways, we will need democratic institutions that are not only capable of regulating capitalism more aggressively, we will also need institutions that challenge the way global capitalism works, the inequalities it produces, and thus the undemocratic conditions it creates. This might seem to be an impossibly difficult task—and it might, indeed, prove to be one—but there are some options to consider, such as democratic firms and democratic investment regimes (see, e.g., Pérotin 2016; Schweickart 2009, 2011).

Democratic firms provide workers with some collective control over their work environments and the economic activities of their firms. The *most* democratic workplaces are those in which workers are also owners of their firms. In these enterprises, worker-owners make all the decisions: they collectively decide how productive resources should be used, how much people should be paid, how many hours each person should be required to work, how profits should be distributed, and when profits should be reinvested in the firms. Democratic firms—like democratic countries—may be structured in many different ways. Large ones might elect worker-owners as executives to run their firms for limited periods of time, while in small firms, worker-owners might make collective decisions through participatory means, such as deliberation and direct voting. Democratic firms represent only a small portion of the businesses in any industrialized economy today, but there are more of them than is commonly thought. As Pérotin (2016) explains: "There exist more than 25,000 workers' co-operatives in Italy, some 18,000 worker cooperatives in Spain, 2,800 in France, about 500 or more in the UK, and probably several hundred in the US, for example" (p. 334). It is possible to imagine whole economies dominated by collectively owned, democratically run firms as opposed to privately owned, publicly traded, and hierarchically structured ones.

Democratic firms would enhance our collective capacities for future-regarding action in several ways. Although democratic firms have to make money to stay in business in competitive markets, they are, as Schweickart (2009) explains, "strikingly different in their orientation toward growth" when compared to capitalist firms (p. 571). One reason is that as capitalist firms grow, the number of people at the top of the hierarchy can—and often does—stay the same. This creates a strong incentive for those at the top to favour growth because they will personally benefit from each extra dollar earned by the company as a whole. In democratic firms run by worker-owners, growth requires additional worker-owners, and each additional dollar earned by a growing firm must be divided by a larger number of workers, unless efficiencies are found. This does not mean that worker-owned firms will not grow—they often do, as the example of the Mondragon Corporation in Spain illustrates—but the imperatives and incentives for growth are much reduced. As Schweickart explains: "However greedy workers may be, they cannot increase their incomes by expanding, unless economies of scale are significant" (p. 572).[2]

Democratic firms would also help support our collective capacities for future-regarding action by reducing overall levels of income inequality, and thereby reducing the threat of democratic capture and the threat of passing inequalities from generation to generation. In 2016, chief executive officers at the 350 largest companies in the United States made, on average, 271 times more than the average workers at those companies (Mischel and Schieder 2017). As Lixin Jaing (2020) explains, this means that "an ordinary American worker would have to toil for almost a year to make what these CEOs made in one day" (p. 192). It is difficult to imagine that worker-owners would elect to pay their executives (if they had them) at such high rates; but even if they did, those executives would be elected to serve for limited periods of time, after which they would rejoin the ranks of the other worker-owners. As such, income inequality *within* democratic firms tends to be dramatically less than in capitalist firms (e.g., Pérotin 2016).

There are also reasons to think that economies dominated by democratic firms would help reduce *overall* levels of income inequality. When a single

[2] Furthermore, instead of seeking to grow their businesses and increase profits, workers in democratic firms might seek innovations and efficiencies for the purposes of reducing the time they must spend working to support their existing living standards. As Schweickart (2009) points out: "Increased leisure is a readily available option in a democratic firm. But not in a capitalist firm" (p. 573).

person owns tens of thousands of coffee shops, for example, money from each shop flows upward to that person. When hundreds of thousands of people own tens of thousands of coffee shops, money made at each shop must be more widely and evenly distributed. In economies dominated by democratic firms there would, on this logic, be a larger, and probably wealthier and more economically secure middle class, along with smaller groups of very wealthy and very poor people.[3] In a society that is economically more equal, it will be more difficult for any single group or class to leverage their financial resources to capture democratic processes for their own near-term purposes. On this account, then, democratic firms—or economies dominated by democratic firms—would help reduce the threat of democratic capture, which is, as explained in Chapter 1, one of the four primary causes of democratic myopia.

Democratic firms do not face the same growth incentives as capitalist ones, and economies that are dominated by worker-owned firms would be more equal in terms of income disparities, but democratic firms would, nevertheless, have reasons to engage in environmentally unsustainable and socially unjust practices if doing so increased their chances of staying in business. There is no reason to think that democratic firms would, for example, be any less willing than capitalist ones to produce cheap plastic packaging if doing so was profitable. More fundamentally, economies dominated by democratic firms would not give societies, as a whole, control over how their productive resources are employed or which collective ends those resources should be directed toward. It would be possible to regulate democratic firms more aggressively in political systems where the threat of democratic capture was mitigated by reductions in income inequalities, but even that would not be enough to give whole societies collective control over how their productive resources are used.

In order to address these problems, Schweickart (2009, 2011) has suggested that democratic firms should be given access to capital from public investment banks. The managers of these banks would be public employees, and they would be given instructions or directives from elected representatives. They would assess the economic viability of business plans, but they

[3] There is evidence that in economic downturns, democratic firms tend to reduce pay and benefits for their employees before opting to lay-off people, whereas hierarchical firms tend to lay-off people before making adjustments to pay and benefits (Pérotin 2016). This means that democratic firms provide more stable employment even during economic downturns, which would also help reduce overall income inequality and instability.

could also be instructed to consider any number of additional criteria, such as whether business plans would help meet specific environmental standards or other long-term societal goals. Schweickart imagines an economic system in which all, or most, firms are democratic, and capital is largely or entirely distributed through public investment banks. This model would give whole societies—through their representatives—more control over how their economic resources are used. It would be a means of *ex ante* regulation to supplement the *post hoc* regulation that would also be required to direct market forces toward collectively intentional goals and objectives. Schweickart's model is not the only means of giving societies more control over the market forces that will shape their collective futures, but it nevertheless provides a concrete illustration of how this might be done. The more general point is that to take control of the market forces that will otherwise shape our futures for us, we will have to make our political *and* economic systems more democratic.

8.3. Digital Democracy

In addition to thinking about how we might make our economies more democratic, we have to think about the future of digital democracy. Given that so many of our political communications and social and economic interactions happen online—or in what Jamie Susskind (2020) has called the "digital lifeworld"—it is likely that we will make at least some of our collective decisions online in the future. Many jurisdictions have experimented with digital democracy (e.g., Simon et al. 2017), but there has been little attention paid to how digital platforms might be used to help make our political and economic systems more future-regarding.[4] This question is worth considering because digital platforms have the potential to (1) be widely inclusive and highly deliberative; (2) operate independently from the short-term dynamics associated with electoral politics; and (3) engage and empower many different types of publics, including those not defined in territorial or geographic terms.

Digital democracy is especially promising with respect to the criterion of inclusion. Mass democracy has traditionally been limited to voting in elections or referendums, but digital platforms make it possible for large numbers of people to interact with each other and make collective decisions

[4] Exceptions include, for example, Bezold (2006) and Ramos (2014).

in other ways. Some jurisdictions, for example, have experimented with what Susskind (2020) calls Wiki Democracy, or digital platforms that allow large numbers of people to write law proposals collectively (e.g., Noveck 2009). This approach was recently used in Brazil, for example, to rewrite laws on the rights of young people and internet users (Simon et al. 2017, pp. 19–20).

Another approach is the DemocracyOS platform, which aims to help voters influence (or control) elected representatives by making it possible for users "to review legislative bills online, add comments and submit a virtual vote to be tallied on the website after polls close" (Serna 2015, p. 103). The Net Party in Argentina, which ran candidates in municipal elections in 2013 and 2015, was created to put the DemocracyOS platform into action. Candidates for the Net Party pre-committed themselves to following the instructions of voters using the platform, an approach that would have turned them into "pure" delegates had any of them been elected.

Hiroki Azuma (2014) has argued that elected representatives should use data from our online activities—data that already exists in the digital lifeworld—to guide public policy decisions. He points out that our online activities reveal our genuine needs, interests, and preferences in finer detail than other processes, such as elections or polling, and that data from our online lives is continuously updated in real time. In this system, all of us—or at least all of those who are active online—would contribute to policymaking processes simply by living and acting in the digital lifeworld. Susskind (2020) has (rightly) questioned whether this model—which he calls Data Democracy—can be considered democratic, but he nevertheless acknowledges that it would be "a really representative system—more representative than any other model of democracy in human history" (p. 248).

In an even more radical proposal, César Hidalgo (2018) has suggested that we could employ digital avatars to make decisions for us in "democratic" processes. In this system—which Hidalgo calls Augmented Democracy—individuals would provide their digital representatives with continually updated information about their likes and dislikes, interests, beliefs, and worldviews more generally. The avatars would use machine-learning algorithms (or artificial intelligence) to make public decisions or recommendations on behalf of their humans. The argument is that these digital representatives would have more insight into the unique combinations of preferences associated with each individual than would be possible in any conventional representative system where a relatively small number of individuals are charged with representing the unique preferences and interests of thousands or millions of individuals at once. Individuals would be empowered to give their digital representatives less or more autonomy, depending on their interest levels or knowledge of particular issues and their confidence in the judgments of their avatars. Hidalgo argues that this system would make it possible for everyone to "participate" in making public decisions even though none of us has the time to participate personally in making the thousands of decisions that must be made daily in complex societies.

If we need more inclusive democratic systems to make our shared futures together, digital democracy—in one form or another—could provide us with levels of inclusion that exceed any possibilities that might be had in conventional political processes. The problem is that many of the processes that have been tried thus far have not been widely inclusive or adequately representative (Simon et al. 2017). As Susskind (2020) points out, digital democratic processes are in danger of becoming the preserve of the "learned and leisured classes" (p. 245).

But inclusion, itself, is not the only criterion: if we want to make our shared futures together in collectively intentional ways, we will need to find ways of deliberating with each other in the digital lifeworld. There are examples of digital tools that encourage public deliberation, such as Iceland's Better Reykjavik and Better Neighbourhoods platforms. The first is a platform for generating policy ideas, and the second is a digital platform for participatory budgeting. Both platforms allow users to propose and justify specific ideas for public improvements or investments, while encouraging others to explain why they support or oppose those ideas. Each month, representatives on the Reykjavik City Council deliberate the 15 most popular ideas proposed on the Better Reykjavik platform and publicly explain whether and why they support or oppose them. The Better Neighbourhoods initiative is a yearly process that coincides with the city's budget cycle. As Simon et al. (2017) explain: "There is no doubt that as a result of Better Reykjavik and Better Neighbourhoods every neighbourhood has seen investment in facilities and infrastructure that would not have been conceived of by local politicians or civil servants" (p. 46).

Unfortunately, many of the more ambitious—and futuristic—forms of digital democracy do not support good deliberative practices. The DemocracyOS platform does not require or encourage individuals to deliberate with each other before giving their representatives instructions—although it could, in principle, be designed to do so. More problematically, the DemocracyOS approach, in its purest form, undermines the possibility of deliberation *between* elected representatives if each representative is precommitted to following instructions from participants on the digital platform. In these circumstances, elected representatives would not be free to adjust their positions or votes based on the arguments made by other elected officials.

Data Democracy, as outlined by Azuma (2014), would sidestep deliberation (and intentionality) completely by severing the link between participation and reflectivity that supports democratic legitimacy (MacKenzie and Moore 2020). In Azuma's model, individuals would contribute to policymaking processes without being aware that they are doing so. As such, although Data Democracy would be widely inclusive, it would not help us make our shared futures together in collectively intentional and reflective ways.

Hidalgo (2018) does not discuss deliberation in his proposal for Augmented Democracy, but it would, in principle, be possible to train digital representatives to deliberate with each other on our behalf. Digital representatives might be particularly adept at deliberation because they would not be affected by the human foibles that often undermine deliberation, such as our partisan commitments or in-group biases (e.g., Achen and Bartels 2016). Digital representatives could be trained to seek common ground among conflicting opinions, integrative solutions to shared problems, economies of moral disagreements, and many other goods that have been associated with productive deliberations (see, e.g., Bächtiger et al. 2018; Gutmann and Thompson 1996; Warren and Mansbridge 2015). Digital representatives could also be trained to think about the future without being subject to the myopias common among humans. In these ways, Augmented Democracy could help support (something like) mass inclusion, large-scale deliberation, and future-regarding collective action. But would it be democracy? Would Augmented Democracy encourage reflective participation or unreflective non-participation? Would it produce outcomes that could be considered democratically legitimate? Would it support or undermine collective agency? Hidalgo's proposal would need to be subject to considerably more critical scrutiny from democratic theorists before it is used to make—and legitimate—public decisions.

Susskind (2020) has identified a number of threats to deliberation in the digital lifeworld, including anonymity, which encourages incivility, and fragmentation processes, which encourage individuals to interact only with others who agree with them. These and other challenges facing deliberation in the digital lifeworld could be addressed by using random selection processes to create inclusive and representative online deliberative forums, or digital deliberative minipublics (DDMPs).

DDMPs could be used to engage thousands—or tens of thousands—of people in making deliberative decisions about their shared futures together. Participants might deliberate with each other in small groups using video conferencing tools, and those groups might communicate with each other through online discussion boards. Facilitators could be used to ensure that good deliberative practices are followed and that the interests of others—such as future others—are adequately considered when collective decisions are made. DDMPs (or something like them) could be combined with other models of digital democracy, such as Wiki Democracy, to ensure that those processes are genuinely inclusive, representative, and deliberative. Another option would be to use video conferencing tools to link face-to-face deliberations in different locations together into larger deliberative forums. This approach was used by the organization AmericaSpeaks to facilitate large-scale, digitally enabled deliberative processes (Lukensmeyer et al. 2005).

The online world—as it exists today—has probably done more to undermine than enhance good public deliberations (see, e.g., Suskind 2020, Chap. 13), but this does not mean that digital tools cannot be used to create inclusive, representative, and productive deliberative spaces for (very) large numbers of people. In principle, the digital world—which *is* our world—makes it possible for whole societies or groups of people to interact with each other, and it thus provides the foundations that are needed for us to make our shared futures together.

Digital platforms can also help support democratic processes that can—or might—operate independently from the short-term dynamics of electoral processes and market imperatives. E-petitions, for example, help minimize the financial and political resources normally required to promote successful citizens' initiatives. In principle, e-petitions can be initiated and successfully promoted by individuals and groups who do not have access to large sums of money or extensive political connections. What is required, instead, are well-developed online connections and policy ideas that others might plausibly support. In this way, e-petitions could help make citizens' initiatives more effective tools for circumventing the short-term dynamics of electoral politics *and* the political influence of wealthy actors with dominant short-term interests.

The DemocracyOS platform would also help make representatives less susceptible to being captured by otherwise powerful interests and actors such as lobbyists (Serna 2015). If elected representatives were (genuinely) committed to following instructions from users on the DemocracyOS platform, lobbyists would have to try to shift public opinions—or dominate the platform—if they wanted to influence legislative votes and policy outcomes.

It is not clear whether mass democracy can be practiced online in ways that are secure, inclusive, adequately representative, deliberative, and democratically legitimate. The digital democratic platforms that have been conceived thus far are either very small scale (e.g., Serna 2015; Simon et al. 2017) or wildly speculative (e.g., Azuma 2014; Hidalgo 2018). It is nevertheless clear that if we want to make our shared futures in collectively intentional ways, digital democracy holds considerable promise. Digital democracy makes it possible, at least in principle, for thousands or millions of people to actively make collective decisions together in deliberative ways, which is something that could not have been imagined before the digital revolution.

8.4. Myopic Ideas and Concepts

I have argued that we will need to make our political institutions more future-regarding if we want to make our shared futures together in collectively intentional ways. In making this argument, I have not said much about education reform, cultural norms, or future-regarding ideas, concepts, or principles more generally. I have adopted an institutional approach because I believe that however difficult it will be to change our political institutions, it would be more difficult still to change our myopic behaviours through education reforms and cultural or conceptual transformations alone. The institutions that I have discussed in this book start with humans as we know them, not as we would like them to be. Future-regarding institutions, as I have defined them, are those that aim to give people tangible (economic or political) reasons to act in future-regarding ways *even if they are not principally committed to doing so.*

Although I am confident that an institutional approach is the right one, any efforts to encourage future-regarding behaviours through other means should also be promoted. The ways that we think about the future will affect what we might be willing to do for our future selves and future others in practical, pragmatic, or concrete terms—and although I think we must leverage institutional mechanisms to encourage and support future-regarding collective actions, this task would be made easier if the people acting within those institutions were a little more future-regarding to begin with.

There are, in fact, numerous concepts and ideas—or ways of thinking—that can either encourage or inhibit future-regarding action. Consider, for example, the famous quote: "We do not inherit the earth from our ancestors; we borrow it from our children"—which has been formulated in different ways and attributed to numerous people (O'Toole 2013). This quote is rhetorically powerful because it challenges notions of temporality that focus on the here and now, and it shifts our gaze to the future. It is politically powerful because it challenges the concept of property—or landownership—that is the foundation of modern capitalist economies. Once we begin to think differently about landownership, once we place the concept in its proper temporal context and recognize that we—as individuals—cannot own land (or anything else) in perpetuity, we also have to think differently about whether we have the right to use the land and the earth as we please to serve our own near-term interests.

A related concept that encourages myopic thinking is the idea of the unembedded individual, which is a foundational concept in Western political philosophy, and the starting point for many thinkers, including Thomas Hobbes, John Locke, Thomas Paine, and John Rawls. According to this concept, it is possible to make sense of our selves as individuals—our interests, needs, wants, convictions, and obligations—outside of our historical, cultural, sociological, political, and economic contexts. This idea is problematic on a number of levels, not least of which is the fact that the unembedded individual does not exist and never has existed. But even if the concept is understood in its most abstract form, the idea of the unembedded individual is problematic because it strips individuals of any reasons they might have to think and act in future-regarding ways. If we think that we can be made sense of *as individuals* outside of our connections to the past and to others within the present—as Hobbes, Paine, and Rawls have implied—we will have few reasons to think about the future beyond our own expected lifetimes.

Indeed, thinkers who adopt this approach have often found that they must (re)connect their abstract individuals to others in order to make sense of whatever intergenerational relations or obligations they might be thought have. Jana Thompson's (2009) theory of "lifetime transcending interests," for example, connects individuals to the future by linking their own personal interests to the actions of contemporaries and future others.

Similarly, John Rawls (1999) felt compelled to introduce "family ties" into his otherwise purely individual-based theory of intergenerational justice, precisely because he could not motivate those who are behind the veil of ignorance to think about the needs of future others without embedding them in a community of others. To "solve" this problem, he chose to embed his otherwise unembedded individuals in family units, presumably because the family is a form of community that is broadly acceptable within the liberal tradition itself. But this conceptual move—which has been rightly criticized as inconsistent with the rest of Rawls's conceptual framework (see, e.g., English 1977)—is a concession that intergenerational relations cannot be maintained if the unembedded individual is used as our primary unit of analysis.

There are many other concepts and ideas that we have to rethink if we are going to make our societies more future-regarding and temporally aware. I have argued elsewhere that the very idea that there are short-term issues and problems in public affairs directs our attention away from the long-term costs, benefits, and consequences associated with *all* of our decisions and non-decisions (MacKenzie 2021).

The concept of permanence also needs to be reconsidered. It is meant to invoke timeless stability, but it can be understood only in relative terms—which is to say in relation to specific timeframes. We normally act, for example, as if states are "permanent" political entities, even though most of the states that exist in the world today are less than 200 years old and none will exist forever. We make this assumption because states, like any collective entity, can continue to "live" into the future as the individuals who make them up are replaced by new individuals. States thus often appear to be permanent—or immortal—from the perspective of any individual living at a particular moment in time, but they are not, in fact, permanent or immortal. The United States did not exist 300 years ago, and it will almost certainly not exist in its current form 500 or 1000 years from now. The fiction of permanence limits our temporal perspectives because it encourages us to think and act only within that relatively brief period of time in which some semblance of permanence might be had.

This book has focused on the institutional requirements for future-regarding collective action, precisely because I do not think that changing our ideas about the future will be enough; we will need to give people tangible reasons and opportunities to think and act in future-regarding ways if we want to make better futures for ourselves and future others. But this does not mean that we should not also strive to confront harmful short-termism at the level of ideas and concepts. These two approaches—the institutional and the ideational—are not, in fact, mutually antagonistic. Karl Marx, for example, argued that our ideas, concepts, and political systems are predicated on our modes of economic production, and, as such, he did not think that we could reform our political and economic systems by simply changing the ideas and concepts that we use to understand them; but nor did he think that ideas, or ways of thinking about the world, were irrelevant to the actions we might (or might not) take to change the social, political, and economic worlds we inhabit. Drawing on this way of thinking—that there are interactions between our material interests and opportunities and the ideas we have about the world—it is apparent that we will have to work on two fronts simultaneously: we will have to change the way that people think about the past and the future before we are likely to make the sort of institutional reforms that would help make our political and economic systems more future-regarding; at the same time, we will have to change the many myopic incentives that people face in our political and economic worlds before we are likely to radically change how we think about the future.

8.5. Prospects for Reform

I have argued that we will have to think creatively—and expansively—about democracy if we are going to make our democratic systems more future-regarding. There are, however, several challenges associated with doing so that threaten to make reforms unlikely. One challenge has to do with striking the right balance between the abstract principles necessary to inform our institutional designs and the details required to make proposals concrete enough to be used by people in the real world. I have made concrete proposals for institutional reforms because I am concerned that working on a purely abstract level will not make the case for reform strongly enough—that it is, indeed, possible, in a practical sense, to make our shared futures together in collectively intentional ways. I have identified abstract principles to guide our institutional designs—inclusiveness, deliberativeness, and independence—but I have also outlined how these design criteria might be put into practice. The danger with this approach is that whenever too many details are provided, people will rightly have very specific critiques of those details. This can lead to productive critical exchanges, but it can also mean that the larger objectives and aims of any reform proposals can get lost in disputes about the details. I have taken this risk in order to illustrate in concrete terms what we will need to do to make our democratic systems more future-regarding. My hope is that readers will take my proposals as detailed points for discussion rather than directives for how I think democracy must be done.

Another challenge has to do with the practical and political difficulties associated with making radical institutional reforms. There is no point advancing detailed reform proposals that would not be achievable in practical terms. The institutions that I discuss—future-regarding constitutional clauses, carefully designed referendums and initiatives, randomly selected legislatures or assemblies, posterity impact statements, democratic workplaces, democratized investment regimes, and various forms of digital democracy—are functional, workable, institutional options: they would radically change the way that our political and economic systems function, and they would give us more collective control over our shared futures, but these institutions would not overburden the political actors who are supposed to operate within them.

The question of *political* difficulty is thornier. There are political and economic barriers, and powerful actors who will resist the democratic reforms that would be required to make our political and economic systems more future-regarding. In the face of such challenges, there are those who argue that political feasibility should be a primary consideration when thinking about future-regarding institutions (e.g., Boston 2017; Smith 2019). If we cannot get the radical reforms needed in the short term, perhaps we can make more modest adjustments to our democratic systems that would help make them a little *more* future-regarding than they currently are—and those reforms could lay the groundwork for more radical reforms in the future. I understand this concern, but I worry that by focusing on reform proposals that are, as Boston (2017) puts it, "practical, plausible, and achievable" (p. 184), we will limit ourselves with respect to what we might actually achieve. If politics is the art of making the seemingly "impossible" possible—and if democratic politics is about shaping expectations, beliefs, and possibilities—we need to be careful about making claims about what is or is not feasible. There are things that are impossible—such as flying by flapping our arms—but feasibility is not the right framework to think about any actions or outcomes that are not literally beyond our grasp. In politics, we should be thinking about the difficulty or relative ease of collective actions or desired outcomes, not about whether our objectives are politically "feasible." The concept of "politics" applies only where there are possibilities for collective action, not where our actions are foreclosed by practical or physical constraints. If future-regarding institutions are urgently needed—as I have argued—we will have to confront whatever political considerations make them difficult to establish, but those difficulties, themselves, should not be considered a reason not to act; and difficulties, more generally, should not be mistaken for "impossibilities" or "infeasibilities."[5]

Indeed, the idea that we should limit ourselves to what appears to be politically "feasible" today will only ensure that we fail to see the full scope of our future potentialities. As Robert Dahl points out:

> Whatever form it takes, the democracy of our successors will not and cannot be the democracy of our predecessors. Nor should it be. For the limits and possibilities of democracy in a world we can already dimly foresee are certain to be radically unlike the limits and possibilities of democracy in any previous time or place. (Dahl 1989, p. 340)

Like Dahl, I encourage people to think creatively and ambitiously about our democratic futures. If we do not allow ourselves to do so, we will guarantee that the democratic futures we think most desirable and necessary will not be achieved.

Furthermore, reforms that appear to be most politically difficult today may become imperative in the near future. It has been suggested, for example, that the climate crisis could make radical institutional reforms necessary. If the crisis gets bad enough—if coastal cities are flooded by rising sea levels; international trade is disrupted by fuel shortages, pandemics, or wars; food systems become unstable; and fresh water becomes increasingly scarce—we may be forced to dramatically, and quickly, reform the way we do things.

[5] I would like to thank Michael Goodhart for raising this point. Indeed, Boston (2017) implicitly recognizes that when we talk about "feasibility" in politics we often mean (or should mean) difficulty not impossibility. As he points out, in focusing on political reforms that might be considered "feasible" he does not wish to "imply that radical, transformative or experimental suggestions should be automatically rejected" only that "their political acceptability will be low, and building a sufficient constituency of support will take time" (p. 184). Such reforms will take time because they will be more difficult politically, not because they are necessarily unfeasible in practical terms. Likewise, Erman and Möller (2013) argue that while we might say that some political outcome or ideal is "likely" or "unlikely," the concept of feasibility is only appropriate when collective actions, outcomes, or ideals are literally impossible, which is not normally the case in the political realm.

The problem is that institutional reforms forced upon us by crises are not likely to produce *better* institutions. Wainwright and Mann (2013) have argued that the climate crisis *could* lead to more responsive, inclusive, and organic (i.e., flexible and reflexive) democratic systems, but they do not see this as the most likely possibility. The more likely scenario, in their view, will be a tightening of the grip of the most authoritarian regimes and leaders. In times of crisis those with power and resources are likely to want to protect themselves and their resources by any means necessary. Furthermore, as Dryzek and Pickering (2019) observe, while crises *could* provide opportunities for overcoming pathological path dependencies that would otherwise be too hard, or too costly, to change, there is a real danger that decisions made in response to crises will introduce new—and largely unexamined or unrecognized—pathological path dependencies (p. 45). In any case, we probably do not want to get to the point of disaster before we decide to do things differently.

I have argued that we will need to make our democratic systems more inclusive and deliberative if we want to make our shared futures together in collectively intentional ways—and that it will, likely, be politically difficult to do so. But we should remember that our existing democratic institutions—elected legislatures, multiparty systems, universal suffrage (or something like it), constitutionally protected human rights, transnational governments (such as the European Union), and federalism—would have looked politically unlikely (although not actually *impossible*) when they were first imagined. Given the political difficulties associated with any institutional reforms, it may take time—and perhaps too much time—to make our democratic systems more future-regarding. It took the United Kingdom, for example, almost 300 years to transition from an absolute monarchy into a parliamentary democracy with universal suffrage. It may take many generations for future-regarding democratic institutions to become established, if they are established at all. I am confident that it is possible to make our democratic systems more future-regarding, but I am worried that we will not have the political will to do so or the luxury of time on our side.

References

Abizadeh, A. (2020). Representation, Bicameralism, Political Equality, and Sortition: Reconstituting the Second Chamber as a Randomly Elected Assembly. *Perspectives on Politics*, 18(1), 1–16.

Achen, C. H., and Bartels, L. M. (2016). *Democracy for Realists: Why Elections Do Not Produce Responsive Government*. Princeton University Press.

Arendt, H. (1951). *The Origins of Totalitarianism*. 2nd ed. Benediction Classics.

Arendt, H. (1958). *The Human Condition*. Doubleday.

Arendt, H. (1961). *Between Past and Future: Eight Exercises in Political Thought*. Penguin Classics.

Aspinwall, L. G. (2005). The Psychology of Future-Oriented Thinking: From Achievement to Proactive Coping, Adaptation, and Aging. *Motivation and Emotion*, 29(4), 203–235.

Attas, D. (2009). A Transgenerational Difference Principle. In A. Gosseries and L. H. Meyer (Eds.), *Intergenerational Justice* (pp. 189–218). Oxford University Press.

Azuma, H. (2014). *General Will 2.0: Rousseau, Freud, Google*. Vertical.

Bachrach, P., and Baratz, M. (1962). Two Faces of Power. *American Political Science Review*, 56(4), 947–952.

Bächtiger, A., Dryzek, J., Mansbridge, J., and Warren, M. E. (2018). Deliberative Democracy: An Introduction. In J. Dryzek, A. Bächtiger, J. Mansbridge, and M. E. Warren (Eds.), *The Oxford Handbook of Deliberative Democracy* (pp. 1–31). Oxford University Press.

Baier, A. (1981). The Rights of Past and Future Persons. In E. Partridge (Ed.), *Responsibilities to Future Generations: Environmental Ethics* (pp. 171–183). Prometheus Books.

Baker, D. E. (1978). State, Regional, and Local Experiments in Anticipatory Democracy: An Overview. In C. Bezold (Ed.), *Anticipatory Democracy: People in the Politics of the Future* (pp. 5–34). Vintage Books.

Ball, T. (1985). The Incoherence of Intergenerational Justice. *Inquiry*, 28(1), 321–337.

Ball, T. (2000). "The Earth Belongs to the Living": Thomas Jefferson and the Problem of Intergenerational Relations. *Environmental Politics*, 9(2), 61–77.

Barber, B. R. (1998). Three Scenarios for the Future of Technology and Strong Democracy. *Political Science Quarterly*, 113(4), 573–589.

Barnett, A., and Carty, P. (2008). *The Athenian Option: Radical Reform for the House of Lords*. Imprint Academic.

Barry, B. (1978). Circumstances of Justice and Future Generations. In R. I. Sikora and B. Barry (Eds.), *Obligations to Future Generations* (pp. 204–248). Temple University Press.

Bartlett, M. (2012, January 10). *How Can Britain Protect the Interests of Future Generations?* Open Democracy UK. https://www.opendemocracy.net/en/opendemocracyuk/how-can-britain-protect-interests-of-future-generations/.

Baumgartner, F. R., and Jones, B. D. (2009). *Agendas and Instability in American Politics*. 2nd Edition. University of Chicago Press.

Beckerman, W. (2006). The Impossibility of a Theory of Intergenerational Justice. In J. Tremmel (Ed.), *Handbook of Intergenerational Justice* (pp. 53–71). Edward Elgar.

Beckerman, W., and Pasek, J. (2001). *Justice, Posterity, and the Environment*. Oxford University Press.

Beerbohm, E. (2015). Is Democratic Leadership Possible? *American Political Science Review*, 109(4), 639–652.

Beeson, M. (2010). The Coming of Environmental Authoritarianism. *Environmental Politics*, 19(2), 276–294.

Bell, D. A. (2016). *The China Model: Political Meritocracy and the Limits of Democracy*. Princeton University Press.

Berkman, M. B., and Plutzer, E. (2004). Gray Peril or Loyal Support? The Effects of the Elderly on Educational Expenditures. *Social Science Quarterly*, 85(5), 1178–1192.

Bernstein, E. (1988). [1899]. Evolutionary Socialism. In D. McLellan (Ed.), *Marxism: Essential Writings* (pp. 76–86). Oxford University Press.

Bezold, C. (Ed.) (1978). *Anticipatory Democracy: People in the Politics of the Future*. Vintage Books.

Bezold, C. (2006). Anticipatory Democracy Revisited. In M. Mannermaa, J. Dator, and P. Tiihonen (Eds.), *Democracy and Futures* (pp. 38–51). Committee for the Future, Parliament of Finland.

Bezold, C. (2019). The History and Future of Anticipatory Democracy and Foresight. *World Futures Review*, 11(3), 273–282.

Bidadanure, J. (2016). Youth Quotas, Diversity, and Long-Termism? Can Young People Act as Proxies for Future Generations? In I. González-Ricoy and A. Gosseries (Eds.), *Institutions for Future Generations* (pp. 266–281). Oxford University Press.

Biddle, B. J. (1986). Recent Developments in Role Theory. *Annual Review of Sociology*, 12, 67–92.

Birnbacher, D. (2009). What Motivates Us to Care for the (Distant) Future? In A. Gosseries and L. H. Meyer (Eds.), *Intergenerational Justice* (pp. 273–300). Oxford University Press.

Blais, A., Carty, R. K., and Fournier, P. (2008). Do Citizens' Assemblies Make Reasoned Choices? In M. E. Warren and H. Pearse (Eds.), *Designing Deliberative Democracy: The British Colombia Citizens' Assembly* (pp. 127–144). Cambridge University Press.

Bohman, J. (1998). The Coming of Age of Deliberative Democracy. *The Journal of Political Philosophy*, 6(4), 400–425.

Boston, J. (2017). *Governing for the Future: Designing Democratic Institutions for a Better Tomorrow*. Emerald.

Bradley, R. B. (1978). Goals for Dallas. In C. Bezold (Ed.), *Anticipatory Democracy: People in the Politics of the Future* (pp. 58–87). Vintage Books.

Braunstein, R. (2004). *Initiative and Referendum Voting: Governing Through Direct Democracy in the United States*. LFB Scholarly Publications.

Brennan, J. (2016). *Against Democracy*. Princeton University Press.

Bula, F. (2010, September 13). For Vancouver Mayor, China Makes an Environmental Leap Forward. *The Globe and Mail*.

Burke, E. (1973) [1790]. *Reflections on the Revolution in France*. Anchor Books.

Burnheim, J. (2014). *Is Democracy Possible: The Alternative to Electoral Politics* (3rd edition). Jump Up Press.

Burns, J. M. (1963). *The Deadlock of Democracy: Four-Party Politics in America*. Prentice-Hall.

Butler, D., and Ranney, A. (1994). *Referendums Around the World: The Growing Use of Direct Democracy*. AEI Press.

Button, J. W. (1992). A Sign of Generational Conflict: The Impact of Florida's Aging Voters on Local School and Tax Referenda. *Social Science Quarterly,* 73(4), 786–797.

Callenbach, E., and Phillips, M. (1985). *A Citizen Legislature.* Banyan Tree Books.

Campbell, B. (2012). Managing Oil Wealth: The Alberta/Canada Model vs. the Norwegian Model. Canadian Centre for Policy Alternatives. http://www.policyalternatives.ca/publications/commentary/managing-oil-wealth

Caney, S. (2016). Political Institutions for the Future: A Fivefold Package. In I. González-Ricoy and A. Gosseries (Eds.), *Institutions for Future Generations* (pp. 135–155). Oxford University Press.

Caney, S. (2018). Justice and Future Generations. *Annual Review of Political Science.* 21, 475–493.

Chambers, S. (1996). *Reasonable Democracy: Jürgen Habermas and the Politics of Discourse.* Cornell University Press.

Chambers, S. (2001). Constitutional Referendums and Democratic Deliberation. In M. Mendelsohn and A. Parkin (Eds.), *Referendum Democracy: Citizens, Elites, and Deliberation in Referendum Campaigns* (pp. 231–255). Palgrave.

Chambers, S. (2003). Deliberative Democratic Theory. *Annual Review of Political Science,* 6(1), 307–326.

Coate, S., and Morris, S. (1999). Policy Persistence. *The American Economic Review,* 89(5), 1327–1336.

Coates, T. (2014, June). The Case for Reparations. *The Atlantic.*

Cohen, J. (1989). Deliberation and Democratic Legitimacy. In A. P. Hamlin and P. Pettit (Eds.), *The Good Polity: Normative Analysis of the State* (pp. 17–34). Blackwell.

Crick, B. (1962). *In Defense of Politics.* University of Chicago Press.

Cronin, T. E. (1989). *Direct Democracy: The Politics of Initiative, Referendum, and Recall.* Harvard University Press.

Dahl, R. A. (1989). *Democracy and Its Critics.* Yale University Press.

Dahl, R. A. (1998). *On Democracy.* Yale University Press.

Dator, J. (1978). The Future of Anticipatory Democracy. In C. Bezold (Ed.), *Anticipatory Democracy: People in the Politics of the Future* (pp. 315–328). Vintage Books.

Dator, J. (1981). Responding to the Future. In D. Douthit (Ed.), *Planning the Good Life for Hawaii* (pp. 62–67). Hawaii Committee for the Humanities.

Dator, J. (2009). The Unholy Trinity, Plus One. *Journal of Futures Studies,* 13(3), 33–48.

Dator, J. (2019). *Jim Dator: A Noticer in Time Selected Work, 1967–2018.* Springer.

De-Shalit, A. (1995). *Why Posterity Matters: Environment Policies and Future Generations.* Routledge.

Dietz, T., Stern, P. S., and Dan, A. (2009). How Deliberation Affects Stated Willingness to Pay for Mitigation of Carbon Dioxide Emissions: An Experiment. *Land Economics,* 85(2), 329–347.

Dobson, A. (1996). Representative Democracy and the Environment. In W. M. Lafferty and J. Meadowcroft (Eds.), *Democracy and the Environment: Problems and Prospects* (pp. 124–139). Edward Elgar.

Dowlen, O. (2008). *The Political Potential of Sortition*
A Study of the Random Selection of Citizens for Public
Office. Imprint Academic.

Dryzek, J. S., Bächtiger, A., and Milewicz, K. (2011). Toward a Deliberative Global Citizens' Assembly. *Global Policy Volume,* 2(1), 33–43.

Dryzek, J. S., and Pickering, J. (2019). *The Politics of the Anthropocene*. Oxford University Press.

Dulic, A., Angel, J., and Sheppard, S. (2016). Designing Futures: Inquiry in Climate Change Communication. *Futures*, 81, 54–67.

Ekeli, K. S. (2005). Giving a Voice to Posterity—Deliberative Democracy and Representation of Future People. *Journal of Agricultural and Environmental Ethics*, 18, 429–450.

Ekeli, K. S. (2007). Green Constitutionalism: The Constitutional Protection of Future Generations. *Ratio Juris*, 20(3), 378–401.

Ekeli, K. S. (2009). Constitutional Experiments: Representing Future Generations Through Submajority Rules. *Journal of Political Philosophy*, 17(4), 440–461.

Elster, J. (1986). The Market and the Forum: Three Varieties of Political Theory. In J. Elster and A. Hylland (Eds.), *Foundations of Social Choice Theory* (pp. 103–132). Cambridge University Press.

Emirbayer, M., and Mische, A. 1998. What Is Agency? *American Journal of Sociology*, 103(4), 962–1023.

English, J. (1977). Justice Between Generations. *Philosophical Studies*, 31(2), 91–104.

Erman, E., and Möller, N. (2013). Three Failed Charges Against Ideal Theory. *Social Theory and Practice*, 39(1), 19–44.

Erreygers, G., and Vandevelde, A. (1997). *Is Inheritance Legitimate? Ethical and Economic Aspects of Wealth Transfers*. Springer-Verlag.

Farrell, D. M., O'Malley, E., and Suiter, J. (2013). Deliberative Democracy in Action Irish-Style: The 2011 We the Citizens Pilot Citizens' Assembly. *Irish Political Studies*, 28(1), 99–113.

Faulkner, W. (1951). *Requiem for a Nun*. Vintage International.

Feffer, J. (2013, August 26). The Disease of Short-Termism. *Hankyoreh*.

Fernandez, R., and Rodrik, D. (1991). Resistance to Reform: Status Quo Bias in the Presence of Individual-Specific Uncertainty. *The American Economic Review*, 81(5), 1146–1155.

Fiorino, D. (2018). *Can Democracy Handle Climate Change?* Polity Press.

Fisher, P. (2008). Is There an Emerging Age Gap in US Politics? *Society*, 45, 504–511.

Fishkin, J. (1995). *The Voice of the People: Public Opinion and Democracy*. Yale University Press.

Fishkin, J. (2009). *When the People Speak: Deliberative Democracy and Public Consultation*. Oxford University Press.

Foucault, M. (1977). *Discipline and Punish: The Birth of the Prison*. Vintage Books.

Foucault, M. (1982). The Subject and Power. *Critical Inquiry*, 8(4), 777–795.

Fournier, P., Van der Kolk, H., Carty, R. K., Blais, A., and Rose, J. (2011). *When Citizens Decide: Lessons from Citizen Assemblies on Electoral Reform*. Oxford University Press.

Fransen, T., Song, R., Stolle, F., and Henderson, G. (2015). *A Closer Look at China's New Climate Plan (INDC)*. World Resources Institute. https://www.wri.org/blog/2015/07/closer-look-chinas-new-climate-plan-indc.

Förster, J., Friedman, R. S., and Liberman, N. (2004). Temporal Construal Effects on Abstract and Concrete Thinking: Consequences for Insight and Creative Cognition. *Journal of Personality and Social Psychology*, 87(2), 177–189.

Fuller, T., Medina, J., and Dougherty, C. (2019, February 25). Can America Still Build Big? A California Rail Projects Raises Doubts. *The New York Times. https://www.nytimes.com/2019/02/25/us/california-high-speed-rail.html*

Gallie, W. B. (1956). Essentially Contested Concepts. *Proceedings of the Aristotelian Society,* 56(1), 167–198.

Gamble, A. (2019). *Politics: Why It Matters.* Polity Press.

Gardiner, S. M. (2009). A Contract on Future Generations? In A. Gosseries and L. H. Meyer (Eds.), *Intergenerational Justice* (pp. 77–118). Oxford University Press.

Gastil, J., and Wright, E. O. (2018). Legislature by Lot: Envisioning Sortition Within a Bicameral System. *Politics & Society,* 46(3), 303–330.

Gastil, J., Burkhalter, S., and Black, L. W. (2007). Do Juries Deliberate? A Study of Deliberation, Individual Difference, and Group Member Satisfaction at a Municipal Courthouse. *Small Group Research,* 38(3), 337–359.

Gastil, J., Knobloch, K. R., Reedy, J., Henkels, M., and Cramer, K. (2018). Assessing the Electoral Impact of the 2010 Oregon Citizens' Initiative Review. *American Politics Research* 46(3), 534–563.

Geyer, R., Jambeck, J. R., and Law, K. L. (2017). Production, Use, and Fate of All Plastics Ever Made. *Science Advances,* 7, 1–5.

Gidley, J. (2017). *The Future: A Very Short Introduction.* Oxford University Press.

Gilens, M. (2012). *Affluence and Influence: Economic Inequality and Political Power in America.* Russell Sage Foundation and Princeton University Press.

Gingrich, N. (1978). The Goals for Georgia Program. In C. Bezold (Ed.), *Anticipatory Democracy: People in the Politics of the Future* (pp. 35–57). Vintage Books.

Glantz, M. H. (1999). Sustainable Development and Creeping Environmental Problems in the Aral Sea Region. In M. H. Glantz (Ed.), *Creeping Environmental Problems and Sustainable Development in the Aral Sea Basin* (pp. 1–25). Cambridge University Press.

González-Ricoy, I. (2016). Constitutionalising Intergenerational Provisions. In I. González-Ricoy and A. Gosseries (Eds.), *Institutions for Future Generations* (pp. 170–183). Oxford University Press.

González-Ricoy, I., and Gosseries, A. (2016). An Introduction. In I. González-Ricoy and A. Gosseries (Eds.), *Institutions for Future Generations* (pp. 3–23). Oxford University Press.

Goodhart, M. E. (2018). *Injustice: Political Theory for the Real World.* Oxford University Press.

Goodin, R. E. (1986). Laundering Preferences. In J. Elster and A. Hylland (Eds.), *Foundations of Social Choice Theory* (pp. 75–102). Cambridge University Press.

Goodin, R. E. (2003). *Reflective Democracy.* Oxford University Press.

Goodin, R. E. (2007). Enfranchising All Affected Interests, and Its Alternatives. *Philosophy & Public Affairs,* 35(1), 40–68.

Gosseries, A. (2007). Should They Honor the Promises of Their Parents' Leaders? *Ethics and International Affairs,* 21(1), 99–125.

Gosseries, A. (2008). On Future Generations' Future Rights. *Journal of Political Philosophy,* 16(4), 446–474.

Gosseries, A., and Meyer, L. H. (Eds.). (2009). *Intergenerational Justice.* Oxford University Press.

Göpel, M., and Pearce, C. (2013). *Guarding Our Future: How to Include Future Generations in Policy Making.* World Future Council.

Gundersen, A. G. (1995). *The Environmental Promise of Democratic Deliberation.* University of Wisconsin Press.

Gutmann, A., and Thompson, D. F. (1996). *Democracy and Disagreement.* Belknap Press of Harvard University Press.

Gutmann, A., and Thompson, D. F. (2004). *Why Deliberative Democracy?* Princeton University Press.

Gutmann, A., and Thompson, D. F. (2018). Reflections on Deliberative Democracy: When Theory Meets Practice. In A. Bächtiger, J. S. Dryzek, J. Mansbridge, and M. E. Warren (Eds.), *Oxford Handbook of Deliberative Democracy* (pp. 900–912). Oxford University Press.

Habermas, J. (2006). *The Divided West.* (C. Cronin, Trans.). Polity.

Hacker, J. S., and Pierson, P. (2010). *Winner-Take-All Politics: How Washington Made the Rich Richer and Turned Its Back on the Middle Class.* Simon & Schuster.

Hanusch, F. (2018). *Democracy and Climate Change.* Routledge.

Harrington, M. (1981). Marxism and Democracy. *PRAXIS International,* 1(1), 6–22.

Haslett, D. W. (1986). Is Inheritance Justified? *Philosophy & Public Affairs,* 15(2), 122–155.

Hawken, P., Lovins, L. H., and Lovins, A. (1999). *Natural Capitalism: Creating the Next Industrial Revolution.* Little, Brown.

Healy, A., and Malhotra, N. (2009). Myopic Voters and Natural Disaster Policy. *American Political Science Review,* 103(3), 387–406.

Heath, J. (2013). The Structure of Intergenerational Cooperation. *Philosophy & Public Affairs,* 41(1), 31–66.

Heath, J. (2014). *Enlightenment 2.0: Restoring Sanity to Our Politics, Our Economy, and Our Lives.* Harper Perennial.

Heilbroner, R. L. (1991). *An Inquiry into the Human Prospect: Looked at Again for the 1990s.* Norton & Company.

Hershfield, H. E. (2011). Future Self-Continuity: How Conceptions of the Future Self Transform Intertemporal Choice. *Annals of the New York Academy of Sciences,* 1235, 30–43.

Heyd, D. (2009). A Value or an Obligation? Rawls on Justice to Future Generations. In A. Gosseries and L. H. Meyer (Eds.), *Intergenerational Justice* (pp. 167–188). Oxford University Press.

Hibbing, J. R., and Theiss-Morse, E. (2002). *Stealth Democracy: Americans' Beliefs About How Government Should Work.* Cambridge University Press.

Hidalgo, C. (2018). *Augmented Democracy* [Video]. TED. https://www.ted.com/talks/cesar_hidalgo_a_bold_idea_to_replace_politicians/discussion?rss=172BB350-0368.

Ignatieff, M. (2001). Human Rights as Politics. In A. Gutmann (Ed.), *Human Rights as Politics and Idolatary* (pp. 3–52). Princeton University Press.

Ilgen, D. R., and Hollenbeck, J. R. (1991). The Structure of Work: Job Design and Roles. In M. D. Dunnette and L. M. Hough (Eds.), *Handbook of Industrial and Organizational Psychology* (pp. 165–207). Consulting Psychologists Press.

Jacobs, A. M. (2011). *Governing for the Long Term: Democracy and the Politics of Investment.* Cambridge University Press.

Jacobs, A. M., and Matthews, J. S. (2012). Why Do Citizens Discount the Future? Public Opinion and the Timing of Policy Consequences. *British Journal of Political Science,* 42(4), 903–935.

Järvensivu, T. (2012). Four Steps to a Growth-Free, Prosperous Finland. *Green European Journal,* 3, 38–42.

Jaspers, K. (1961). *The Future of Mankind.* University of Chicago Press.

Jefferson, T. (1999) [1789]. Letter to James Madison. In J. Appleby and T. Ball (Eds.), *Jefferson: Political Writings* (pp. 36–38). Cambridge University Press.

Jefferson, T. (1999) [1813]. Letter to John Wayles Eppes. In J. Appleby and T. Ball (Eds.), *Jefferson: Political Writings* (pp. 598–604). Cambridge University Press.

Jeffords, C., and Minkler, L. (2016). Do Constitutions Matter? The Effects of Constitutional Environmental Rights Provisions on Environmental Outcomes. *Kyklos*, 69(2), 294–335.

Jenni, K. E., and Loewenstein, G. (1997). Explaining the "Identification Victim" Effect. *Journal of Risk and Uncertainty*, 14(3), 235–257.

Jiang, L. (2020). Changes in Organizational Inequality. In B. J. Hoffman, M. K. Shoss, and L. A. Wegman (Eds.), *Cambridge Handbook of the Changing Nature of Work* (pp. 192–213). Cambridge University Press.

Johnson, D., and Levin, S. (2009). The Tragedy of Cognition: Psychological Biases and Environmental Inaction. *Current Science*, 97(11), 1593–1603.

Jones, B. D., and Baumgartner, F. R. (2005). *The Politics of Attention: How Government Prioritizes Problems*. University of Chicago Press.

Jones, B. D., and Baumgartner, F. R. (2012). From There to Here: Punctuated Equilibrium to the General Punctuation Thesis to a Theory of Government Information Processing. *Policy Studies Journal*, 40(1), 1–20.

Jones, N., O'Brien, M., and Ryan, T. (2018). Representation of Future Generations in United Kingdom Policy-Making. *Futures*, 102, 153–163.

Kahneman, D. (2011). *Thinking, Fast and Slow*. Farrar, Straus and Giroux.

Kim, H., Schnall, S., and White, M. P. (2013). Similar Psychological Distance Reduces Temporal Discounting. *Personality and Social Psychology Bulletin*, 39(8), 1005–1016.

Knight, J., and Johnson, J. P. (1997). What Sort of Equality Does Deliberative Democracy Require? In J. Bohman and J. Johnson (Eds.), *Deliberative Democracy: Essays on Reason and Politics* (pp. 279–320). MIT Press.

Krosnick, J. A., Holbrook, A. L., Lowe, L., and Visser, P. S. (2006). The Origins and Consequences of Democratic Citizens' Policy Agendas: A Study of Popular Concern About Global Warming. *Climatic Change*, 77, 7–43.

Landemore, H. (2015). Inclusive Constitution-Making: The Icelandic Experiment. *Journal of Political Philosophy*, 23(2), 166–191.

Laslett, P., and Fishkin, J. S. (1992). *Philosophy, Politics, and Society, Sixth Series: Justice Between Age Groups and Generations*. Yale University Press.

Levitsky, S., and Ziblatt, D. (2018). *How Democracies Die*. Crown.

Lewis, Jeff. (2019, June 9). Ottawa Moves to Ban Single-Use Plastics as Part of Waste-Reduction Efforts. *The Globe and Mail*.

Lewis-Beck, M. S., and Stegmaier, M. (2019). Economic Voting. In R. D. Congleton, B. Grofman and S. Voigt (Eds.), *The Oxford Handbook of Public Choice, Volume 1* (pp. 247–265). Oxford University Press.

Lindblom, C. E. (1982). The Market as Prison. *The Journal of Politics*, 44(2), 323–336.

Lippmann, W. (1914). *Drift and Mastery: An Attempt to Diagnose the Current Unrest*. M. Kennerley.

Lippmann, W. (1922). *Public Opinion*. Harcourt, Brace.

Lukensmeyer, C. J., Goldman, J., Brigham, S., Gastil, J., and Levine, P. (2005). A Town Meeting for the Twenty-First Century. In J. Gastil and P. Levine (Eds.), *Deliberative Democracy Handbook: Strategies for Effective Civic Engagement in the 21st Century* (pp. 154–163). Jossey-Bass.

Lukes, S. (2005). *Power: A Radical View*. 2nd Edition. Palgrave MacMillan.

Lupia, A., and Norton, A. (2017). Inequality Is Always in the Room: Language & Power in Deliberative Democracy. *Daedalus*, 146(3), 64–76.

Lyons, O. (1980). An Iroquois Perspective. In C. Vecsey, & R. Venables (Eds.), *American Indian Environments: Ecological Issues in Native American History*, (pp. 173–174). Syracuse University Press.

MacKenzie, M. K. (2016a). Institutional Design and Sources of Short-Termism. In I. Gonzalez-Ricoy and A. Gosseries (Eds.), *Institutions for Future Generations* (pp. 24–48). Oxford University Press.

MacKenzie, M. K. (2016b.) A General-Purpose, Randomly Selected Chamber. In I. González-Ricoy and A. Gosseries (Eds.), *Institutions for Future Generations* (pp. 282–298). Oxford University Press.

MacKenzie, M. K. (2021). There is No Such Thing as a Short-Term Issue. *Futures*, 125, Article 102652.

MacKenzie, M. K., and Caluwaerts, D. (2021). Paying for the Future: Deliberation and Support for Climate Action Policies. *Journal of Environmental Policy & Planning*. Online First, pp. 1–15.

MacKenzie, M. K., and Moore, A. (2020). Democratic Non-Participation. *Polity*, 52(3), 430–459.

MacKenzie, M. K., and O'Doherty, K. (2011). Deliberating Future Issues: Minipublics and Salmon Genomics. *Journal of Public Deliberation*, 6(1), 15–32.

Manin, B. (1997). *The Principles of Representative Government*. Cambridge University Press.

Mann, G. and Wainwright, J. (2018). *Climate Leviathan*. Verso.

Mansbridge, J. (1999). Everyday Talk in the Deliberative System. In S. Macedo (Eds.), *Deliberative Politics: Essays on Democracy and Disagreement* (pp. 211–242). Oxford University Press.

Mansbridge, J. (2012). On the Importance of Getting Things Done. *PS: Political Science & Politics*, 45(1), 1–8.

Mansbridge, J., Bohman, J., Chambers, S., Estlund, D., Føllesdal, A., Fung, A., Lafont, C., Manin, B., and Martí, J. L. (2010). The Place of Self-Interest and the Role of Power in Deliberative Democracy. *Journal of Political Philosophy*, 18(1), 64–100.

Marx, K. (1906) [1867]. *Capital: A Critique of Political Economy*. The Modern Library.

Marx, K. (2000) [1852]. The 18th Brumaire of Louis Bonaparte. In D. McLellan (Eds.), *Karl Marx: Selected Writings* (pp. 329–355). Oxford University Press.

Matravers, M., and Meyer, L. (2011). Introduction: Democracy, Equality, and Justice. In M. Matravers and L. Meyer (Eds.), *Democracy, Equality, and Justice* (pp. 1–16). Routledge.

Mayer, J. (2016). *Dark Money: The Hidden History of the Billionaires Behind the Rise of the Radical Right*. Doubleday.

Mazor, J. (2010). Liberal Justice, Future People, and Natural Resource Conservation. *Philosophy & Public Affairs*, 38(4), 380–408.

McCaffery, E. J. (1994). The Uneasy Case for Wealth Transfer Taxation. *The Yale Law Journal*, 104(283), 284–365.

McCormick, J. P. (2006). Contain the Wealthy and Patrol the Magistrates: Restoring Elite Accountability to Popular Government. *American Political Science Review*, 100(2), 147–163.

McCormick, J. P. (2011). *Machiavellian Democracy*. Cambridge University Press.

Mead, G. H. (1937). *Philosophy of the Present*. Open Court.

McNeill, J. R., and Engelke, P. (2016). *The Great Acceleration: Environmental History of the Anthropocene Since 1945*. Belknap Press.

Mendelberg, T. (2002). The Deliberative Citizen: Theory and Evidence. In M. D. Carpini, L. Huddy, and R. Y. Shapiro (Eds.), *Research in Micropolitics, Volume 6: Political Decision Making, Deliberation and Participation* (pp. 151–193). Elsever Press.

Mendelsohn, M., and Parkin, A. (2001). *Referendum Democracy: Citizens, Elites and Deliberation in Referendum Campaigns*. Palgrave MacMillan.

Mercier, H., and Landemore, H. (2012). Reasoning Is for Arguing: Understanding the Successes and Failures of Deliberation. *Political Psychology,* 33(2), 243–258.

Meyer, L. H. (2016). *Intergenerational Justice*. Stanford Encyclopedia of Philosophy. plato.stanford.edu/entries/justice-intergenerational/.

Meyer, L. H., and Roser, D. (2009). Enough for the Future. In A. Gosseries and L. H. Meyer (Eds.), *Intergenerational Justice* (pp. 219–248). Oxford University Press.

Mill, J. S. (1978) [1859] *On Liberty.* Hackett Publishing Company.

Mill, J. S. (1861). *Considerations on Representative Government*. Floating Press.

Milman, O., and Chang, A., (2021, February 2). How Biden Is Reversing Trump's Assault on the Environment. *The Guardian*. https://www.theguardian.com/us-news/2021/feb/02/biden-trump-environment-climate-crisis

Mishel, L., and Schieder, J. (2017). *CEO Pay Remains High Relative to the Pay of Typical Workers and High Wage Earners*. Economic Policy Institute. https://www.epi.org/publication/ceo-pay-remains-high-relative-to-the-pay-of-typical-workers-and-high-wage-earners/.

Montesquieu, C. L. S. du. (1952) [1748]. *The Spirit of the Laws*. Hafner.

Montfort, N. (2017). *The Future*. MIT Press.

Moore, A. (2017). *Critical Elitism: Deliberation, Democracy, and the Problem of Expertise*. Cambridge University Press.

Mosher, M. (2010, September 2–5). Out of Time: A Typology of Political Action. American Political Science Association Annual Meeting, Washington DC.

Müller, H. (2004). Arguing, Bargaining and All That: Communicative Action, Rationalist Theory and the Logic of Appropriateness in International Relations. *European Journal of International Relations* 10(3), 395–435.

Mutz, D. C. (2006). *Hearing the Other Side: Deliberative Versus Participatory Democracy*. Cambridge University Press.

Mutz, D. C. (2008). Is Deliberative Democracy a Falsifiable Theory? *Annual Review of Political Science,* 11(1), 521–538.

Njuguna, J. K. (2018). The Efficacy of the Ban on Use of Plastic Bags in Kenya. *The Journal of Conflict Management and Sustainable Development,* 2(1), 91–101.

Norwegian Ministry of Finance. (2003). The Report from the Graver Committee: Responsible Investments. https://www.regjeringen.no/en/dokumenter/ Report-on-ethical-guidelines/id420232/ at § 5.4.

Noveck, B. S. (2009). *Wiki Government: How Technology Can Make Government Better, Democracy Stronger, and Citizens More Powerful*. Brookings Institute Press.

O'Doherty, K. C., MacKenzie, M. K., Badulescu, D., and Burgess, M. M. (2013). Explosives, Genomics, and the Environment: Conducting Public Deliberation on Topics of Complex Science and Social Controversy. *SAGE Open,* 3, 1–17.

O'Flynn, I. (2007). Divided Societies and Deliberative Democracy. *British Journal of Political Science,* 37(4), 731–751.

O'Sullivan, J. (2011). Sustainability, Seventh Generation. In J. Newman (Ed.), *Green Ethics and Philosophy: An A-to-Z Guide* (pp. 755–761). Sage.

O'Toole, G. (2013). *We Do Not Inherit the Earth from Our Ancestors; We Borrow It from Our Children*. Quote Investigator. https://quoteinvestigator.com/2013/01/22/borrow-earth/.

Olson, M. (1965). *The Logic of Collective Action: Public Goods and the Theory of Groups*. Harvard University Press.

Ophuls, W. (2011). *Plato's Revenge Politics in the Age of Ecology*. MIT Press.

Ophuls, W., and Boyan, A. S. (1992). *Ecology and the Politics of Scarcity Revisited: The Unraveling of the American Dream*. Freeman.

Owen, D., and Smith, G. (2018). Sortition, Rotation, and Mandate: Conditions for Political Equality and Deliberative Reasoning. *Politics & Society*, 46(3), 419–434.

Pahl, S., Sheppard, S., Boomsma, C., and Groves, C. (2014). Perceptions of Time in Relation to Climate Change. *WIREs: Climate Change*, 5(3), 375–388.

Paine, T. (1973) [1791]. *The Rights of Man*. Anchor Books.

Parfit, D. (1984). *Reasons and Persons*. Clarendon Press.

Parker, L. (2019, April). Plastic Bag Bans Are Spreading. But Are They Truly Effective? *National Geographic*.

Parkinson, J., and Mansbridge, J. (2012). *Deliberative Systems*. Cambridge University Press.

Partridge, E. (1981). Why Care About the Future? In E. Partridge (Ed.), *Responsibilities to Future Generations: Environmental Ethics* (pp. 203–220). Prometheus Books.

Patomäki, H., and Teivainen, T. (2004). *A Possible World: Democratic Transformations of Global Institutions*. Zed Books.

Perotin, V. (2016). Democratic Firms: Assets for the Long Term. In I. González-Ricoy and A. Gosseries (Eds.), *Institutions for Future Generations* (pp. 331–351). Oxford University Press.

Pettit, P. (1997). *Republicanism: A Theory of Freedom and Government*. Clarendon Press.

Pierson, P. (2004). *Politics in Time: History, Institutions, and Social Analysis*. Princeton University Press.

Pitkin, H. F. (1967). *The Concept of Representation*. Berkeley: University of California Press.

Pitkin, H. F. (1981). Justice: On Relating Private and Public. *Political Theory*, 9(3), 327–352.

Plato. (1992). *Republic*. (G. M. A. Grube, Trans.). Hackett.

Plumer, B. (2010, August). Fossil-Fuel Subsidies Still Dominate. *The New Republic*.

Polak, F. L. (1973). *The Image of the Future*. (E. Boulding, Trans.). Jossey-Bass.

Popovich, N., Albeck-Pipka, L., and Pierre-Louis, K. (2021, January 20). 85 Environmental Rules Being Rolled Back Under Trump. *The New York Times*. https://www.nytimes.com/interactive/2020/climate/trump-environment-rollbacks-list.html

Przeworski, A. (1999). Minimalist Conception of Democracy: A Defense. In I. Shapiro and C. Hacker-Cordón (Eds.), *Democracy's Value* (pp. 23–55). Cambridge University Press.

Qvortrup, M. (2007). *The Politics of Participation: From Athens to E-Democracy*. Manchester University Press.

Ramos, J. M. (2014). Anticipatory Governance: Traditions and Trajectories for Strategic Design. *Journal of Futures Studies*, 19(1), 35–52.

Randers, J. (2012). *2052: A Global Forecast for the Next Forty Years*. Chelsea Green.

Rankin, J. (2019, March 27). European Parliament Votes to Ban Single-Use Plastics. *The Guardian*.

Ratner, R. S. (2008). Communicative Rationality in the Citizens' Assembly and Referendum Processes. In M. E. Warren and H. Pearse (Eds.) *Designing Deliberative*

Democracy: The British Columbia Citizens' Assembly (pp. 145–165). Cambridge University Press.

Rawls, J. (1971). *A Theory of Justice*. Belknap Press of Harvard University Press.

Rawls, J. (1993). *Political Liberalism*. Columbia University Press.

Rawls, J. (1999). *A Theory of Justice: Revised Edition*. Belknap Press of Harvard University Press.

Read, D., and Read, N. L. (2004). Time Discounting Over the Lifespan. *Organizational Behavior and Human Decision Processes*, 94(1), 22–32.

Read, R. (2012). *Guardians of the Future*. Green House.

Reid, C. (2015). *Roads Were Not Built for Cars: How Cyclists Were the First to Push for Good Roads & Became the Pioneers of Motoring*. Island Press.

Reid, D. (2019). Norway's $1 Trillion Sovereign Wealth Fund Grows Despite a Volatile Quarter for Markets. https://www.cnbc.com/2019/08/21/norways-1-trillion-sovereign-wealth-fund-enjoys-returns-on-stocks-and-bonds.html

Rhodebeck, L. A. (1993). The Politics of Greed? Political Preferences Among the Elderly. *The Journal of Politics*, 55(2), 342–364.

Ridley, M. (2010). *The Rational Optimist: How Posterity Evolves*. Harper Collins.

Risse, T. (2018). Arguing and Deliberation in International Relations. In A. Bächtiger, J. S. Dryzek, J. Mansbridge, and M. E. Warren (Eds.), *The Oxford Handbook of Deliberative Democracy* (pp. 518–534). Oxford University Press.

Runciman, D. (2013). *The Confidence Trap: A History of Democracy in Crisis from World War I to the Present*. Princeton University Press.

Runciman, D. (2018). *How Democracy Ends*. Basic Book, Hachette Book Group.

Sanders, L. M. (1997). Against Deliberation. *Political Theory*, 25(3), 347–376.

Saward, M. (1996). Must Democrats Be Green? In B. Doherty & M. de-Geus (Eds.), *Democracy and Green Political Thought: Sustainability, Rights and Citizenship* (pp. 79–96). Routledge.

Saward, M. (1998). *The Terms of Democracy*. Polity Press.

Scheffler, S. (2013). *Death and the Afterlife*. Oxford University Press.

Scheffler, S. (2018). *Why Worry About Future Generations*. Oxford University Press.

Scheuerman, W. E. (2004). *Liberal Democracy and the Social Acceleration of Time*. Johns Hopkins University Press.

Scheuerman, W. E. (2008). Global Governance without Global Government? *Political Theory*, 36(1), 133–151.

Schlesinger, A. M., Jr. (1999). *The Cycles of American History*. Houghton Mifflin.

Schroth, O., Angel, J., Sheppard, S., and Dulic, A. (2014). Visual Climate Change Communication: From Iconography to Locally Framed 3d Visualization. *Environmental Communication*, 8(4), 413–432.

Schumpeter, J. A. (2006) [1942]. *Capitalism, Socialism and Democracy*. Routledge.

Schweickart, D. (2009). Is Sustainable Capitalism an Oxymoron? *Perspectives on Global Development and Technology*, 8(2–3), 559–580.

Schweickart, D. (2011). *After Capitalism*. Rowman & Littlefield.

Sen, A. (1999). *Development as Freedom*. Anchor Books.

Serna, A. (2015). Partido de la Red and DemocracyOS. *Americas Quarterly*, 9(2), 103.

Setälä, M., and Smith, G. (2018). Mini-Publics and Deliberative Democracy. In A. Bächtiger, J. Dryzek, J. Mansbridge, and M. E. Warren (Eds.), *The Oxford Handbook of Deliberative Democracy* (pp. 300–314). Oxford University Press.

Shapiro, I. 1999. Enough of Deliberation: Politics Is About Interests and Power. In S. Macedo (Ed.), *Deliberative Politics: Essays on Democracy and Disagreement* (pp. 28–38). Oxford University Press.

Shearman, D., and Smith, J. W. (2007). *The Climate Change Challenge and the Failure of Democracy*. Praeger.

Sheppard, S. (2012). *Visualizing Climate Change: A Guide to Visual Communication of Climate Change and Developing Local Solutions*. Routledge.

Shoham, S. (2010). *Future Intelligence*. Bertelsmann Stiftung.

Shoham, S., and Lamay, N. (2006). Commission for Future Generations in the Knesset: Lessons Learnt. In J. Tremmel (Eds.), *Handbook of Intergenerational Justice* (pp. 244–281). Edward Elgar.

Sikora, R. I., and Barry, B. (Eds.). (1978). *Obligations to Future Generations*. Temple University Press.

Simon, J., Bass, T., and Boelman, V., and Mulgan, G. (2017). *Digital Democracy: The Tools Transforming Political Engagement*. Nesta. https://www.nesta.org.uk/report/digital-democracy-the-tools-transforming-political-engagement/.

Siu, A. (2017). Deliberation and the Challenge of Inequality. *Daedelus*, 146(3), 119–128.

Smith, G. (2003). *Deliberative Democracy and the Environment*. Routledge.

Smith, G. (2009). *Democratic Innovations: Designing Institutions for Citizen Participation*. Cambridge University Press.

Smith, G. (2019). Enhancing the Legitimacy of Offices for Future Generations: The Case for Public Participation. *Political Studies*, Online First: https://doi.org/10.1177/0032321719885100.

Speth, J. G. (2008). *The Bridge at the Edge of the World: Capitalism, the Environment, and Crossing from Crisis to Sustainability*. Yale University Press.

Spitz, E. (1984). *Majority Rule*. Chatham House.

Steffen, W., Crutzen, P. J., and McNeill, J. R. (2007). The Anthropocene: Are Humans Now Overwhelming the Great Forces of Nature. *AMBIO: A Journal of the Human Environment*, 36(8), 614–621.

Stein, T. (1998). Does the Constitutional and Democratic System Work? The Ecological Crisis as a Challenge to the Political Order of Constitutional Democracy. *Constellations*, 4(3), 420–449.

Steinberg, L., Graham, S., O'Brian, L., Woolard, J., Cauffman, E., and Banich, M. (2009). Age Differences in Future Orientation and Delay Discounting. *Child Development*, 80(1), 28–44.

Steiner, H., and Vallentyne, P. (2009). Libertarian Theories of Intergenerational Justice. In A. Gosseries and L. H. Meyer (Eds.), *Intergenerational Justice* (pp. 50–76). Oxford University Press.

Steiner, J. (2012). *The Foundations of Deliberative Democracy: Empirical Research and Normative Implications*. Cambridge University Press.

Steiner, J., Bächtiger, A., Spörndli, M. R., and Steenbergen, M. (2004). *Deliberative Politics in Action: Analyzing Parliamentary Discourse*. Cambridge University Press.

Stigler, R. L. (1978). Alternatives for Washington. In C. Bezold (Ed.), *Anticipatory Democracy: People in the Politics of the Future* (pp. 88–99). Vintage Books.

Strijbos, J., Martens, R. L., Jochems, W. M. G., and Broers, N. J. (2004). The Effect of Functional Roles on Group Efficiency: Using Multilevel Modeling and Content Analysis to Investigate Computer-Supported Collaboration in Small Groups. *Small Group Research*, 35(2), 195–229.

Sumner, L. W. (1978). Classical Utilitarianism and the Population Optimum. In R. I. Sikora and B. Barry (Eds.), *Obligations to Future Generations* (pp. 91–111). Temple University Press.

Sunstein, C. R. (2002). The Law of Group Polarization. *Journal of Political Philosophy*, 10(2), 175–195.

Susskind, J. (2020). *Future Politics: Living Together in a World Transformed by Tech*. Oxford University Press.

Thaler, R. H., and Sunstein, C. R. (2008). *Nudge: Improving Decisions About Health, Wealth, and Happiness*. Yale University Press.

Theobald, R. (1978). The Deeper Implications of Citizen Participation. In C. Bezold (Ed.), *Anticipatory Democracy: People in the Politics of the Future* (pp. 303–314). Vintage Books.

Thompson, D. F. (2005). Democracy in Time: Popular Sovereignty and Temporal Representation. *Constellations*, 12(2), 245–261.

Thompson, D. F. (2010). Representing Future Generations: Political Presentism and Democratic Trusteeship. *Critical Review of International Social and Political Philosophy*, 13(1), 17–37.

Thompson, D. F. (2016). Democratic Trusteeship: Institutions to Protect the Future of the Democratic Process. In I. González-Ricoy and A. Gosseries (Eds.), *Institutions for Future Generations* (pp. 184–197). Oxford University Press.

Thompson, J. (2009). *Intergenerational Justice: Rights and Responsibilities in an Intergenerational Polity*. Routledge.

Thompson, T. H. (1981). Are We Obligated to Future Others? In E. Partridge (Ed.), *Responsibilities to Future Generations: Environmental Ethics* (pp. 195–202). Prometheus Books.

Tocqueville, A. de. (1835). *Democracy in America*. Saunders and Otley.

Toffler, A. (1970). *Future Shock*. Bantam Books.

Toffler, A. (1978). Introduction on Future-Conscious Politics. In C. Bezold (Ed.), *Anticipatory Democracy: People in the Politics of the Future* (pp. xi–xxvi). Vintage Books.

Tonn, B. E. (1991). The Court of Generations: A Proposed Amendment to the US Constitution. *Futures*, 23(5), 482–498.

Tonn, B. E. (1996). A Design for Future-Oriented Government. *Futures*, 28(5), 413–431.

Tremmel, J. (2006). Establishing Intergenerational Justice in National Constitutions. In J. Tremmel (Eds.), *Handbook of Intergenerational Justice* (pp. 187–214). Edward Elgar.

Tremmel, J. (2009). *A Theory of Intergenerational Justice*. Earthscan.

Tremmel, J. (2015). Parliaments and Future Generations: The Four-Power-Model. In D. Birnbacher and M. Thorseth (Eds.), *The Politics of Sustainability: Philosophical Perspectives* (pp. 212–233). Routledge.

Tremmel, J. (2019). Whose Constitution? Constitutional Self-Determination and Generational Change. *Ratio Juris*, 32(1), 49–75.

Tufte, E. R. (1978). *Political Control of the Economy*. Princeton University Press.

Tännsjö, T. (2007). *Future People, the All Affected Principle, and the Limits of the Aggregation Model of Democracy*. [Unpublished Manuscript]. Stockholm University.

UNFCCC. (2021). United Nations Framework Convention on Climate Change. https://unfccc.int/resource/bigpicture/#content-the-paris-agreemen.

Van Parijs, P. (1998). The Disfranchisement of the Elderly, and Other Attempts to Secure Intergenerational Justice. *Philosophy & Public Affairs*, 27(4), 292–333.

Van Reybrouck, D. (2019, April 25). Belgium's Democratic Experiment Europe's Smallest Federal Entity Is Setting a Big Precedent. *Politico*.

Vernon, R. (2016). *Justice Back and Forth: Duties to the Past and Future*. University of Toronto Press.

Vowles, J. (1995). The Politics of Electoral Reform in New Zealand. *International Political Science Review*, 16(1), 95–115.

Vuori, J. A. (2015). Strange Encounters: Past, Present, and Future Conceivable Life. In R. Van Munster and C. Sylvest (Eds.), *Documenting World Politics: A Critical Companion to IR and Non-Fiction Film* (pp. 183–198). Routledge.

Wainwright, J., and Mann, G. (2013). Climate Leviathan. *Antipode*, 45(1), 1–22.

Warren, M. E. (2007). Institutionalizing Deliberative Democracy. In S. W. Rosenberg (Eds.), *Deliberation Participation, and Democracy: Can the People Govern?* (pp. 272–289). Palgrave MacMillan.

Warren, M. E. (2008). Citizen Representatives. In M. E. Warren and H. Pearse (Eds.), *Designing Deliberative Democracy: The British Colombia Citizens' Assembly* (pp. 50–69). Cambridge University Press.

Warren, M. E. (2017). A Problem-Based Approach to Democratic Theory. *American Political Science Review*, 111(1), 39–53.

Warren, M. E. (2019, August 29–September 1). The Future of Deliberative Democracy in Light of Its Expanding Engagements. American Political Science Association Annual Meeting, Washington DC.

Warren, M. E., and Pearse, H. (Eds.). (2008). *Designing Deliberative Democracy: The British Columbia Citizens' Assembly*. Cambridge University Press.

Warren, M. E., and Mansbridge, J. (2015). Deliberative Negotiation. In J. Mansbridge and C. J. Martin (Eds.), *Political Negotiation: A Handbook* (pp. 141–198). Brookings Institution Press.

Watts, J. (2018, April 25). Eight Months On, Is the World's Most Drastic Plastic Bag Ban Working? *The Guardian*.

Weber, E. U. (2006). Experience-Based and Description-Based Perceptions of Long-Term Risk: Why Global Warming Does Not Scare Us (yet). *Climatic Change*, 77(1), 103–120.

Winters, J. A. (2011). *Oligarchy*. Cambridge University Press.

Winters, J. A., and Page, B. I. (2009). Oligarchy in the United States? *Perspectives on Politics*, 7(4), 731–751.

Wollstonecraft, M. (1993) [1792]. *A Vindication of the Rights of Men*. Oxford University Press.

York, E., and Cornwell, B. (2006). Status on Trial: Social Characteristics and Influence in the Jury Room. *Social Forces*, 85(1), 455–477.

Young, I. M. (2000). *Inclusion and Democracy*. Oxford University Press.

Zakaras, A. (2010). Lot and Democratic Representation: A Modest Proposal. *Constellations*, 17(3), 455–471.

Index

For the benefit of digital users, indexed terms that span two pages (e.g., 52–53) may, on occasion, appear on only one of those pages.